Legal Aid, Sentencing and Punishment of Offenders Act 2012

CHAPTER 10

CONTENTS

PART 1

LEGAL AID

Provision of legal aid

Remands to youth detention accommodation

Supplementary

CHAPTER 4

RELEASE ON LICENCE ETC

Calculation of days to be served

Release

Further release after recall

Other provisions about release

Life sentence prisoners

Application and transitional provision

CHAPTER 9

OFFENCES

PART 4

FINAL PROVISIONS

Legal Aid, Sentencing and Punishment of Offenders Act 2012

2012 CHAPTER 10

An Act to make provision about legal aid; to make further provision about funding legal services; to make provision about costs and other amounts awarded in civil and criminal proceedings; to make provision about referral fees in connection with the provision of legal services; to make provision about sentencing offenders, including provision about release on licence or otherwise; to make provision about the collection of fines and other sums; to make provision about bail and about remand otherwise than on bail; to make provision about the employment, payment and transfer of persons detained in prisons and other institutions; to make provision about penalty notices for disorderly behaviour and cautions; to make provision about the rehabilitation of offenders; to create new offences of threatening with a weapon in public or on school premises and of causing serious injury by dangerous driving; to create a new offence relating to squatting; to increase penalties for offences relating to scrap metal dealing and to create a new offence relating to payment for scrap metal; and to amend section 76 of the Criminal Justice and Immigration Act 2008. [1st May 2012]

BE IT ENACTED by the Queen's most Excellent Majesty, by and with the advice and consent of the Lords Spiritual and Temporal, and Commons, in this present Parliament assembled, and by the authority of the same, as follows:—

PART 1

LEGAL AID

Provision of legal aid

1 Lord Chancellor's functions

(1) The Lord Chancellor must secure that legal aid is made available in accordance with this Part.

(2) In this Part "legal aid" means—
 (a) civil legal services required to be made available under section 9 or 10 or paragraph 3 of Schedule 3 (civil legal aid), and
 (b) services consisting of advice, assistance and representation required to be made available under section 13, 15 or 16 or paragraph 4 or 5 of Schedule 3 (criminal legal aid).

(3) The Lord Chancellor may secure the provision of—
 (a) general information about the law and the legal system, and
 (b) information about the availability of advice about, and assistance in connection with, the law and the legal system.

(4) The Lord Chancellor may do anything which is calculated to facilitate, or is incidental or conducive to, the carrying out of the Lord Chancellor's functions under this Part.

(5) Nothing in this Part affects the powers that the Lord Chancellor has otherwise than under this Part.

2 Arrangements

(1) The Lord Chancellor may make such arrangements as the Lord Chancellor considers appropriate for the purposes of carrying out the Lord Chancellor's functions under this Part.

(2) The Lord Chancellor may, in particular, make arrangements by—
 (a) making grants or loans to enable persons to provide services or facilitate the provision of services,
 (b) making grants or loans to individuals to enable them to obtain services, and
 (c) establishing and maintaining a body to provide services or facilitate the provision of services.

(3) The Lord Chancellor may by regulations make provision about the payment of remuneration by the Lord Chancellor to persons who provide services under arrangements made for the purposes of this Part.

(4) If the Lord Chancellor makes arrangements for the purposes of this Part that provide for a court, tribunal or other person to assess remuneration payable by the Lord Chancellor, the court, tribunal or person must assess the remuneration in accordance with the arrangements and, if relevant, with regulations under subsection (3).

(5) The Lord Chancellor may make different arrangements, in particular, in relation to—
 (a) different areas in England and Wales,
 (b) different descriptions of case, and
 (c) different classes of person.

3 Standards of service

(1) The Lord Chancellor may set and monitor standards in relation to services made available under this Part.

(2) The Lord Chancellor may, in particular, make arrangements for the accreditation of persons providing, or wishing to provide, such services by—

(a) the Lord Chancellor, or

(b) persons authorised by the Lord Chancellor.

(3) Arrangements for accreditation must include—

(a) arrangements for monitoring services provided by accredited persons, and

(b) arrangements for withdrawing accreditation where the services provided are unsatisfactory.

(4) The Lord Chancellor may impose charges in connection with—

(a) accreditation,

(b) monitoring services provided by accredited persons, and

(c) authorising accreditation by others.

(5) Persons authorised by the Lord Chancellor may, in accordance with the terms of their authorisation, impose charges in connection with—

(a) accreditation, and

(b) monitoring services provided by accredited persons.

4 Director of Legal Aid Casework

(1) The Lord Chancellor must designate a civil servant as the Director of Legal Aid Casework ("the Director").

(2) The Lord Chancellor must make arrangements for the provision to the Director by civil servants or other persons (or both) of such assistance as the Lord Chancellor considers appropriate.

(3) The Director must—

(a) comply with directions given by the Lord Chancellor about the carrying out of the Director's functions under this Part, and

(b) have regard to guidance given by the Lord Chancellor about the carrying out of those functions.

(4) But the Lord Chancellor—

(a) must not give a direction or guidance about the carrying out of those functions in relation to an individual case, and

(b) must ensure that the Director acts independently of the Lord Chancellor when applying a direction or guidance under subsection (3) in relation to an individual case.

(5) The Lord Chancellor must publish any directions and guidance given under this section.

(6) Directions and guidance under this section may be revised or withdrawn from time to time.

5 Delegation

(1) The following functions of the Lord Chancellor may be exercised by, or by employees of, a person authorised by the Lord Chancellor for that purpose—

(a) securing the provision of information under section 1(4), and

(b) setting and monitoring standards under section 3.

(2) Regulations may provide for a function of the Lord Chancellor under regulations made under this Part to be exercisable by, or by employees of, a person authorised by the Lord Chancellor for that purpose.

(3) The functions conferred on the Director by this Part may be exercised by, or by employees of, a person authorised by the Director for that purpose.

(4) Regulations may provide for a function of the Director under regulations made under this Part to be exercisable by, or by employees of, a person authorised by the Director for that purpose.

(5) A direction given by the Lord Chancellor under section 4 about the carrying out of the Director's functions may, in particular, require the Director—

(a) to authorise, or not to authorise, a person to carry out a function specified in the direction, or

(b) to authorise, or not to authorise, a person specified, or of a description specified, in the direction to carry out such a function.

(6) Regulations under subsection (2) or (4) may provide that a function may be exercised—

(a) wholly or to a limited extent;

(b) generally or in particular cases or areas;

(c) unconditionally or subject to conditions.

(7) An authorisation given for the purposes of this section or regulations under this section may provide that a function may be exercised—

(a) wholly or to a limited extent;

(b) generally or in particular cases or areas;

(c) unconditionally or subject to conditions.

(8) In the case of an authorisation given for the purposes of regulations under this section, subsection (7) is subject to the provisions of the regulations.

6 Authorisations

(1) An authorisation given for the purposes of section 5 or regulations under that section—

(a) may specify its duration,

(b) may specify or describe the authorised person,

(c) may be varied or revoked at any time by the person who gave it, and

(d) does not prevent the Lord Chancellor, the Director or another person from exercising the function to which the authorisation relates.

(2) Anything done or omitted to be done by or in relation to a person authorised under section 5(1) or regulations under section 5(2) (or an employee of such a person) in, or in connection with, the exercise or purported exercise of the function concerned is to be treated for all purposes as done or omitted to be done by the Lord Chancellor.

(3) Anything done or omitted to be done by or in relation to a person authorised under section 5(3) or regulations under section 5(4) (or an employee of such a person) in, or in connection with, the exercise or purported exercise of the function concerned is to be treated for all purposes as done or omitted to be done by the Director.

(4) Subsections (2) and (3)—

(a) do not affect the rights and liabilities of the authorised person or the Lord Chancellor under any arrangements made between them,

(b) do not prevent any civil proceedings which could otherwise be brought by or against the authorised person (or an employee of that person) from being brought,

(c) do not apply for the purposes of criminal proceedings brought in respect of anything done or omitted to be done by the authorised person (or an employee of that person), and

(d) do not make the Lord Chancellor or the Director liable under section 6 of the Human Rights Act 1998 in respect of any act or omission of an authorised person if the act or omission is of a private nature.

(5) Where—

(a) an authorisation given for the purposes of section 5 or regulations under that section is revoked, and

(b) at the time of the revocation so much of any contract made between the authorised person and the Lord Chancellor as relates to the exercise of the function is subsisting,

the authorised person is entitled to treat the contract as repudiated by the Lord Chancellor (and not as frustrated by reason of the revocation).

(6) In this section "authorised person" means a person authorised for the purposes of section 5 or regulations under that section.

7 Annual report

(1) As soon as reasonably practicable after the end of each financial year, the Director must prepare an annual report for the financial year.

(2) The annual report must state how the Director has carried out the functions of the office in the financial year.

(3) The Director must send a copy of the report to the Lord Chancellor.

(4) The Lord Chancellor must—

(a) lay the copy of the report before Parliament, and

(b) arrange for it to be published.

(5) In this section "financial year" means—

(a) the period beginning on the day on which section 4 comes into force and ending on the following 31 March, and

(b) each successive period of 12 months.

Civil legal aid

8 Civil legal services

(1) In this Part "legal services" means the following types of services—

(a) providing advice as to how the law applies in particular circumstances,

(b) providing advice and assistance in relation to legal proceedings,

(c) providing other advice and assistance in relation to the prevention of disputes about legal rights or duties ("legal disputes") or the settlement or other resolution of legal disputes, and

(d) providing advice and assistance in relation to the enforcement of decisions in legal proceedings or other decisions by which legal disputes are resolved.

(2) The services described in subsection (1) include, in particular, advice and assistance in the form of—

(a) representation, and

(b) mediation and other forms of dispute resolution.

(3) In this Part "civil legal services" means any legal services other than the types of advice, assistance and representation that are required to be made available under sections 13, 15 and 16 (criminal legal aid).

9 General cases

(1) Civil legal services are to be available to an individual under this Part if—

(a) they are civil legal services described in Part 1 of Schedule 1, and

(b) the Director has determined that the individual qualifies for the services in accordance with this Part (and has not withdrawn the determination).

(2) The Lord Chancellor may by order—

(a) add services to Part 1 of Schedule 1, or

(b) vary or omit services described in that Part,

(whether by modifying that Part or Part 2, 3 or 4 of the Schedule).

10 Exceptional cases

(1) Civil legal services other than services described in Part 1 of Schedule 1 are to be available to an individual under this Part if subsection (2) or (4) is satisfied.

(2) This subsection is satisfied where the Director—

(a) has made an exceptional case determination in relation to the individual and the services, and

(b) has determined that the individual qualifies for the services in accordance with this Part,

(and has not withdrawn either determination).

(3) For the purposes of subsection (2), an exceptional case determination is a determination—

(a) that it is necessary to make the services available to the individual under this Part because failure to do so would be a breach of—

(i) the individual's Convention rights (within the meaning of the Human Rights Act 1998), or

(ii) any rights of the individual to the provision of legal services that are enforceable EU rights, or

(b) that it is appropriate to do so, in the particular circumstances of the case, having regard to any risk that failure to do so would be such a breach.

(4) This subsection is satisfied where—

(a) the services consist of advocacy in proceedings at an inquest under the Coroners Act 1988 into the death of a member of the individual's family,

(b) the Director has made a wider public interest determination in relation to the individual and the inquest, and

(c) the Director has determined that the individual qualifies for the services in accordance with this Part,

(and neither determination has been withdrawn).

(5) For the purposes of subsection (4), a wider public interest determination is a determination that, in the particular circumstances of the case, the provision of advocacy under this Part for the individual for the purposes of the inquest is likely to produce significant benefits for a class of person, other than the individual and the members of the individual's family.

(6) For the purposes of this section an individual is a member of another individual's family if—

(a) they are relatives (whether of the full blood or half blood or by marriage or civil partnership),

(b) they are cohabitants (as defined in Part 4 of the Family Law Act 1996), or

(c) one has parental responsibility for the other.

11 Qualifying for civil legal aid

(1) The Director must determine whether an individual qualifies under this Part for civil legal services in accordance with—

(a) section 21 (financial resources) and regulations under that section, and

(b) criteria set out in regulations made under this paragraph.

(2) In setting the criteria, the Lord Chancellor—

(a) must consider the circumstances in which it is appropriate to make civil legal services available under this Part, and

(b) must, in particular, consider the extent to which the criteria ought to reflect the factors in subsection (3).

(3) Those factors are—

(a) the likely cost of providing the services and the benefit which may be obtained by the services being provided,

(b) the availability of resources to provide the services,

(c) the appropriateness of applying those resources to provide the services, having regard to present and likely future demands for the provision of civil legal services under this Part,

(d) the importance for the individual of the matters in relation to which the services would be provided,

(e) the nature and seriousness of the act, omission, circumstances or other matter in relation to which the services are sought,

(f) the availability to the individual of services provided other than under this Part and the likelihood of the individual being able to make use of such services,

(g) if the services are sought by the individual in relation to a dispute, the individual's prospects of success in the dispute,

(h) the conduct of the individual in connection with services made available under this Part or an application for such services,

(i) the conduct of the individual in connection with any legal proceedings or other proceedings for resolving disputes about legal rights or duties, and

(j) the public interest.

(4) In setting the criteria, the Lord Chancellor must seek to secure that, in cases in which more than one form of civil legal service could be provided for an individual, the individual qualifies under this Part for the form of service which in all the circumstances is the most appropriate having regard to the criteria.

(5) The criteria must reflect the principle that, in many disputes, mediation and other forms of dispute resolution are more appropriate than legal proceedings.

(6) Regulations under subsection (1)(b) may provide that no criteria apply in relation to a prescribed description of individual or services.

12 Determinations

(1) A determination by the Director that an individual qualifies under this Part for civil legal services must specify—

(a) the type of services, and

(b) the matters in relation to which the services are to be available.

(2) Regulations may make provision about the making and withdrawal of determinations under sections 9 and 10.

(3) Regulations under subsection (2) may, in particular, include—

(a) provision about the form and content of determinations and applications for determinations,

(b) provision permitting or requiring applications and determinations to be made and withdrawn in writing, by telephone or by other prescribed means,

(c) provision setting time limits for applications and determinations,

(d) provision for a determination to be disregarded for the purposes of this Part if made in response to an application that is made otherwise than in accordance with the regulations,

(e) provision about conditions which must be satisfied by an applicant before a determination is made,

(f) provision about the circumstances in which a determination may or must be withdrawn,

(g) provision requiring information and documents to be provided,

(h) provision requiring individuals who are the subject of a determination to be informed of the reasons for making or withdrawing the determination, and

(i) provision for giving information to individuals who do not qualify for civil legal services under this Part about alternative ways of obtaining or funding civil legal services.

(4) The circumstances prescribed under subsection (3)(f) may, in particular, relate to whether the individual who is the subject of the determination has complied with requirements imposed by or under this Part.

(5) Regulations under subsection (2) must make provision establishing procedures for the review of determinations under sections 9 and 10 and of the withdrawal of such determinations.

(6) Regulations under subsection (2) may make provision for appeals to a court, tribunal or other person against such determinations and against the withdrawal of such determinations.

Criminal legal aid

13 Advice and assistance for individuals in custody

(1) Initial advice and initial assistance are to be available under this Part to an individual who is arrested and held in custody at a police station or other premises if the Director has determined that the individual qualifies for such advice and assistance in accordance with this Part (and has not withdrawn the determination).

(2) The Director must make a determination under this section having regard, in particular, to the interests of justice.

(3) A determination under this section must specify the type of advice or assistance (or both) to be available under this Part.

(4) Regulations may make provision about the making and withdrawal of determinations under this section.

(5) Regulations under subsection (4) may, in particular, include—
 (a) provision about the form and content of determinations and applications for determinations,
 (b) provision permitting or requiring applications and determinations to be made and withdrawn in writing, by telephone or by other prescribed means,
 (c) provision setting time limits for applications and determinations,
 (d) provision for a determination to be disregarded for the purposes of this Part if made in response to an application that is made otherwise than in accordance with the regulations,
 (e) provision about conditions which must be satisfied by an applicant before a determination is made,
 (f) provision about the circumstances in which a determination may or must be withdrawn,
 (g) provision requiring information and documents to be provided, and
 (h) provision requiring individuals who are the subject of a determination to be informed of the reasons for making or withdrawing the determination.

(6) The circumstances prescribed under subsection (5)(f) may, in particular, relate to whether the individual who is the subject of the determination has complied with requirements imposed by or under this Part.

(7) For the purposes of this section, in relation to an individual who is in custody—
 "initial advice" means advice as to how the law in relation to a matter relevant to the individual's arrest applies in particular circumstances and as to the steps that might be taken having regard to how it applies;

"initial assistance" means assistance in taking any of those steps which the individual might reasonably take while in custody, including assistance in the form of advocacy.

(8) The Lord Chancellor may by regulations provide that prescribed advice or assistance is not initial advice or initial assistance for the purposes of this section.

14 Criminal proceedings

In this Part "criminal proceedings" means—

(a) proceedings before a court for dealing with an individual accused of an offence,

(b) proceedings before a court for dealing with an individual convicted of an offence, including proceedings in respect of a sentence or order,

(c) proceedings for dealing with an individual under the Extradition Act 2003,

(d) proceedings for binding an individual over to keep the peace or to be of good behaviour under section 115 of the Magistrates' Courts Act 1980 and for dealing with an individual who fails to comply with an order under that section,

(e) proceedings on an appeal brought by an individual under section 44A of the Criminal Appeal Act 1968 (appeal in case of death of appellant),

(f) proceedings on a reference under section 36 of the Criminal Justice Act 1972 on a point of law following the acquittal of an individual on indictment,

(g) proceedings for contempt committed, or alleged to have been committed, by an individual in the face of a court, and

(h) such other proceedings, before any court, tribunal or other person, as may be prescribed.

15 Advice and assistance for criminal proceedings

(1) Regulations may provide that prescribed advice and assistance is to be available under this Part to an individual described in subsection (2) if—

(a) prescribed conditions are met, and

(b) the Director has determined that the individual qualifies for such advice and assistance in accordance with the regulations (and has not withdrawn the determination).

(2) Those individuals are—

(a) individuals who are involved in investigations which may lead to criminal proceedings (other than individuals arrested and held in custody at a police station or other premises),

(b) individuals who are before a court, tribunal or other person in criminal proceedings, and

(c) individuals who have been the subject of criminal proceedings.

(3) When making the regulations, the Lord Chancellor must have regard, in particular, to the interests of justice.

(4) The regulations must require the Director to make determinations under the regulations having regard, in particular, to the interests of justice.

(5) The regulations may require the Director to make such determinations in accordance with—
  (a) section 21 (financial resources) and regulations under that section, and
  (b) criteria set out in the regulations.

(6) The regulations may make provision about the making and withdrawal of determinations under the regulations.

(7) The regulations may, in particular, include—
  (a) provision about the form and content of determinations and applications for determinations,
  (b) provision permitting or requiring applications and determinations to be made and withdrawn in writing, by telephone or by other prescribed means,
  (c) provision setting time limits for applications and determinations,
  (d) provision for a determination to be disregarded for the purposes of this Part if made in response to an application that is made otherwise than in accordance with the regulations,
  (e) provision about conditions which must be satisfied by an applicant before a determination is made,
  (f) provision about the circumstances in which a determination may or must be withdrawn,
  (g) provision requiring information and documents to be provided, and
  (h) provision requiring individuals who are the subject of a determination to be informed of the reasons for making or withdrawing the determination.

(8) The circumstances prescribed under subsection (7)(f) may, in particular, relate to whether the individual who is the subject of the determination has complied with requirements imposed by or under this Part.

(9) The regulations may provide for the review of, or appeals to a court, tribunal or other person against, a decision by the Director—
  (a) that the interests of justice do not require advice or assistance to be made available to an individual under the regulations, or
  (b) that criteria prescribed under subsection (5)(b) are not met.

(10) In this section "assistance" includes, in particular, assistance in the form of advocacy.

16 Representation for criminal proceedings

(1) Representation for the purposes of criminal proceedings is to be available under this Part to an individual if—
  (a) the individual is a specified individual in relation to the proceedings, and
  (b) the relevant authority has determined (provisionally or otherwise) that the individual qualifies for such representation in accordance with this Part (and has not withdrawn the determination).

(2) Representation for the purposes of criminal proceedings is to be available under this Part to an individual if—
  (a) the proceedings involve the individual resisting an appeal to the Crown Court otherwise than in an official capacity, and

(b) the relevant authority has determined (provisionally or otherwise) that the individual qualifies for such representation in accordance with this Part (and has not withdrawn the determination).

(3) Where an individual qualifies under this Part for representation for the purposes of criminal proceedings ("the principal proceedings"), representation is also to be available to the individual for the purposes of—

(a) any related bail proceedings, and

(b) any preliminary or incidental proceedings.

(4) Regulations may—

(a) make provision specifying whether proceedings are or are not to be regarded as preliminary or incidental for the purposes of subsection (3), and

(b) make provision for exceptions from subsection (3).

(5) Regulations under subsection (4)(b) may, in particular, make exceptions for proceedings taking place more than a prescribed period of time before or after the principal proceedings.

(6) In this section—

"the relevant authority", in relation to a specified individual and criminal proceedings, means the person who is authorised by or under section 18, 19 or 20 to determine (provisionally or otherwise) whether the individual qualifies under this Part for representation for the purposes of the proceedings;

"specified individual" means—

(a) in relation to criminal proceedings mentioned in any of paragraphs (a) to (g) of section 14, an individual mentioned in that paragraph in relation to those proceedings, and

(b) in relation to criminal proceedings prescribed by regulations under section 14(h), a description of individual specified in the regulations in relation to those proceedings.

17 Qualifying for representation

(1) The relevant authority must determine whether an individual qualifies under this Part for representation for the purposes of criminal proceedings (whether provisionally or otherwise) in accordance with—

(a) section 21 (financial resources) and regulations under that section, and

(b) the interests of justice.

(2) In deciding what the interests of justice consist of for the purposes of such a determination, the following factors must be taken into account—

(a) whether, if any matter arising in the proceedings is decided against the individual, the individual would be likely to lose his or her liberty or livelihood or to suffer serious damage to his or her reputation,

(b) whether the determination of any matter arising in the proceedings may involve consideration of a substantial question of law,

(c) whether the individual may be unable to understand the proceedings or to state his or her own case,

(d) whether the proceedings may involve the tracing, interviewing or expert cross-examination of witnesses on behalf of the individual, and

(e) whether it is in the interests of another person that the individual be represented.

(3) The Lord Chancellor may by order amend subsection (2) by adding or varying a factor.

(4) Regulations may prescribe circumstances in which making representation available to an individual for the purposes of criminal proceedings is to be taken to be in the interests of justice for the purposes of a determination under section 16.

(5) In this section "the relevant authority", in relation to an individual and criminal proceedings, means the person who is authorised by or under section 18, 19 or 20 to determine (provisionally or otherwise) whether the individual qualifies under this Part for representation for the purposes of the proceedings.

18 Determinations by Director

(1) The Director is authorised to determine whether an individual qualifies under this Part for representation for the purposes of criminal proceedings, except in circumstances in which a court is authorised to make the determination under regulations under section 19.

(2) A determination by the Director under section 16 must specify the criminal proceedings.

(3) Regulations may make provision about the making and withdrawal of determinations by the Director under that section.

(4) Regulations under subsection (3) may, in particular, include—

(a) provision about the form and content of determinations and applications for determinations,

(b) provision permitting or requiring applications and determinations to be made and withdrawn in writing, by telephone or by other prescribed means,

(c) provision setting time limits for applications and determinations,

(d) provision for a determination to be disregarded for the purposes of this Part if made in response to an application that is made otherwise than in accordance with the regulations,

(e) provision about conditions which must be satisfied by an applicant before a determination is made,

(f) provision about the circumstances in which a determination may or must be withdrawn,

(g) provision requiring information and documents to be provided,

(h) provision requiring individuals who are the subject of a determination to be informed of the reasons for making or withdrawing the determination, and

(i) provision for the review of a decision by the Director that the interests of justice do not require representation to be made available, or to continue to be made available, to an individual under this Part for the purposes of criminal proceedings.

(5) The circumstances prescribed under subsection (4)(f) may, in particular, relate to whether the individual who is the subject of the determination has complied with requirements imposed by or under this Part.

(6) An appeal lies to such court, tribunal or other person as may be prescribed against a decision by the Director that the interests of justice do not require representation to be made available, or to continue to be made available, to an individual under this Part for the purposes of criminal proceedings, subject to subsection (7).

(7) Regulations may provide for exceptions from subsection (6).

(8) This section does not authorise the Director to make a provisional determination and accordingly—
   (a) references in this section to a determination do not include a provisional determination, and
   (b) references in this section to a decision do not include a decision made as part of such a determination.

19 Determinations by court

(1) Regulations may—
   (a) provide that a court before which criminal proceedings take place, or are to take place, is authorised to determine whether an individual qualifies under this Part for representation for the purposes of criminal proceedings of a prescribed description, and
   (b) make provision about the making and withdrawal of such determinations by a court.

(2) The regulations may, in particular, include—
   (a) provision about the form and content of determinations and applications for determinations,
   (b) provision permitting or requiring applications and determinations to be made and withdrawn in writing, by telephone or by other prescribed means,
   (c) provision setting time limits for applications and determinations,
   (d) provision enabling a court to determine that an individual qualifies under this Part for representation for the purposes of criminal proceedings before another court,
   (e) provision for the powers of a magistrates' court of any area under the regulations to be exercised by a single justice of the peace for the area, and
   (f) provision about the circumstances in which a determination may or must be withdrawn.

(3) The circumstances prescribed under subsection (2)(f) may, in particular, relate to whether the individual who is the subject of the determination has complied with requirements imposed by or under this Part.

(4) The regulations must provide that, subject to prescribed exceptions, an appeal lies to such court, tribunal or other person as may be prescribed against a decision by a court that the interests of justice do not require representation to be made available, or to continue to be made available, to an individual under this Part for the purposes of criminal proceedings.

(5) The regulations may include consequential provision modifying an Act or instrument.

(6) Regulations under this section may not authorise a court to make a provisional determination and accordingly—

(a) references in this section to a determination do not include a provisional determination, and

(b) references in this section to a decision do not include a decision made as part of such a determination.

20 Provisional determinations

(1) Regulations may provide that the Director or a court may make a provisional determination that an individual qualifies under this Part for representation for the purposes of criminal proceedings where—

(a) the individual is involved in an investigation which may result in criminal proceedings,

(b) the determination is made for the purposes of criminal proceedings that may result from the investigation, and

(c) any prescribed conditions are met.

(2) The regulations may, in particular, include—

(a) provision about the stage in an investigation at which a provisional determination may be made,

(b) provision about the making and withdrawal of provisional determinations, including provision equivalent to that described in section 18(4)(a) to (i) and (5),

(c) provision about the circumstances in which a provisional determination is to cease to be provisional, and

(d) provision about the circumstances in which a provisional determination is to be treated as if it were a determination made by the Director or a court in reliance on section 18 or 19.

(3) In this Part, as it applies in connection with a provisional determination made under regulations under this section as to whether an individual qualifies for representation for the purposes of criminal proceedings, references to proceedings include criminal proceedings that may result from the investigation concerned.

Financial resources

21 Financial resources

(1) A person may not make a relevant determination that an individual qualifies under this Part for services unless the person has determined that the individual's financial resources are such that the individual is eligible for the services (and has not withdrawn the determination).

(2) Regulations may—

(a) make provision about when an individual's financial resources are such that the individual is eligible under this Part for services, and

(b) make provision for exceptions from subsection (1).

(3) Regulations may provide that an individual is to be treated, for the purposes of regulations under subsection (2), as having or not having financial resources of a prescribed description.

(4) Regulations under subsection (3) may, in particular, provide that the individual is to be treated as having prescribed financial resources of a person of a prescribed description.

(5) Regulations may make provision about the making and withdrawal of determinations under this section.

(6) Regulations under subsection (5) may, in particular, include—
- (a) provision about the form and content of determinations,
- (b) provision permitting or requiring determinations to be made and withdrawn in writing, by telephone or by other prescribed means,
- (c) provision setting time limits for determinations,
- (d) provision about conditions which must be satisfied before a determination is made,
- (e) provision about the circumstances in which a determination may or must be withdrawn,
- (f) provision requiring information and documents to be provided,
- (g) provision requiring individuals who are the subject of a determination to be informed of the reasons for making or withdrawing the determination, and
- (h) provision for the review of a determination in respect of an individual's financial resources.

(7) The circumstances prescribed under subsection (6)(e) may, in particular, relate to whether the individual who is the subject of the determination has complied with requirements imposed by or under this Part.

(8) In this section "relevant determination" means a determination that is required to be carried out in accordance with this section by—
- (a) section 11 or 17, or
- (b) regulations under section 15 or paragraph 4 of Schedule 3.

22 Information about financial resources

(1) The relevant authority may make an information request to—
- (a) the Secretary of State,
- (b) a relevant Northern Ireland Department, or
- (c) the Commissioners for Her Majesty's Revenue and Customs ("the Commissioners").

(2) An information request may be made only for the purposes of facilitating a determination about an individual's financial resources for the purposes of this Part.

(3) An information request made to the Secretary of State or a relevant Northern Ireland Department under this section may request the disclosure of some or all of the following information—
- (a) a relevant individual's full name and any previous names;
- (b) a relevant individual's address and any previous addresses;
- (c) a relevant individual's date of birth;
- (d) a relevant individual's national insurance number;
- (e) a relevant individual's benefit status at a time specified in the request;
- (f) information of a prescribed description.

(4) An information request made to the Commissioners under this section may request the disclosure of some or all of the following information—
   (a) whether or not a relevant individual is employed or was employed at a time specified in the request;
   (b) the name and address of the employer;
   (c) whether or not a relevant individual is carrying on a business, trade or profession or was doing so at a time specified in the request;
   (d) the name under which it is or was carried on;
   (e) the address of any premises used for the purposes of carrying it on;
   (f) a relevant individual's national insurance number;
   (g) a relevant individual's benefit status at a time specified in the request;
   (h) information of a prescribed description.

(5) The information that may be prescribed under subsections (3)(f) and (4)(h) includes, in particular, information relating to—
   (a) prescribed income of a relevant individual for a prescribed period, and
   (b) prescribed capital of a relevant individual.

(6) Information may not be prescribed under subsection (4)(h) without the Commissioners' consent.

(7) The Secretary of State, the relevant Northern Ireland Departments and the Commissioners may disclose to the relevant authority information specified in an information request made under this section.

(8) In this section—

"benefit status", in relation to an individual, means whether or not the individual is in receipt of a prescribed benefit or benefits and, if so—
   (a) which benefit or benefits the individual is receiving,
   (b) whether the individual is entitled to the benefit or benefits alone or jointly,
   (c) in prescribed cases, the amount the individual is receiving by way of the benefit (or each of the benefits) ("the benefit amount"), and
   (d) in prescribed cases, where the benefit consists of a number of elements, what those elements are and the amount included in respect of each element in calculating the benefit amount;

"the relevant authority" means—
   (a) a prescribed person, or
   (b) in relation to circumstances for which no person is prescribed, the Director;

"a relevant individual", in relation to an information request for the purposes of a determination about an individual's financial resources, means—
   (a) that individual, and
   (b) any other individual whose financial resources are or may be relevant for the purposes of the determination;

"relevant Northern Ireland Department" means the Department for Social Development in Northern Ireland or the Department of Finance and Personnel in Northern Ireland.

Contributions and costs

23 Payment for services

(1) An individual to whom services are made available under this Part is not to be required to make a payment in connection with the provision of the services, except where regulations provide otherwise.

(2) The regulations may, in particular, provide that in prescribed circumstances an individual must do one or more of the following—

(a) pay the cost of the services;

(b) pay a contribution in respect of the cost of the services of a prescribed amount;

(c) pay a prescribed amount in respect of administration costs.

(3) The regulations may, in particular, provide that where—

(a) civil legal services are provided to an individual under this Part in relation to a dispute, and

(b) prescribed conditions are met,

the individual must pay a prescribed amount which may exceed the cost of the civil legal services provided.

(4) The regulations may, in particular, make provision about the determination of the cost of services for the purposes of the regulations.

(5) The regulations may, in particular—

(a) provide for an individual's liability under the regulations to make a payment to change or cease in prescribed circumstances,

(b) provide for an individual's liability under the regulations to arise on a determination by a prescribed person,

(c) provide for such a determination to be varied or withdrawn by a prescribed person, and

(d) provide for the review of such a determination in respect of an individual's liability to make a payment.

(6) The regulations may, in particular, provide that an individual is to be treated, for the purposes of the regulations, as having or not having financial resources of a prescribed description.

(7) Regulations under subsection (6) may, in particular, provide that the individual is to be treated as having prescribed financial resources of a person of a prescribed description.

(8) The regulations may, in particular, include provision for an amount to be payable entirely or partly—

(a) by periodical payments;

(b) by one or more lump sums;

(c) out of income;

(d) out of capital.

(9) The regulations may, in particular, include—

(a) provision requiring information and documents to be provided,

(b) provision about the time and manner in which payments must be made,

(c) provision about the person to whom payments must be made, and

(d) provision about what that person must do with the payments.

(10) The regulations may, in particular, make provision for the payment by an individual of interest, on such terms as may be prescribed, in respect of—

(a) a loan made to the individual under this Part,

(b) a payment in connection with the provision of services which is not required by the regulations to be made by the individual until after the time when the services are provided, and

(c) so much of a payment as remains unpaid after the time when it is required by the regulations to be made by the individual.

(11) The regulations—

(a) must make provision for the repayment to an individual of any amount in excess of the individual's liability under the regulations or under section 24, and

(b) may make provision for the payment of interest on the excess.

(12) In this section—

"administration costs" means costs in connection with the administration of legal aid, including the administration of charges arising under section 25;

"prescribed amount" includes an amount calculated in a prescribed manner.

24 Enforcement

(1) Regulations may make provision about the enforcement of an obligation to make a payment imposed under section 23.

(2) The regulations may, in particular, make provision for costs incurred in connection with the enforcement of an individual's obligation to make a payment to be recovered from the individual.

(3) Regulations under this section may, in particular—

(a) provide that overdue amounts are recoverable summarily as a civil debt;

(b) provide that overdue amounts are recoverable as if they were payable under an order of the High Court or a county court, if the court in question so orders on the application of the person to whom the amounts are due.

(4) Regulations under this section may include provision requiring information and documents to be provided.

(5) Schedule 2 (criminal legal aid: motor vehicle orders) has effect.

25 Charges on property in connection with civil legal services

(1) Where civil legal services are made available to an individual under this Part, the amounts described in subsection (2) are to constitute a first charge on—

(a) any property recovered or preserved by the individual in proceedings, or in any compromise or settlement of a dispute, in connection with which the services were provided (whether the property is recovered or preserved for the individual or another person), and

(b) any costs payable to the individual by another person in connection with such proceedings or such a dispute.

(2) Those amounts are—

(a) amounts expended by the Lord Chancellor in securing the provision of the services (except to the extent that they are recovered by other means), and

(b) other amounts payable by the individual in connection with the services under section 23 or 24.

(3) Regulations may make provision for exceptions from subsection (1).

(4) Regulations may make provision about the charge under subsection (1) including, in particular—

(a) provision as to whether the charge is in favour of the Lord Chancellor or a person by whom the services were made available,

(b) provision modifying the charge for the purposes of its application in prescribed cases or circumstances, and

(c) provision about the enforcement of the charge.

(5) Regulations under subsection (4)(c) may, in particular, include—

(a) provision requiring amounts recovered by the individual in proceedings or as part of a compromise or settlement of a dispute, and costs payable to the individual, to be paid to the Lord Chancellor or a person by whom the services were made available,

(b) provision about the time and manner in which the amounts must be paid,

(c) provision about what the Lord Chancellor or the person by whom the services were made available must do with the amounts,

(d) provision for the payment of interest on all or part of the amounts,

(e) provision for the payment to the individual concerned of any amount in excess of the amounts described in subsection (2), and

(f) provision for the enforcement of requirements described in paragraph (a).

(6) Regulations under this section may include provision requiring information and documents to be provided.

26 Costs in civil proceedings

(1) Costs ordered against an individual in relevant civil proceedings must not exceed the amount (if any) which it is reasonable for the individual to pay having regard to all the circumstances, including—

(a) the financial resources of all of the parties to the proceedings, and

(b) their conduct in connection with the dispute to which the proceedings relate.

(2) In subsection (1) "relevant civil proceedings", in relation to an individual, means—

(a) proceedings for the purposes of which civil legal services are made available to the individual under this Part, or

(b) if such services are made available to the individual under this Part for the purposes of only part of proceedings, that part of the proceedings.

(3) Regulations may make provision for exceptions from subsection (1).

(4) In assessing for the purposes of subsection (1) the financial resources of an individual to whom civil legal services are made available, the following must not be taken into account, except so far as prescribed—
(a) the individual's clothes and household furniture, and
(b) the implements of the individual's trade.

(5) Subject to subsections (1) to (4), regulations may make provision about costs in relation to proceedings for the purposes of which civil legal services are made available under this Part.

(6) Regulations under subsection (5) may, in particular, make provision—
(a) specifying the principles to be applied in determining the amount of any costs which may be awarded against a party to whom civil legal services are made available under this Part,
(b) limiting the circumstances in which, or the extent to which, an order for costs may be enforced against such a party,
(c) as to the cases in which, and the extent to which, such a party may be required to give security for costs and the manner in which it is to be given,
(d) requiring the payment by the Lord Chancellor of the whole or part of any costs incurred by a party to whom civil legal services are not made available under this Part,
(e) specifying the principles to be applied in determining the amount of costs which may be awarded to a party to whom civil legal services are made available under this Part,
(f) as to the court, tribunal or other person by whom the amount of any costs is to be determined, and
(g) as to the extent to which any determination of that amount is to be final.

(7) Regulations may provide that an individual is to be treated, for the purposes of subsection (1) or regulations under subsection (3) or (5), as having or not having financial resources of a prescribed description (but such regulations have effect subject to subsection (4)).

(8) Regulations under subsection (7) may, in particular, provide that the individual is to be treated as having prescribed financial resources of a person of a prescribed description.

(9) Regulations under this section may include provision requiring information and documents to be provided.

Providers of services etc

27 Choice of provider of services etc

(1) The Lord Chancellor's duty under section 1(1) does not include a duty to secure that, where services are made available to an individual under this Part, they are made available by the means selected by the individual.

(2) The Lord Chancellor may discharge that duty, in particular, by arranging for the services to be provided by telephone or by other electronic means.

(3) The Lord Chancellor's duty under section 1(1) does not include a duty to secure that, where services are made available to an individual under this Part,

they are made available by a person selected by the individual, subject to subsections (4) to (10).

(4) An individual who qualifies under this Part for representation for the purposes of criminal proceedings by virtue of a determination under section 16 may select any representative or representatives willing to act for the individual, subject to regulations under subsection (6).

(5) Where an individual exercises that right, representation by the selected representative or representatives is to be available under this Part for the purposes of the proceedings.

(6) Regulations may provide that in prescribed circumstances—

(a) the right conferred by subsection (4) is not to apply in cases of prescribed descriptions,

(b) an individual who has been provided with advice or assistance in accordance with section 13 or regulations under section 15 by a person selected by the individual is to be taken to have selected that person under subsection (4),

(c) the right conferred by subsection (4) is not to include a right to select a representative of a prescribed description,

(d) that right is to select only a representative located in a prescribed area or of a prescribed description,

(e) that right is to select not more than a prescribed number of representatives to act at any one time, and

(f) that right is not to include a right to select a representative in place of a representative previously selected.

(7) Regulations under subsection (6)(b) may prescribe circumstances in which an individual is to be taken to have selected a person to provide advice or assistance.

(8) Regulations may provide that in prescribed circumstances the Lord Chancellor is not required to make available representation for an individual by a prescribed representative.

(9) Provision made under subsection (8) does not prejudice any right of the individual to select another representative.

(10) The circumstances which may be prescribed under this section include that a determination has been made by a prescribed person.

28 Position of providers of services

(1) The fact that services provided for an individual are or could be provided under arrangements made for the purposes of this Part does not affect—

(a) the relationship between the individual and the person by whom the services are provided,

(b) any privilege arising out of that relationship, or

(c) any right which the individual may have to be indemnified by another person in respect of expenses incurred by the individual,

except to the extent that regulations provide otherwise.

(2) A person who provides services under arrangements made for the purposes of this Part must not take any payment in respect of the services apart from—

(a) payment made in accordance with the arrangements, and

(b) payment authorised by the Lord Chancellor to be taken.

(3) Regulations may provide that the withdrawal of a determination that an individual qualifies for prescribed services under this Part does not affect the right of any person who has provided such services to the individual under arrangements made for the purposes of this Part to remuneration for work done before the date of the withdrawal.

29 Code of conduct

(1) The Lord Chancellor must publish a code of conduct to be observed by the following persons when providing services to an individual under arrangements made for the purposes of this Part—
(a) civil servants, and
(b) employees of a body established and maintained by the Lord Chancellor.

(2) The code must include—
(a) duties to avoid discrimination,
(b) duties to protect the interests of the individuals for whom services are provided,
(c) duties to courts and tribunals,
(d) duties to avoid conflicts of interest,
(e) duties of confidentiality, and
(f) duties on persons who are members of a professional body to comply with the rules of the body.

(3) The Lord Chancellor must lay the code, and any revision of the code, before Parliament.

(4) The persons described in subsection (1)(a) and (b) are not subject to the direction of the Lord Chancellor when providing services to an individual under arrangements made for the purposes of this Part.

30 Position of other parties, courts and tribunals

(1) Except as expressly provided by regulations, any rights conferred by or under this Part on an individual for whom services are provided under this Part for the purposes of proceedings do not affect—
(a) the rights or liabilities of other parties to the proceedings, or
(b) the principles on which the discretion of a court or tribunal is normally exercised.

(2) Regulations may make provision about the procedure of a court or tribunal in relation to services made available under this Part.

(3) Regulations under subsection (2) may, in particular, authorise the exercise of the functions of a court or tribunal by—
(a) a member or officer of that court or tribunal, or
(b) another court or tribunal.

Supplementary

31 Legal aid for legal persons

Schedule 3 (legal aid for legal persons) has effect.

32 Foreign law

(1) The civil legal services described in Part 1 of Schedule 1 do not include services relating to any law other than the law of England and Wales, except—
   (a) where express provision to the contrary is made by or under Part 1 of Schedule 1;
   (b) where such law is relevant for determining any issue relating to the law of England and Wales;
   (c) in other circumstances specified by the Lord Chancellor by order.

(2) A determination by the Director or a court under section 13, 15 or 16 that an individual qualifies for advice, assistance or representation under this Part does not impose a duty on the Lord Chancellor to secure that services relating to any law other than the law of England and Wales are made available, except—
   (a) where such law is relevant for determining any issue relating to the law of England and Wales;
   (b) in other circumstances specified by the Lord Chancellor by order.

(3) The Lord Chancellor may not make an order under subsection (1) or (2) unless the Lord Chancellor considers—
   (a) that it is necessary to make the order because failure to do so would result in a breach of—
      (i) an individual's Convention rights (within the meaning of the Human Rights Act 1998), or
      (ii) any rights of an individual to the provision of legal services that are enforceable EU rights, or
   (b) that it is appropriate to make the order having regard to any risk that failure to do so would result in such a breach.

33 Restriction on disclosure of information about financial resources

(1) A person to whom information is disclosed under section 22 or this subsection may disclose the information to any person to whom its disclosure is necessary or expedient in connection with facilitating a determination in respect of an individual's financial resources that is required under section 21.

(2) A person to whom such information is disclosed must not—
   (a) disclose the information other than in accordance with subsection (1), or
   (b) use the information other than for the purpose of facilitating a determination described in subsection (1).

(3) Subsection (2) does not prevent—
   (a) the disclosure of information in accordance with an enactment or an order of a court,
   (b) the disclosure of information for the purposes of the investigation or prosecution of an offence (or suspected offence) under the law of

England and Wales or Northern Ireland or any other jurisdiction, except where regulations otherwise provide,

(c) the disclosure of information for the purposes of instituting, or otherwise for the purposes of, proceedings before a court, or

(d) the disclosure of information which has previously been lawfully disclosed to the public.

(4) A person who discloses or uses information in contravention of this section is guilty of an offence and liable—

(a) on conviction on indictment, to imprisonment for a term not exceeding 2 years or a fine (or both);

(b) on summary conviction—

(i) in England and Wales, to imprisonment for a term not exceeding 12 months or a fine not exceeding the statutory maximum (or both), and

(ii) in Northern Ireland, to imprisonment for a term not exceeding 6 months or a fine not exceeding the statutory maximum (or both).

(5) It is a defence for a person charged with an offence under this section to prove that the person reasonably believed that the disclosure or use was lawful.

(6) In this section "enactment" includes—

(a) an enactment contained in subordinate legislation (within the meaning of the Interpretation Act 1978), and

(b) an enactment contained in, or in an instrument made under, an Act or Measure of the National Assembly for Wales or Northern Ireland legislation.

(7) In relation to an offence under this section committed before the commencement of section 154(1) of the Criminal Justice Act 2003, the reference in subsection (4)(b)(i) to 12 months has effect as if it were a reference to 6 months.

34 Restriction on disclosure of other information

(1) This section applies to information that is provided—

(a) to the Lord Chancellor, the Director, a court, a tribunal or any other person on whom functions are imposed or conferred by or under this Part, and

(b) in connection with the case of an individual seeking or receiving services provided under arrangements made for the purposes of this Part.

(2) Such information must not be disclosed, subject to the exceptions in section 35.

(3) A person who discloses information in contravention of this section is guilty of an offence and liable on summary conviction to a fine not exceeding level 4 on the standard scale.

(4) It is a defence for a person charged with an offence under this section to prove that the person reasonably believed that the disclosure was lawful.

(5) Proceedings for an offence under this section may not be brought without the consent of the Director of Public Prosecutions.

(6) Nothing in this section applies to information if—
(a) it is provided to a person providing services under arrangements made for the purposes of this Part, and
(b) it is provided by or on behalf of an individual seeking or receiving the services.

(7) Nothing in this section applies to information to which section 33 applies.

35 Exceptions from restriction under section 34

(1) Section 34(2) does not prevent the disclosure of information—
(a) for the purpose of enabling or assisting the Lord Chancellor or the Secretary of State for Justice to carry out their functions (whether conferred or imposed by an Act or otherwise),
(b) for the purpose of enabling or assisting the Director to carry out functions imposed or conferred on the Director by or under this Part, or
(c) for the purpose of enabling or assisting a court, tribunal or other person on whom functions are imposed or conferred by or under this Part to carry out those functions.

(2) Section 34(2) does not prevent—
(a) the disclosure of information in accordance with the law of England and Wales or an order of a court,
(b) the disclosure of information for the purposes of the investigation or prosecution of an offence (or suspected offence) under the law of England and Wales or any other jurisdiction, except where regulations otherwise provide,
(c) the disclosure of information for the purposes of instituting, or otherwise for the purposes of, proceedings before a court,
(d) the disclosure of information which has previously been lawfully disclosed to the public, or
(e) the disclosure of information for the purpose of facilitating the proper performance by a tribunal of disciplinary functions.

(3) Section 34(2) does not prevent the disclosure of—
(a) information in the form of a summary or collection of information that is framed so that information relating to an individual cannot be ascertained from it, or
(b) information about the amount of any grant, loan or other payment made to a person by the Lord Chancellor under arrangements made for the purposes of this Part.

(4) Section 34(2) does not prevent the disclosure of information for any purpose—
(a) with the consent of the individual in connection with whose case it was provided, and
(b) if the information was provided other than by that individual, with the consent of the person who provided the information.

(5) Section 34(2) does not prevent the disclosure of information after the end of the restricted period if—
(a) the disclosure is by a person who is a public authority for the purposes of the Freedom of Information Act 2000 or who is acting on behalf of such a person, and

(b) the information is not held by the public authority on behalf of another person.

(6) The restricted period is the period of 100 years beginning with the end of the calendar year in which a record containing the information was first created by a person to whom the information was provided in connection with a case described in section 34(1)(b).

36 Misrepresentation

(1) This section applies where a person—

(a) intentionally fails to comply with a requirement imposed by or under this Part to provide documents or information, or

(b) in providing documents or information in accordance with such a requirement, makes a statement or representation knowing or believing it to be false.

(2) The person is guilty of an offence and liable on summary conviction to a fine not exceeding level 4 on the standard scale.

(3) Proceedings in respect of an offence under this section may (despite anything in the Magistrates' Courts Act 1980) be brought at any time within the period of 6 months beginning with the date on which evidence sufficient in the opinion of the prosecutor to justify a prosecution comes to the prosecutor's knowledge.

(4) Subsection (3) does not authorise the commencement of proceedings for an offence more than 2 years after the date on which the offence was committed.

(5) A county court is to have jurisdiction to hear and determine an action brought by the Lord Chancellor to recover loss sustained by reason of—

(a) the failure by a person to comply with a requirement imposed by or under this Part to provide documents or information, or

(b) a false statement or false representation made by a person in providing documents or information in accordance with such a requirement.

37 Status of Director and Lord Chancellor

(1) The Director is to carry out the functions of the office on behalf of the Crown.

(2) Service as the Director is service in the civil service of the State.

(3) The Lord Chancellor is to be treated as a corporation sole—

(a) for all purposes relating to the acquisition, holding, management and disposal of property and interests in property under this Part, and

(b) for all other purposes relating to the Lord Chancellor's functions in connection with legal aid and other functions under this Part.

(4) An instrument in connection with the acquisition, holding, management or disposal by the Lord Chancellor of property or an interest in property under this Part or for a purpose mentioned in subsection (3)(b) may be executed on the Lord Chancellor's behalf by a person authorised by the Lord Chancellor for that purpose.

(5) Any such instrument purporting to have been executed by the Lord Chancellor or on the Lord Chancellor's behalf is to be received in evidence and, unless the contrary is proved, to be treated as having been so executed.

38 Abolition of Legal Services Commission

(1) The Legal Services Commission ceases to exist.

(2) Schedule 4 (transfer of employees and property etc of Legal Services Commission) has effect.

(3) The Lord Chancellor must, as soon as practicable after subsection (1) comes into force—
   (a) prepare a report on how the Legal Services Commission has carried out its functions in the final period,
   (b) lay a copy of the report before Parliament, and
   (c) once it has been laid, publish the report.

(4) The Lord Chancellor must, as soon as practicable after subsection (1) comes into force—
   (a) prepare a statement of accounts for the Legal Services Commission for the final period, and
   (b) send a copy of the statement to the Comptroller and Auditor General.

(5) The Comptroller and Auditor General must—
   (a) examine, certify and report on the statement, and
   (b) arrange for a copy of the statement and the report to be laid before Parliament.

(6) In this section—
   "the final period" means the period—
      (a) beginning with end of the last financial year for which the Legal Services Commission produced a report and accounts in accordance with paragraphs 14 and 16 of Schedule 1 to the Access to Justice Act 1999, and
      (b) ending immediately before the day on which subsection (1) comes into force;
   "financial year" means a period of 12 months ending with 31 March.

39 Consequential and transitional provision

(1) Schedule 5 (legal aid: consequential amendments) has effect.

(2) Where the Lord Chancellor considers it appropriate as part of the arrangements for effecting the transition from the operation of Part 1 of the Access to Justice Act 1999 to the operation of this Part of this Act, the Lord Chancellor may by regulations make provision requiring or enabling prescribed 1999 Act services to be made available to individuals or other persons under this Part for a period specified or described in the regulations.

(3) In subsection (2) "1999 Act services" means services which, immediately before the day on which the first regulations under that subsection come into force, may be funded under Part 1 of the Access to Justice Act 1999.

(4) Where the Lord Chancellor considers it appropriate for the Legal Services Commission to cease to exist before this Part is brought fully into force, the Lord Chancellor may by regulations make provision for the purpose of requiring or enabling the Lord Chancellor and the Director, or persons authorised by the Lord Chancellor or the Director, to carry out LSC functions for a period specified or described in the regulations.

(5) In subsection (4) "LSC functions" means functions conferred or imposed on the Legal Services Commission by or under Part 1 of the Access to Justice Act 1999.

(6) Regulations under subsection (4) may not include provision requiring or enabling the Lord Chancellor—

(a) to take decisions about whether services should be funded in individual cases, or

(b) to give directions or guidance about the carrying out of functions under Part 1 of the Access to Justice Act 1999 in relation to individual cases.

(7) Regulations under this section—

(a) may amend, repeal, revoke or otherwise modify Part 1 of the Access to Justice Act 1999, this Part of this Act, any other Act and any instrument made under an Act;

(b) may describe a period, in particular, by reference to the coming into force of a provision of this Part of this Act or the repeal of a provision of Part 1 of the Access to Justice Act 1999.

(8) The requirement for regulations under this section to specify or describe a period does not prevent the making of further regulations under this section.

(9) The powers to make regulations under this section are without prejudice to the generality of the powers to make regulations under the other provisions of this Part and under section 149.

(10) In this section "Act" includes an Act or Measure of the National Assembly for Wales.

40 Northern Ireland: information about financial resources

Schedule 6 (Northern Ireland: information about financial resources) has effect.

41 Orders, regulations and directions

(1) Orders, regulations and directions under this Part—

(a) may make different provision for different cases, circumstances or areas,

(b) may make provision generally or only for specified cases, circumstances or areas, and

(c) may make provision having effect for a period specified or described in the order, regulations or direction.

(2) They may, in particular, make provision by reference to—

(a) services provided for the purposes of proceedings before a particular court, tribunal or other person,

(b) services provided for a particular class of individual, or

(c) services provided for individuals selected by reference to particular criteria or on a sampling basis.

(3) Orders and regulations under this Part—

(a) may provide for a person to exercise a discretion in dealing with any matter,

(b) may make provision by reference to a document produced by any person, and

(c) may make consequential, supplementary, incidental, transitional or saving provision.

(4) Orders and regulations under this Part are to be made by statutory instrument.

(5) A statutory instrument containing an order or regulations under this Part is subject to annulment in pursuance of a resolution of either House of Parliament, unless it is an instrument described in subsection (6) or (9).

(6) A statutory instrument containing an order or regulations listed in subsection (7) (whether alone or with other provision) may not be made unless a draft of the instrument has been laid before, and approved by a resolution of, each House of Parliament.

(7) Those orders and regulations are—

(a) orders under section 9;

(b) regulations under section 11(1)(b), other than regulations in respect of which the Lord Chancellor has made an urgency statement;

(c) regulations under section 13(8);

(d) orders under section 17(3);

(e) regulations under section 18(7);

(f) regulations under section 19;

(g) regulations under section 20;

(h) regulations under section 22;

(i) regulations under section 26(3) or (6)(b) or (d);

(j) regulations under section 27(6)(a) or (8);

(k) regulations under section 39 that amend or repeal a provision of an Act (as defined in that section), other than regulations revoking such regulations or inserting or repealing provision previously repealed or inserted by such regulations;

(l) regulations under paragraph 5(9) of Schedule 3;

(m) regulations under paragraph 11 of Schedule 4 that amend or repeal a provision of an Act (as defined in that Schedule).

(8) An urgency statement is a statement that the Lord Chancellor considers that it is desirable for the regulations to come into force without delay for the reasons given in the statement.

(9) Where a statutory instrument contains regulations under section 11(1)(b) in respect of which the Lord Chancellor has made an urgency statement—

(a) the regulations may not come into force before the instrument and the statement are laid before Parliament, and

(b) the regulations cease to have effect at the end of the period of 120 days beginning with the day on which the instrument is made unless the instrument is approved by a resolution of each House of Parliament before the end of that period.

(10) In reckoning the period of 120 days no account is to be taken of any time—

(a) during which Parliament is dissolved or prorogued, or

(b) during which both Houses are adjourned for more than 4 days.

(11) Where regulations cease to have effect under subsection (9) that does not affect—

(a) anything previously done in reliance on the regulations, or

(b) the making of further regulations.

42 Interpretation

(1) In this Part—

"advocacy" means the exercise of a right of audience before a court, tribunal or other person;

"civil legal services" has the meaning given in section 8;

"civil servant" means an individual employed in the civil service of the State;

"criminal proceedings" has the meaning given in section 14;

"the Director" means the Director of Legal Aid Casework;

"functions" includes powers and duties;

"legal aid" has the meaning given in section 1;

"legal proceedings" means proceedings before a court or tribunal;

"legal services" has the meaning given in section 8;

"modify", in relation to an Act or instrument, includes amend, repeal or revoke and related terms are to be interpreted accordingly;

"prescribed" means prescribed by regulations (except in Schedule 6) and related terms are to be interpreted accordingly;

"regulations" means regulations made by the Lord Chancellor (except in Schedule 6);

"remuneration" includes disbursements;

"representation" means representation for the purposes of proceedings and includes—

(a) the advice and assistance which is usually given by a representative in the steps preliminary or incidental to proceedings, and

(b) subject to any time limits which may be prescribed, advice and assistance as to any appeal.

(2) In this Part references to proceedings are to be interpreted in accordance with section 20(3).

43 Crown application

This Part binds the Crown.

PART 2

LITIGATION FUNDING AND COSTS

Payments for legal services in civil cases

44 Conditional fee agreements: success fees

(1) In section 58 of the Courts and Legal Services Act 1990 (conditional fee agreements), in subsection (2)—

(a) omit "and" after paragraph (a), and

(b) after paragraph (b) insert "and

(c) references to a success fee, in relation to a conditional fee agreement, are to the amount of the increase."

(2) After subsection (4) of that section insert—

"(4A) The additional conditions are applicable to a conditional fee agreement which—

(a) provides for a success fee, and

(b) relates to proceedings of a description specified by order made by the Lord Chancellor for the purposes of this subsection.

(4B) The additional conditions are that—

(a) the agreement must provide that the success fee is subject to a maximum limit,

(b) the maximum limit must be expressed as a percentage of the descriptions of damages awarded in the proceedings that are specified in the agreement,

(c) that percentage must not exceed the percentage specified by order made by the Lord Chancellor in relation to the proceedings or calculated in a manner so specified, and

(d) those descriptions of damages may only include descriptions of damages specified by order made by the Lord Chancellor in relation to the proceedings."

(3) In section 58A of that Act (conditional fee agreements: supplementary), in subsection (5) after "section 58(4)" insert ", (4A) or (4B)".

(4) For subsection (6) of that section substitute—

"(6) A costs order made in proceedings may not include provision requiring the payment by one party of all or part of a success fee payable by another party under a conditional fee agreement."

(5) In section 120(4) of that Act (regulations and orders subject to parliamentary approval) after "58(4)," insert "(4A) or (4B),".

(6) The amendment made by subsection (4) does not prevent a costs order including provision in relation to a success fee payable by a person ("P") under a conditional fee agreement entered into before the day on which that subsection comes into force ("the commencement day") if—

(a) the agreement was entered into specifically for the purposes of the provision to P of advocacy or litigation services in connection with the matter that is the subject of the proceedings in which the costs order is made, or

(b) advocacy or litigation services were provided to P under the agreement in connection with that matter before the commencement day.

45 Damages-based agreements

(1) Section 58AA of the Courts and Legal Services Act 1990 (damages-based agreements) is amended as follows.

(2) In subsection (1) omit "relates to an employment matter and".

(3) In subsection (2)—

(a) after "But" insert "(subject to subsection (9))", and

(b) omit "relates to an employment matter and".

(4) Omit subsection (3)(b).

(5) After subsection (4)(a) insert—

"(aa) must not relate to proceedings which by virtue of section 58A(1) and (2) cannot be the subject of an enforceable conditional fee agreement or to proceedings of a description prescribed by the Lord Chancellor;".

(6) In subsection (4)(b), at the beginning insert "if regulations so provide,".

(7) In subsection (4)(d) for "has provided prescribed information" substitute "has complied with such requirements (if any) as may be prescribed as to the provision of information".

(8) After subsection (6) insert—

"(6A) Rules of court may make provision with respect to the assessment of costs in proceedings where a party in whose favour a costs order is made has entered into a damages-based agreement in connection with the proceedings."

(9) After subsection (7) insert—

"(7A) In this section (and in the definitions of "advocacy services" and "litigation services" as they apply for the purposes of this section) "proceedings" includes any sort of proceedings for resolving disputes (and not just proceedings in a court), whether commenced or contemplated."

(10) After subsection (8) insert—

"(9) Where section 57 of the Solicitors Act 1974 (non-contentious business agreements between solicitor and client) applies to a damages-based agreement other than one relating to an employment matter, subsections (1) and (2) of this section do not make it unenforceable.

(10) For the purposes of subsection (9) a damages-based agreement relates to an employment matter if the matter in relation to which the services are provided is a matter that is, or could become, the subject of proceedings before an employment tribunal."

(11) In the heading of that section omit "relating to employment matters".

(12) In section 120(4) of that Act (regulations and orders subject to parliamentary approval) for "58AA" substitute "58AA(4)".

(13) The amendments made by subsections (1) to (11) do not apply in relation to an agreement entered into before this section comes into force.

46 Recovery of insurance premiums by way of costs

(1) In the Courts and Legal Services Act 1990, after section 58B insert—

"58C Recovery of insurance premiums by way of costs

(1) A costs order made in favour of a party to proceedings who has taken out a costs insurance policy may not include provision requiring the payment of an amount in respect of all or part of the premium of the policy, unless such provision is permitted by regulations under subsection (2).

(2) The Lord Chancellor may by regulations provide that a costs order may include provision requiring the payment of such an amount where—

(a) the order is made in favour of a party to clinical negligence proceedings of a prescribed description,

(b) the party has taken out a costs insurance policy insuring against the risk of incurring a liability to pay for one or more expert reports in respect of clinical negligence in connection with the proceedings (or against that risk and other risks),

(c) the policy is of a prescribed description,

(d) the policy states how much of the premium relates to the liability to pay for an expert report or reports in respect of clinical negligence ("the relevant part of the premium"), and

(e) the amount is to be paid in respect of the relevant part of the premium.

(3) Regulations under subsection (2) may include provision about the amount that may be required to be paid by the costs order, including provision that the amount must not exceed a prescribed maximum amount.

(4) The regulations may prescribe a maximum amount, in particular, by specifying—

(a) a percentage of the relevant part of the premium;

(b) an amount calculated in a prescribed manner.

(5) In this section—

"clinical negligence" means breach of a duty of care or trespass to the person committed in the course of the provision of clinical or medical services (including dental or nursing services);

"clinical negligence proceedings" means proceedings which include a claim for damages in respect of clinical negligence;

"costs insurance policy", in relation to a party to proceedings, means a policy insuring against the risk of the party incurring a liability in those proceedings;

"expert report" means a report by a person qualified to give expert advice on all or most of the matters that are the subject of the report;

"proceedings" includes any sort of proceedings for resolving disputes (and not just proceedings in court), whether commenced or contemplated."

(2) In the Access to Justice Act 1999, omit section 29 (recovery of insurance premiums by way of costs).

(3) The amendments made by this section do not apply in relation to a costs order made in favour of a party to proceedings who took out a costs insurance policy in relation to the proceedings before the day on which this section comes into force.

47 Recovery where body undertakes to meet costs liabilities

(1) In the Access to Justice Act 1999, omit section 30 (recovery where body undertakes to meet costs liabilities).

(2) The repeal made by subsection (1) does not apply in relation to a costs order made in favour of a person to whom a body gave an undertaking before the day on which this section comes into force if the undertaking was given specifically in respect of the costs of other parties to proceedings relating to the matter which is the subject of the proceedings in which the costs order is made.

48 Sections 44 and 46 and diffuse mesothelioma proceedings

(1) Sections 44 and 46 may not be brought into force in relation to proceedings relating to a claim for damages in respect of diffuse mesothelioma until the Lord Chancellor has—

(a) carried out a review of the likely effect of those sections in relation to such proceedings, and

(b) published a report of the conclusions of the review.

(2) In this section "diffuse mesothelioma" has the same meaning as in the Pneumoconiosis etc (Workers' Compensation) Act 1979.

49 Divorce etc proceedings: orders for payment in respect of legal services

(1) In section 22 of the Matrimonial Causes Act 1973 (maintenance pending suit)—

(a) number the existing provision subsection (1), and

(b) after that subsection insert—

"(2) An order under this section may not require a party to a marriage to pay to the other party any amount in respect of legal services for the purposes of the proceedings.

(3) In subsection (2) "legal services" has the same meaning as in section 22ZA."

(2) After that section insert—

"22ZA Orders for payment in respect of legal services

(1) In proceedings for divorce, nullity of marriage or judicial separation, the court may make an order or orders requiring one party to the marriage to pay to the other ("the applicant") an amount for the purpose of enabling the applicant to obtain legal services for the purposes of the proceedings.

(2) The court may also make such an order or orders in proceedings under this Part for financial relief in connection with proceedings for divorce, nullity of marriage or judicial separation.

(3) The court must not make an order under this section unless it is satisfied that, without the amount, the applicant would not reasonably be able to obtain appropriate legal services for the purposes of the proceedings or any part of the proceedings.

(4) For the purposes of subsection (3), the court must be satisfied, in particular, that—

(a) the applicant is not reasonably able to secure a loan to pay for the services, and

(b) the applicant is unlikely to be able to obtain the services by granting a charge over any assets recovered in the proceedings.

(5) An order under this section may be made for the purpose of enabling the applicant to obtain legal services of a specified description, including legal services provided in a specified period or for the purposes of a specified part of the proceedings.

(6) An order under this section may—

(a) provide for the payment of all or part of the amount by instalments of specified amounts, and

(b) require the instalments to be secured to the satisfaction of the court.

(7) An order under this section may direct that payment of all or part of the amount is to be deferred.

(8) The court may at any time in the proceedings vary an order made under this section if it considers that there has been a material change of circumstances since the order was made.

(9) For the purposes of the assessment of costs in the proceedings, the applicant's costs are to be treated as reduced by any amount paid to the applicant pursuant to an order under this section for the purposes of those proceedings.

(10) In this section "legal services", in relation to proceedings, means the following types of services—

(a) providing advice as to how the law applies in the particular circumstances,

(b) providing advice and assistance in relation to the proceedings,

(c) providing other advice and assistance in relation to the settlement or other resolution of the dispute that is the subject of the proceedings, and

(d) providing advice and assistance in relation to the enforcement of decisions in the proceedings or as part of the settlement or resolution of the dispute,

and they include, in particular, advice and assistance in the form of representation and any form of dispute resolution, including mediation.

(11) In subsections (5) and (6) "specified" means specified in the order concerned."

50 Divorce etc proceedings: matters to be considered by court making legal services order

After section 22ZA of the Matrimonial Causes Act 1973 insert—

"22ZB Matters to which court is to have regard in deciding how to exercise power under section 22ZA

(1) When considering whether to make or vary an order under section 22ZA, the court must have regard to—

(a) the income, earning capacity, property and other financial resources which each of the applicant and the paying party has or is likely to have in the foreseeable future,

(b) the financial needs, obligations and responsibilities which each of the applicant and the paying party has or is likely to have in the foreseeable future,

(c) the subject matter of the proceedings, including the matters in issue in them,

(d) whether the paying party is legally represented in the proceedings,

(e) any steps taken by the applicant to avoid all or part of the proceedings, whether by proposing or considering mediation or otherwise,

(f) the applicant's conduct in relation to the proceedings,

(g) any amount owed by the applicant to the paying party in respect of costs in the proceedings or other proceedings to which both the applicant and the paying party are or were party, and

(h) the effect of the order or variation on the paying party.

(2) In subsection (1)(a) "earning capacity", in relation to the applicant or the paying party, includes any increase in earning capacity which, in the opinion of the court, it would be reasonable to expect the applicant or the paying party to take steps to acquire.

(3) For the purposes of subsection (1)(h), the court must have regard, in particular, to whether the making or variation of the order is likely to—

(a) cause undue hardship to the paying party, or

(b) prevent the paying party from obtaining legal services for the purposes of the proceedings.

(4) The Lord Chancellor may by order amend this section by adding to, omitting or varying the matters mentioned in subsections (1) to (3).

(5) An order under subsection (4) must be made by statutory instrument.

(6) A statutory instrument containing an order under subsection (4) may not be made unless a draft of the instrument has been laid before, and approved by a resolution of, each House of Parliament.

(7) In this section "legal services" has the same meaning as in section 22ZA."

51 Divorce etc proceedings: orders for sale of property

In section 24A(1) of the Matrimonial Causes Act 1973 (orders for sale of property), after "makes" insert "an order under section 22ZA or makes".

52 Dissolution etc proceedings: orders for payment in respect of legal services

(1) Part 8 of Schedule 5 to the Civil Partnership Act 2004 (maintenance pending outcome of dissolution etc proceedings) is amended as follows.

(2) In the heading of that Part after "Maintenance" insert "and other payments".

(3) Before paragraph 38 insert—

"*Maintenance orders*".

(4) In that paragraph—

(a) number the existing provision sub-paragraph (1), and

(b) after that sub-paragraph insert—

"(2) An order under this paragraph may not require one civil partner to pay to the other any amount in respect of legal services for the purposes of the proceedings.

(3) In sub-paragraph (2) "legal services" has the same meaning as in paragraph 38A."

(5) After that paragraph insert—

"*Orders in respect of legal services*

38A (1) In proceedings for a dissolution, nullity or separation order, the court may make an order or orders requiring one civil partner to pay to the other ("the applicant") an amount for the purpose of enabling the applicant to obtain legal services for the purposes of the proceedings.

(2) The court may also make such an order or orders in proceedings under this Schedule for financial relief in connection with proceedings for a dissolution, nullity or separation order.

(3) The court must not make an order under this paragraph unless it is satisfied that, without the amount, the applicant would not reasonably be able to obtain appropriate legal services for the purposes of the proceedings or any part of the proceedings.

(4) For the purposes of sub-paragraph (3), the court must be satisfied, in particular, that—

(a) the applicant is not reasonably able to secure a loan to pay for the services, and

(b) the applicant is unlikely to be able to obtain the services by granting a charge over any assets recovered in the proceedings.

(5) An order under this paragraph may be made for the purpose of enabling the applicant to obtain legal services of a specified description, including legal services provided in a specified period or for the purposes of a specified part of the proceedings.

(6) An order under this paragraph may—

(a) provide for the payment of all or part of the amount by instalments of specified amounts, and

(b) require the instalments to be secured to the satisfaction of the court.

(7) An order under this paragraph may direct that payment of all or part of the amount is to be deferred.

(8) The court may at any time in the proceedings vary an order made under this paragraph if it considers that there has been a material change of circumstances since the order was made.

(9) For the purposes of the assessment of costs in the proceedings, the applicant's costs are to be treated as reduced by any amount paid to the applicant pursuant to an order under this section for the purposes of those proceedings.

(10) In this paragraph "legal services", in relation to proceedings, means the following types of services—

(a) providing advice as to how the law applies in the particular circumstances,

(b) providing advice and assistance in relation to the proceedings,

(c) providing other advice and assistance in relation to the settlement or other resolution of the dispute that is the subject of the proceedings, and

(d) providing advice and assistance in relation to the enforcement of decisions in the proceedings or as part of the settlement or resolution of the dispute,

and they include, in particular, advice and assistance in the form of representation and any form of dispute resolution, including mediation.

(11) In sub-paragraphs (5) and (6) "specified" means specified in the order concerned."

53 Dissolution etc proceedings: matters to be considered by court making legal services order

After paragraph 38A of Schedule 5 to the Civil Partnership Act 2004 insert—

"38B(1) When considering whether to make or vary an order under paragraph 38A, the court must have regard to—

(a) the income, earning capacity, property and other financial resources which each of the applicant and the paying party has or is likely to have in the foreseeable future,

(b) the financial needs, obligations and responsibilities which each of the applicant and the paying party has or is likely to have in the foreseeable future,

(c) the subject matter of the proceedings, including the matters in issue in them,

(d) whether the paying party is legally represented in the proceedings,

(e) any steps taken by the applicant to avoid all or part of the proceedings, whether by proposing or considering mediation or otherwise,

(f) the applicant's conduct in relation to the proceedings,

(g) any amount owed by the applicant to the paying party in respect of costs in the proceedings or other proceedings to which both the applicant and the paying party are or were party, and

(h) the effect of the order or variation on the paying party.

(2) In sub-paragraph (1)(a) "earning capacity", in relation to the applicant or the paying party, includes any increase in earning capacity which, in the opinion of the court, it would be reasonable to expect the applicant or the paying party to take steps to acquire.

(3) For the purposes of sub-paragraph (1)(h), the court must have regard, in particular, to whether the making or variation of the order is likely to—

(a) cause undue hardship to the paying party, or

(b) prevent the paying party from obtaining legal services for the purposes of the proceedings.

(4) The Lord Chancellor may by order amend this paragraph by adding to, omitting or varying the matters mentioned in sub-paragraphs (1) to (3).

(5) An order under sub-paragraph (4) must be made by statutory instrument.

(6) A statutory instrument containing an order under sub-paragraph (4) may not be made unless a draft of the instrument has been laid before, and approved by a resolution of, each House of Parliament.

(7) In this paragraph "legal services" has the same meaning as in paragraph 38A."

54 Dissolution etc proceedings: orders for sale of property

(1) Paragraph 10(1)(a) of Schedule 5 to the Civil Partnership Act 2004 (sale of property orders) is amended as follows.

(2) Omit the "or" at the end of sub-paragraph (i).

(3) After sub-paragraph (ii) insert—

"(iii) an order under paragraph 38A for a payment in respect of legal services, or".

Offers to settle

55 Payment of additional amount to successful claimant

(1) Rules of court may make provision for a court to order a defendant in civil proceedings to pay an additional amount to a claimant in those proceedings where—

(a) the claim is a claim for (and only for) an amount of money,

(b) judgment is given in favour of the claimant,

(c) the judgment in respect of the claim is at least as advantageous as an offer to settle the claim which the claimant made in accordance with rules of court and has not withdrawn in accordance with those rules, and

(d) any prescribed conditions are satisfied.

(2) Rules made under subsection (1) may include provision as to the assessment of whether a judgment is at least as advantageous as an offer to settle.

(3) In subsection (1) "additional amount" means an amount not exceeding a prescribed percentage of the amount awarded to the claimant by the court (excluding any amount awarded in respect of the claimant's costs).

(4) The Lord Chancellor may by order provide that rules of court may make provision for a court to order a defendant in civil proceedings to pay an amount calculated in a prescribed manner to a claimant in those proceedings where—

(a) the claim is or includes a non-monetary claim,

(b) judgment is given in favour of the claimant,

(c) the judgment in respect of the claim is at least as advantageous as an offer to settle the claim which the claimant made in accordance with rules of court and has not withdrawn in accordance with those rules, and

(d) any prescribed conditions are satisfied.

(5) An order under subsection (4) must provide for the amount to be calculated by reference to one or more of the following—

(a) any costs ordered by the court to be paid to the claimant by the defendant in the proceedings;

(b) any amount awarded to the claimant by the court in respect of so much of the claim as is for an amount of money (excluding any amount awarded in respect of the claimant's costs);

(c) the value of any non-monetary benefit awarded to the claimant.

(6) An order under subsection (4)—

(a) must provide that rules made under the order may include provision as to the assessment of whether a judgment is at least as advantageous as an offer to settle, and

(b) may provide that such rules may make provision as to the calculation of the value of a non-monetary benefit awarded to a claimant.

(7) Conditions prescribed under subsection (1)(d) or (4)(d) may, in particular, include conditions relating to—

(a) the nature of the claim;

(b) the amount of money awarded to the claimant;

(c) the value of the non-monetary benefit awarded to the claimant.

(8) Orders under this section are to be made by the Lord Chancellor by statutory instrument.

(9) A statutory instrument containing an order under this section is subject to annulment in pursuance of a resolution of either House of Parliament.

(10) Rules of court and orders made under this section may make different provision in relation to different cases.

(11) In this section—

"civil proceedings" means proceedings to which rules of court made under the Civil Procedure Act 1997 apply;

"non-monetary claim" means a claim for a benefit other than an amount of money;

"prescribed" means prescribed by order made by the Lord Chancellor.

Referral fees

56 Rules against referral fees

(1) A regulated person is in breach of this section if—
  (a) the regulated person refers prescribed legal business to another person and is paid or has been paid for the referral, or
  (b) prescribed legal business is referred to the regulated person, and the regulated person pays or has paid for the referral.

(2) A regulated person is also in breach of this section if in providing legal services in the course of prescribed legal business the regulated person—
  (a) arranges for another person to provide services to the client, and
  (b) is paid or has been paid for making the arrangement.

(3) Section 59 defines "regulated person".

(4) "Prescribed legal business" means business that involves the provision of legal services to a client, where—
  (a) the legal services relate to a claim or potential claim for damages for personal injury or death,
  (b) the legal services relate to any other claim or potential claim for damages arising out of circumstances involving personal injury or death, or
  (c) the business is of a description specified in regulations made by the Lord Chancellor.

(5) There is a referral of prescribed legal business if—
  (a) a person provides information to another,
  (b) it is information that a provider of legal services would need to make an offer to the client to provide relevant services, and
  (c) the person providing the information is not the client;

and "relevant services" means any of the legal services that the business involves.

(6) "Legal services" means services provided by a person which consist of or include legal activities (within the meaning of the Legal Services Act 2007) carried on by or on behalf of that person; and a provider of legal services is a person authorised to carry on a reserved legal activity within the meaning of that Act.

(7) "Client"—
  (a) where subsection (4)(a) applies, means the person who makes or would make the claim;
  (b) where subsection (4)(c) applies, has the meaning given by the regulations.

(8) Payment includes any form of consideration whether any benefit is received by the regulated person or by a third party (but does not include the provision of hospitality that is reasonable in the circumstances).

57 Effect of rules against referral fees

(1) The relevant regulator must ensure that it has appropriate arrangements for monitoring and enforcing the restrictions imposed on regulated persons by section 56.

(2) A regulator may make rules for the purposes of subsection (1).

(3) The rules may in particular provide for the relevant regulator to exercise in relation to anything done in breach of that section any powers (subject to subsections (5) and (6)) that the regulator would have in relation to anything done by the regulated person in breach of another restriction.

(4) Where the relevant regulator is the Financial Services Authority, section 58 applies instead of subsections (1) to (3) (and (7) to (9)).

(5) A breach of section 56—
 (a) does not make a person guilty of an offence, and
 (b) does not give rise to a right of action for breach of statutory duty.

(6) A breach of section 56 does not make anything void or unenforceable, but a contract to make or pay for a referral or arrangement in breach of that section is unenforceable.

(7) Subsection (8) applies in a case where—
 (a) a referral of prescribed legal business has been made by or to a regulated person, or
 (b) a regulated person has made an arrangement as mentioned in section 56(2)(a),

and it appears to the regulator that a payment made to or by the regulated person may be a payment for the referral or for making the arrangement (a "referral fee").

(8) Rules under subsection (2) may provide for the payment to be treated as a referral fee unless the regulated person shows that the payment was made—
 (a) as consideration for the provision of services, or
 (b) for another reason,

and not as a referral fee.

(9) For the purposes of provision made by virtue of subsection (8) a payment that would otherwise be regarded as consideration for the provision of services of any description may be treated as a referral fee if it exceeds the amount specified in relation to services of that description in regulations made by the Lord Chancellor.

58 Regulation by FSA

(1) The Treasury may make regulations to enable the Financial Services Authority, where it is the relevant regulator, to take action for monitoring and enforcing compliance with the restrictions imposed on regulated persons by section 56.

(2) The regulations may apply, or make provision corresponding to, any of the provisions of the Financial Services and Markets Act 2000 with or without modification.

(3) Those provisions include in particular—

(a) provisions as to investigations, including powers of entry and search and criminal offences;

(b) provisions for the grant of an injunction in relation to a contravention or anticipated contravention;

(c) provisions giving Ministers or the Financial Services Authority powers to make subordinate legislation;

(d) provisions for the Financial Services Authority to charge fees.

(4) The regulations may make provision corresponding to the provision that may be made by virtue of section 57(7) to (9) (but as if the reference to the Lord Chancellor were a reference to the Treasury).

(5) The power to make regulations under this section is subject to section 57(5) and (6).

59 Regulators and regulated persons

(1) In relation to a referral of business within section 56(4)(a)—

(a) a regulator is any person listed in column 1 below;

(b) a regulated person is any person listed in column 2;

(c) a regulator in column 1 is the relevant regulator in relation to the corresponding person in column 2.

1. Regulator	*2. Regulated person*
the Financial Services Authority	an authorised person (within the meaning of the Financial Services and Markets Act 2000) of a description specified in regulations made by the Treasury
the Claims Management Regulator	a person authorised by the Regulator under section 5(1)(a) of the Compensation Act 2006 to provide regulated claims management services
the General Council of the Bar	a person authorised by the Council to carry on a reserved legal activity within the meaning of the Legal Services Act 2007
the Law Society	a person authorised by the Society to carry on a reserved legal activity within the meaning of the Legal Services Act 2007
a regulatory body specified for the purposes of this subsection in regulations made by the Lord Chancellor	a person of a description specified in the regulations in relation to the body

(2) In relation to a referral of prescribed legal business of any other kind—

(a) a regulator is any person listed in column 1 below and specified in relation to business of that kind in regulations made by the Lord Chancellor;

(b) a regulated person is any person specified in accordance with column 2 in relation to business of that kind;

(c) a person specified under paragraph (a) in relation to business of that kind is the relevant regulator in relation to a person specified in accordance with the corresponding entry in column 2 in relation to business of that kind.

1. Regulator	*2. Regulated person*
the Financial Services Authority	an authorised person (within the meaning of the Financial Services and Markets Act 2000) of a description specified in regulations made by the Treasury
the Claims Management Regulator	a person who is authorised by the Regulator under section 5(1)(a) of the Compensation Act 2006 to provide regulated claims management services and is of a description specified in regulations made by the Lord Chancellor
an approved regulator for the purposes of Part 3 of the Legal Services Act 2007 (approved legal activities);	a person who is authorised by the regulator to carry on a reserved legal activity and is of a description specified in regulations made by the Lord Chancellor
a licensing authority for the purposes of Part 5 of that Act (alternative business structures)	a person who is licensed by the authority to carry on a reserved legal activity and is of a description specified in regulations made by the Lord Chancellor

60 Referral fees: regulations

(1) This section applies to any regulations under sections 56 to 59.

(2) The regulations are to be made by statutory instrument.

(3) The power to make the regulations includes power to make consequential, supplementary, incidental, transitional, transitory or saving provision.

(4) A statutory instrument containing the regulations may not be made unless a draft of the instrument has been laid before, and approved by a resolution of, each House of Parliament.

Pro bono representation

61 Payments in respect of pro bono representation before the Supreme Court

(1) In section 194 of the Legal Services Act 2007 (power for certain courts to order losing party to make payment to charity where other party is represented pro bono) in subsection (10) for the definition of "civil court" substitute—

""civil court" means—

(a) the Supreme Court when it is dealing with a relevant civil appeal,

(b) the civil division of the Court of Appeal,

(c) the High Court, or

(d) any county court;

"relevant civil appeal" means an appeal to the Supreme Court—

(a) from the High Court in England and Wales under Part 2 of the Administration of Justice Act 1969,

(b) from the Court of Appeal under section 40(2) of the Constitutional Reform Act 2005, or

(c) under section 13 of the Administration of Justice Act 1960 (appeal in cases of contempt of court) other than an appeal from an order or decision made in the exercise of jurisdiction to punish for criminal contempt of court;".

(2) This section applies in relation to appeals to the Supreme Court only where the decision, order or judgment that is the subject of the appeal is made or given on or after the day on which this section comes into force.

Costs in criminal cases

62 Costs in criminal cases

(1) Schedule 7 (costs in criminal cases) has effect.

(2) Schedule 8 (costs in criminal cases: service courts) has effect.

PART 3

SENTENCING AND PUNISHMENT OF OFFENDERS

CHAPTER 1

SENTENCING

General

63 Duty to consider compensation order

(1) In section 130 of the Powers of Criminal Courts (Sentencing) Act 2000 (compensation orders against convicted persons), after subsection (2) insert—

"(2A) A court must consider making a compensation order in any case where this section empowers it to do so."

(2) In section 175 of the Armed Forces Act 2006 (service compensation orders), after subsection (7) insert—

"(7A) The court must consider making a service compensation order in any case where it has power to do so."

64 Duty to give reasons for and to explain effect of sentence

(1) The Criminal Justice Act 2003 is amended as follows.

(2) For section 174 substitute—

"174 Duty to give reasons for and to explain effect of sentence

(1) A court passing sentence on an offender has the duties in subsections (2) and (3).

(2) The court must state in open court, in ordinary language and in general terms, the court's reasons for deciding on the sentence.

(3) The court must explain to the offender in ordinary language—

(a) the effect of the sentence,

(b) the effects of non-compliance with any order that the offender is required to comply with and that forms part of the sentence,

(c) any power of the court to vary or review any order that forms part of the sentence, and

(d) the effects of failure to pay a fine, if the sentence consists of or includes a fine.

(4) Criminal Procedure Rules may—

(a) prescribe cases in which either duty does not apply, and

(b) make provision about how an explanation under subsection (3) is to be given.

(5) Subsections (6) to (8) are particular duties of the court in complying with the duty in subsection (2).

(6) The court must identify any definitive sentencing guidelines relevant to the offender's case and—

(a) explain how the court discharged any duty imposed on it by section 125 of the Coroners and Justice Act 2009 (duty to follow guidelines unless satisfied it would be contrary to the interests of justice to do so);

(b) where the court was satisfied it would be contrary to the interests of justice to follow the guidelines, state why.

(7) Where, as a result of taking into account any matter referred to in section 144(1) (guilty pleas), the court imposes a punishment on the offender which is less severe than the punishment it would otherwise have imposed, the court must state that fact.

(8) Where the offender is under 18 and the court imposes a sentence that may only be imposed in the offender's case if the court is of the opinion mentioned in—

(a) section 1(4)(a) to (c) of the Criminal Justice and Immigration Act 2008 and section 148(1) of this Act (youth rehabilitation order with intensive supervision and surveillance or with fostering), or

(b) section 152(2) of this Act (discretionary custodial sentence),

the court must state why it is of that opinion.

(9) In this section "definitive sentencing guidelines" means sentencing guidelines issued by the Sentencing Council for England and Wales under section 120 of the Coroners and Justice Act 2009 as definitive guidelines, as revised by any subsequent guidelines so issued."

(3) In section 270 (duty to give reasons)—

(a) for subsection (1) substitute—

"(1) Subsection (2) applies where a court makes an order under section 269(2) or (4).", and

(b) in subsection (2) for "In stating its reasons" substitute "In complying with the duty under section 174(2) to state its reasons for deciding on the order made,".

(4) In the Armed Forces Act 2006—

(a) in section 252 (duty to give reasons and explain sentence), omit subsection (2);

(b) in section 253 (duties in complying with section 252), omit subsections (1)(a), (c) and (d) and (2)(b) and (d) to (h).

(5) In consequence of the amendments made by this section omit—

(a) paragraph 9(6) of Schedule 1 to the Violent Crime Reduction Act 2006;

(b) paragraph 80 of Schedule 4 to the Criminal Justice and Immigration Act 2008;

(c) paragraph 24 of Schedule 25 to that Act;

(d) paragraph 84 of Schedule 21 to the Coroners and Justice Act 2009.

65 Sentencing where there is aggravation related to transgender identity

(1) The Criminal Justice Act 2003 is amended as follows.

(2) Section 146 (increase in sentence for aggravation related to disability or sexual orientation) is amended as follows.

(3) In the heading, for "or sexual orientation" substitute ", sexual orientation or transgender identity".

(4) In subsection (2)(a)—

(a) after sub-paragraph (i) omit "or";

(b) at the end insert—

"(iii) the victim being (or being presumed to be) transgender, or".

(5) In subsection (2)(b)—

(a) after sub-paragraph (i) omit "or";

(b) at the end insert ", or

(iii) by hostility towards persons who are transgender."

(6) After subsection (5) insert—

"(6) In this section references to being transgender include references to being transsexual, or undergoing, proposing to undergo or having undergone a process or part of a process of gender reassignment."

(7) Schedule 21 (determination of minimum term in relation to mandatory life sentence) is amended as follows.

(8) For paragraph 3 substitute—

"3 For the purposes of this Schedule—

(a) an offence is aggravated by sexual orientation if it is committed in circumstances mentioned in section 146(2)(a)(i) or (b)(i);

(b) an offence is aggravated by disability if it is committed in circumstances mentioned in section 146(2)(a)(ii) or (b)(ii);

(c) an offence is aggravated by transgender identity if it is committed in circumstances mentioned in section 146(2)(a)(iii) or (b)(iii)."

(9) In paragraph 5(2)(g) (30 year starting point), after "aggravated by sexual orientation" insert ", disability or transgender identity".

(10) Section 241 of the Armed Forces Act 2006 (increase in sentence for aggravation related to disability or sexual orientation) is amended as follows.

(11) In the heading, for "or sexual orientation" substitute ", sexual orientation or transgender identity".

(12) In subsection (2)(a)—

(a) after sub-paragraph (i) omit "or";

(b) at the end insert—

"(iii) the victim being (or being presumed to be) transgender, or".

(13) In subsection (2)(b)—

(a) after sub-paragraph (i) omit "or";

(b) at the end insert ", or

(iii) by hostility towards persons who are transgender."

(14) After subsection (5) insert—

"(6) In this section references to being transgender include references to being transsexual, or undergoing, proposing to undergo or having undergone a process or part of a process of gender reassignment."

Community orders

66 Duration of community order

(1) In section 177 of the Criminal Justice Act 2003 (general provisions about community orders), in subsection (5) (requirement for order to specify date on which requirements must have been complied with)—

(a) after the first "date" insert "("the end date")", and

(b) omit the words from "; and" to the end of the subsection.

(2) After that subsection insert—

"(5A) If a community order imposes two or more different requirements falling within subsection (1), the order may also specify a date by which each of those requirements must have been complied with; and the last of those dates must be the same as the end date.

(5B) Subject to section 200(3) (duration of community order imposing unpaid work requirement), a community order ceases to be in force on the end date."

(3) In Schedule 8 to that Act (breach, revocation or amendment of community order), in paragraph 9 (powers of magistrates' court in case of breach)—

(a) in sub-paragraph (3), for the words from "but may" to the end of the sub-paragraph substitute "but may only amend the order to substitute a later date for that specified under section 177(5) in accordance with sub-paragraphs (3ZA) and (3ZB)", and

(b) after that sub-paragraph insert—

"(3ZA) A date substituted under sub-paragraph (3)—

(a) may not fall outside the period of six months beginning with the date previously specified under section 177(5);

(b) subject to that, may fall more than three years after the date of the order.

(3ZB) The power under sub-paragraph (3) to substitute a date may not be exercised in relation to an order if that power or the power in paragraph 10(3) to substitute a date has previously been exercised in relation to that order.

(3ZC) A date substituted under sub-paragraph (3) is to be treated as having been specified in relation to the order under section 177(5)."

(4) In that Schedule, in paragraph 10 (powers of Crown Court in case of breach)—

(a) in sub-paragraph (3), for the words from "but may" to the end of the sub-paragraph substitute "but may only amend the order to substitute a later date for that specified under section 177(5) in accordance with sub-paragraphs (3ZA) and (3ZB)", and

(b) after that sub-paragraph insert—

"(3ZA) A date substituted under sub-paragraph (3)—

(a) may not fall outside the period of six months beginning with the date previously specified under section 177(5);

(b) subject to that, may fall more than three years after the date of the order.

(3ZB) The power under sub-paragraph (3) to substitute a date may not be exercised in relation to an order if that power or the power under paragraph 9(3) to substitute a date has previously been exercised in relation to that order.

(3ZC) A date substituted under sub-paragraph (3) is to be treated as having been specified in relation to the order under section section 177(5)."

(5) In that Schedule, after paragraph 19 insert—

"Extension of order

19A (1) The appropriate court may, on the application of the offender or the responsible officer, amend a community order by substituting a later date for that specified under section 177(5).

(2) A date substituted under sub-paragraph (1)—

(a) may not fall outside the period of six months beginning with the date previously specified under section 177(5);

(b) subject to that, may fall more than three years after the date of the order.

(3) The power under sub-paragraph (1) may not be exercised in relation to an order if it has previously been exercised in relation to that order.

(4) A date substituted under sub-paragraph (1) is to be treated as having been specified in relation to the order under section 177(5).

(5) In this paragraph "the appropriate court" has the same meaning as in paragraph 16."

67 Breach of community order

(1) Schedule 8 to the Criminal Justice Act 2003 (breach, revocation or amendment of community order) is amended as follows.

(2) In paragraph 9 (powers of magistrates' court in case of breach), in sub-paragraph (1)—

(a) in the opening words, for "must" substitute "may", and

(b) after paragraph (a) insert—

"(aa) by ordering the offender to pay a fine of an amount not exceeding £2,500;".

(3) In that paragraph, after sub-paragraph (3A) insert—

"(3B) A fine imposed under sub-paragraph (1)(aa) is to be treated, for the purposes of any enactment, as being a sum adjudged to be paid by a conviction."

(4) In sub-paragraph (6) of that paragraph, for the words from "be required to" to "or (c)," substitute "have the power to deal with the offender under sub-paragraph (1)(a), (aa), (b) or (c),".

(5) In paragraph 10 (powers of Crown Court in case of breach), in sub-paragraph (1)—

(a) in the opening words, for "must" substitute "may", and

(b) after paragraph (a) insert—

"(aa) by ordering the offender to pay a fine of an amount not exceeding £2,500;".

(6) In that paragraph, after sub-paragraph (3A) insert—

"(3B) A fine imposed under sub-paragraph (1)(aa) is to be treated, for the purposes of any enactment, as being a sum adjudged to be paid by a conviction."

(7) After paragraph 11 insert—

"Power to amend amounts of fines

11A (1) The Secretary of State may by order amend any sum for the time being specified in paragraph 9(1)(aa) or 10(1)(aa).

(2) The power conferred by sub-paragraph (1) may be exercised only if it appears to the Secretary of State that there has been a change in the value of money since the relevant date which justifies the change.

(3) In sub-paragraph (2), "the relevant date" means—

(a) if the sum specified in paragraph 9(1)(aa) or 10(1)(aa) (as the case may be) has been substituted by an order under sub-paragraph (1), the date on which the sum was last so substituted;

(b) otherwise, the date on which section 67 of the Legal Aid, Sentencing and Punishment of Offenders Act 2012 (which inserted this paragraph) came into force.

(4) An order under sub-paragraph (1) (a "fine amendment order") must not have effect in relation to any community order made in respect of an offence committed before the fine amendment order comes into force."

Suspended sentence orders

68 Changes to powers to make suspended sentence order

(1) In section 189 of the Criminal Justice Act 2003 (suspended sentences of imprisonment), for subsection (1) substitute—

"(1) If a court passes a sentence of imprisonment for a term of least 14 days but not more than 2 years, it may make an order providing that the sentence of imprisonment is not to take effect unless—

(a) during a period specified in the order for the purposes of this paragraph ("the operational period") the offender commits another offence in the United Kingdom (whether or not punishable with imprisonment), and

(b) a court having power to do so subsequently orders under paragraph 8 of Schedule 12 that the original sentence is to take effect.

(1A) An order under subsection (1) may also provide that the offender must comply during a period specified in the order for the purposes of this subsection ("the supervision period") with one or more requirements falling within section 190(1) and specified in the order.

(1B) Where an order under subsection (1) contains provision under subsection (1A), it must provide that the sentence of imprisonment will also take effect if—

(a) during the supervision period the offender fails to comply with a requirement imposed under subsection (1A), and

(b) a court having power to do so subsequently orders under paragraph 8 of Schedule 12 that the original sentence is to take effect."

(2) In subsection (2) of that section (application of subsection (1) where consecutive sentences imposed), for the words from "does not exceed" to the end of the subsection substitute "does not exceed 2 years".

(3) In subsection (3) of that section (length of supervision period and operational period), after "supervision period" insert "(if any)".

(4) In subsection (4) of that section (supervision period not to end later than operational period), at the beginning insert "Where an order under subsection (1) imposes one or more community requirements,".

(5) In subsection (7)(c) of that section (meaning of "community requirement"), for "(1)(a)" substitute "(1A)".

(6) Schedule 9 (changes to powers to make suspended sentence orders: consequential and transitory provision) has effect.

(7) The amendments and modifications made by this section and that Schedule apply in relation to offences committed before or after the coming into force of any provision of this section or that Schedule.

69 Fine for breach of suspended sentence order

(1) Schedule 12 to the Criminal Justice Act 2003 (breach or amendment of suspended sentence order, and effect of further conviction) is amended as follows.

(2) In paragraph 8 (powers of court in case of breach or conviction)—

(a) in sub-paragraph (2), after paragraph (b) insert—

"(ba) the court may order the offender to pay a fine of an amount not exceeding £2,500,",

(b) after sub-paragraph (4) insert—

"(4ZA) A fine imposed under sub-paragraph (2)(ba) is to be treated, for the purposes of any enactment, as being a sum adjudged to be paid by a conviction.", and

(c) in sub-paragraph (6), after "(b)" insert ", (ba)".

(3) After paragraph 12 insert—

"Power to amend amount of fine

12A (1) The Secretary of State may by order amend the sum for the time being specified in paragraph 8(2)(ba).

(2) The power conferred by sub-paragraph (1) may be exercised only if it appears to the Secretary of State that there has been a change in the value of money since the relevant date which justifies the change.

(3) In sub-paragraph (2), "the relevant date" means—

(a) if the sum specified in paragraph 8(2)(ba) has been substituted by an order under sub-paragraph (1), the date on which the sum was last so substituted;

(b) otherwise, the date on which section 69 of the Legal Aid, Sentencing and Punishment of Offenders Act 2012 (which inserted this paragraph) came into force.

(4) An order under sub-paragraph (1) (a "fine amendment order") must not have effect in relation to any suspended sentence order made in respect of an offence committed before the fine amendment order comes into force."

Requirements under community orders and suspended sentence orders

70 Programme requirement

(1) In section 177(2) of the Criminal Justice Act 2003 (community orders: restrictions relating to particular requirements) omit paragraph (c) (which refers to section 202(4) and (5) of that Act).

(2) In section 190(2) of that Act (suspended sentence orders: restrictions relating to particular requirements) omit paragraph (c) (which refers to section 202(4) and (5) of that Act).

(3) Section 202 of that Act (orders imposing programme requirements) is amended as follows.

(4) In subsection (1) (meaning of "programme requirement")—

(a) after "participate" insert "in accordance with this section", and

(b) for the words from "specified in the order" to the end of the subsection substitute "on the number of days specified in the order."

(5) Omit subsections (4) and (5) (requirements to be met before court includes a programme requirement in a relevant order).

(6) In subsection (6) (effect of programme requirement)—

(a) in the opening words, for "requirement to attend an accredited programme" substitute "programme requirement", and

(b) in paragraph (a), for "at the place specified in the order" substitute "that is from time to time specified by the responsible officer at the place that is so specified".

(7) In subsection (7) (requirement for place providing programme requirement to be approved) for "in an order" substitute "by a responsible officer".

(8) In consequence of subsection (5), omit paragraph 86 of Schedule 4 to the Criminal Justice and Immigration Act 2008.

71 Curfew requirement

(1) Section 204 of the Criminal Justice Act 2003 (orders imposing curfew requirements) is amended as follows.

(2) In subsection (2) (order may not specify curfew period of more than twelve hours) for "twelve" substitute "sixteen".

(3) In subsection (3) (order may not specify curfew periods outside period of six months from making of order) for "six" substitute "twelve".

72 Foreign travel prohibition requirement

(1) In section 177 of the Criminal Justice Act 2003 (community orders), in subsection (1), after paragraph (g) insert—

"(ga) a foreign travel prohibition requirement (as defined by section 206A),".

(2) In subsection (4) of that section (power to impose electronic monitoring requirement), after "a residence requirement," insert "a foreign travel prohibition requirement,".

(3) In section 190 of that Act (imposition of requirements by suspended sentence order), in subsection (1), after paragraph (g) insert—

"(ga) a foreign travel prohibition requirement (as defined by section 206A),".

(4) In subsection (4) of that section (power to impose electronic monitoring requirement), after "a residence requirement," insert "a foreign travel prohibition requirement,".

(5) After section 206 of that Act insert—

"206A Foreign travel prohibition requirement

(1) In this Part "foreign travel prohibition requirement", in relation to a relevant order, means a requirement prohibiting the offender from travelling, on a day or days specified in the order, or for a period so specified—

(a) to any country or territory outside the British Islands specified or described in the order,

(b) to any country or territory outside the British Islands other than a country or territory specified or described in the order, or

(c) to any country or territory outside the British Islands.

(2) A day specified under subsection (1) may not fall outside the period of 12 months beginning with the day on which the relevant order is made.

(3) A period specified under that subsection may not exceed 12 months beginning with the day on which the relevant order is made."

(6) In section 305(1) of that Act (interpretation of Part 12), at the appropriate place insert—

""foreign travel prohibition requirement", in relation to a community order or suspended sentence order, has the meaning given by section 206A;".

73 Mental health treatment requirement

(1) Section 207 of the Criminal Justice Act 2003 (mental health treatment requirement) is amended as follows.

(2) In subsection (3)(a) (requirement for court to be satisfied as to offender's mental condition on evidence of registered medical practitioner)—

(a) omit the words from ", on the evidence" to "1983,", and

(b) in sub-paragraph (ii), for "that Act" substitute "the Mental Health Act 1983".

(3) Omit subsection (5) (application of section 54(2) and (3) of the Mental Health Act 1983 to proof of offender's mental condition).

74 Drug rehabilitation requirement

(1) In section 209 of the Criminal Justice Act 2003 (drug rehabilitation requirements) omit subsection (3) (requirement for treatment and testing period to be at least six months).

(2) In section 211(2) of that Act (powers of court at review hearing)—

(a) at the end of paragraph (a) insert "and", and

(b) omit paragraph (b) and the "and" at the end of that paragraph.

(3) In section 223(3) of that Act (power to amend specified periods of time), omit paragraph (c).

75 Alcohol treatment requirement

(1) In section 212 of the Criminal Justice Act 2003 (alcohol treatment requirement) omit subsection (4) (requirement for alcohol treatment requirement to have effect for at least six months).

(2) In section 223(3) of that Act (power to amend specified periods of time), omit paragraph (d).

76 Alcohol abstinence and monitoring requirement

(1) After section 212 of the Criminal Justice Act 2003 insert—

"212A Alcohol abstinence and monitoring requirement

(1) In this Part "alcohol abstinence and monitoring requirement", in relation to a relevant order, means a requirement—

(a) that, subject to such exceptions (if any) as are specified—

(i) the offender must abstain from consuming alcohol throughout a specified period, or

(ii) the offender must not consume alcohol so that at any time during a specified period there is more than a specified level of alcohol in the offender's body, and

(b) that the offender must, for the purpose of ascertaining whether the offender is complying with provision under paragraph (a), submit during the specified period to monitoring in accordance with specified arrangements.

(2) A period specified under subsection (1)(a) must not exceed 120 days.

(3) If the Secretary of State by order prescribes a minimum period for the purposes of subsection (1)(a), a period specified under that provision must be at least as long as the period prescribed.

(4) The level of alcohol specified under subsection (1)(a)(ii) must be that prescribed by the Secretary of State by order for the purposes of that provision (and a requirement under that provision may not be imposed unless such an order is in force).

(5) An order under subsection (4) may prescribe a level—
  (a) by reference to the proportion of alcohol in any one or more of an offender's breath, blood, urine or sweat, or
  (b) by some other means.

(6) The arrangements for monitoring specified under subsection (1)(b) must be consistent with those prescribed by the Secretary of State by order (and an alcohol abstinence and monitoring requirement may not be imposed unless such an order is in force).

(7) An order under subsection (6) may in particular prescribe—
  (a) arrangements for monitoring by electronic means;
  (b) arrangements for monitoring by other means of testing.

(8) A court may not include an alcohol abstinence and monitoring requirement in a relevant order unless the following conditions are met.

(9) The first condition is that—
  (a) the consumption of alcohol by the offender is an element of the offence for which the order is to be imposed or an associated offence, or
  (b) the court is satisfied that the consumption of alcohol by the offender was a factor that contributed to the commission of that offence or an associated offence.

(10) The second condition is that the court is satisfied that the offender is not dependent on alcohol.

(11) The third condition is that the court does not include an alcohol treatment requirement in the order.

(12) The fourth condition is that the court has been notified by the Secretary of State that arrangements for monitoring of the kind to be specified are available in the local justice area to be specified.

(13) In this section—
  "alcohol" includes anything containing alcohol;
  "specified", in relation to a relevant order, means specified in the order."

(2) In section 177 of that Act (community orders), in subsection (1), after paragraph (j) insert—
  "(ja) an alcohol abstinence and monitoring requirement (as defined by section 212A),".

(3) In subsection (2) of that section (limitations on power to impose community order)—
  (a) omit the "and" at the end of paragraph (f), and
  (b) at the end of paragraph (g) insert ", and
    (h) section 212A(8) to (12) (alcohol abstinence and monitoring requirement)."

(4) In section 190 of that Act (imposition of requirements by suspended sentence order), in subsection (1), after paragraph (j) insert—
  "(ja) an alcohol abstinence and monitoring requirement (as defined by section 212A),".

(5) In subsection (2) of that section (limitations on power to impose requirements by suspended sentence order)—

(a) omit the "and" at the end of paragraph (f), and

(b) at the end of paragraph (g) insert ", and

(h) section 212A(8) to (12) (alcohol abstinence and monitoring requirement)."

(6) In section 215 of that Act (electronic monitoring requirement), after subsection (4) insert—

"(5) An electronic monitoring requirement may not be included in a relevant order for the purposes of securing the electronic monitoring of the offender's compliance with an alcohol abstinence and monitoring requirement.

(6) Subsection (5) does not prevent the inclusion of an electronic monitoring requirement in a relevant order which includes an alcohol abstinence and monitoring requirement where this is for the purpose of securing the electronic monitoring of an offender's compliance with a requirement other than the alcohol abstinence and monitoring requirement."

(7) In section 223(3) of that Act (provisions to which powers to amend periods of time apply), after paragraph (b) insert—

"(ba) section 212A(2) (alcohol abstinence and monitoring requirement)".

(8) In section 305(1) of that Act (interpretation of Part 12), at the appropriate place insert—

""alcohol abstinence and monitoring requirement", in relation to a community order or suspended sentence order, has the meaning given by section 212A;".

(9) In Schedule 9 to that Act (transfer of community orders to Scotland or Northern Ireland)—

(a) in paragraph 1(5), after "require" insert "an alcohol abstinence and monitoring requirement or", and

(b) in paragraph 3, after sub-paragraph (4) insert—

"(4A) The court may not by virtue of sub-paragraph (1) or (3) require an alcohol abstinence and monitoring requirement to be complied with in Northern Ireland."

(10) In Schedule 13 to that Act (transfer of suspended sentence orders to Scotland or Northern Ireland)—

(a) in paragraph 1(5), after "require" insert "an alcohol abstinence and monitoring requirement or", and

(b) in paragraph 6, after sub-paragraph (4) insert—

"(4A) The court may not by virtue of sub-paragraph (1) or (3) require an alcohol abstinence and monitoring requirement to be complied with in Northern Ireland."

(11) In the Armed Forces Act 2006—

(a) in section 180 (transfer of service community order to Scotland or Northern Ireland), in subsection (2), after "3(1)" insert "and (4A)", and

(b) in section 204 (transfer of suspended sentence order to Scotland or Northern Ireland), in subsection (2), for "6(5)" substitute "6(4A) and (5)".

77 Piloting of alcohol abstinence and monitoring requirements

(1) The Secretary of State may by order provide for the coming into force of section 76.

(2) The Secretary of State may not make an order under subsection (1) with the effect that section 76 is in force for the whole of England and Wales (a "general commencement order") without having previously made a piloting order.

(3) Subsection (2) does not prevent an order under subsection (1) from bringing section 76 into force for the purpose only of making orders under section 212A or 223 of the Criminal Justice Act 2003 or rules under section 222 of that Act (and such an order is not a general commencement order for the purposes of this section).

(4) A "piloting order" is an order under subsection (1) with the effect that section 76 is force only—

(a) in relation to the area or areas specified in the order, and

(b) for the period specified in the order,

but otherwise for all purposes, or for all purposes other than application by the Armed Forces Act 2006.

(5) If, having made one or more piloting orders, the Secretary of State decides to make a general commencement order, the Secretary of State may by order—

(a) amend section 76 so as to enable the general commencement order to bring it into force with those amendments;

(b) amend or repeal any provision of this Act in consequence of provision made under paragraph (a).

(6) Amendments under subsection (5)(a)—

(a) may confer power on the Secretary of State to make an order or rules;

(b) may not enable a court to provide for an alcohol abstinence and monitoring requirement to be complied with in Scotland or Northern Ireland.

(7) If, having made one or more piloting orders, the Secretary of State decides not to make a general commencement order, the Secretary of State may by order—

(a) repeal section 76;

(b) amend the Criminal Justice Act 2003 so as to reverse the effect of that section on that Act;

(c) make other consequential amendments or repeals.

(8) An order under this section may make transitional, transitory or saving provision (including, in the case of a piloting order, provision relating to section 76 ceasing to be in force at the end of the period specified in the order).

(9) An order under this section is to be made by statutory instrument.

(10) A statutory instrument containing—

(a) a general commencement order, or

(b) an order under subsection (5) or (7),

may not be made unless a draft of the instrument has been laid before, and approved by a resolution of, each House of Parliament.

Overseas community orders and service community orders

78 Overseas community orders and service community orders

(1) Section 182 of the Armed Forces Act 2006 (general provisions about overseas community orders) is amended as follows.

(2) In subsection (1)(a) (requirements that may be imposed by overseas community orders), after "Act)" insert "(but see subsection (1A) below)".

(3) After subsection (1) insert—

"(1A) The order may not include a requirement mentioned in section 177(1)(ga) (a foreign travel prohibition requirement) or (ja) (an alcohol abstinence and monitoring requirement)."

(4) In subsection (4) (application of section 177(5) and (6) of the Criminal Justice Act 2003 to overseas community orders), after "(5)" insert ", (5A), (5B)".

(5) In section 322 of that Act (financial penalty enforcement orders), in the definition of "financial penalty" in subsection (4), after "including" insert "a fine imposed by the Court Martial or the Service Civilian Court under paragraph 10(1)(aa) of Schedule 8 to the 2003 Act by virtue of section 184 and Part 2 of Schedule 5 (breach etc of overseas community order) or".

(6) In Part 1 of Schedule 5 to that Act (breach, revocation and amendment of service community orders), in paragraph 1(2) (provisions of Schedule 8 to the Criminal Justice Act 2003 that do not apply to such orders), after "18(4)," insert "19A(5),".

(7) Part 2 of Schedule 5 to that Act (breach, revocation and amendment of overseas community orders) is amended as follows.

(8) In paragraph 10(2)(b) (provisions of Schedule 8 to the Criminal Justice Act 2003 that do not apply to such orders), after "19," insert "19A(5),".

(9) After paragraph 14 insert—

"14A(1) The following provisions apply where the Court Martial or the Service Civilian Court imposes a fine under paragraph 10(1)(aa) of that Schedule as applied by this Part of this Schedule.

(2) Section 251 of this Act (power to order payment of fine by instalments) applies in relation to the fine as it applies in relation to a fine imposed by a court for a service offence.

(3) Where the offender is aged under 18 when the fine is imposed and has a service parent or service guardian (within the meaning of section 268 of this Act), subsections (2) to (4) of that section (payment of fine by service parent or service guardian) apply in relation to the fine as they apply in relation to a fine imposed in the circumstances mentioned in subsection (1) of that section.

(4) In the application of subsection (2) of section 268 by virtue of sub-paragraph (3) of this paragraph, the reference in that subsection to

the time of conviction is to be read as a reference to the time the fine is imposed.

(5) Section 269(2) of this Act (power of court to make financial statement order before making order under section 268) does not apply in relation to an order under section 268 which is made by virtue of sub-paragraph (3) of this paragraph."

(10) In Schedule 6 to that Act (overseas community orders imposed on young offenders), in paragraph 5 (modification of drug rehabilitation requirement in relation to such offenders), omit sub-paragraph (4) (which disapplies section 209(3) of the Criminal Justice Act 2003).

Youth sentences

79 Referral orders for young offenders

(1) In section 16(1)(c) of the Powers of Criminal Courts (Sentencing) Act 2000 (duty or power to refer a young offender to a youth offender panel not to apply if court proposes to discharge the offender absolutely) for "absolutely" substitute ", whether absolutely or conditionally,".

(2) In section 17 of that Act (the referral conditions)—

(a) in subsection (2) at the end of paragraph (a) insert "and",

(b) in that subsection omit paragraph (c) and the word "and" immediately before it, and

(c) omit subsections (2A) to (2D).

(3) In consequence of the amendment made by subsection (2)(c) omit paragraph 12(3), (4) and (5) of Schedule 17 to the Coroners and Justice Act 2009.

(4) The amendments made by this section do not apply in relation to any sentence passed in relation to an offence committed before the coming into force of this section.

80 Breach of detention and training order

(1) The Powers of Criminal Courts (Sentencing) Act 2000 is amended as follows.

(2) In section 104 (breach of detention and training order), in subsection (3) (penalties for breach), for paragraph (a) and the "or" at the end of that paragraph substitute—

"(a) order the offender to be detained, in such youth detention accommodation as the Secretary of State may determine, for such period, not exceeding the maximum period found under subsection (3A) below, as the court may specify;

(aa) order the offender to be subject to such period of supervision, not exceeding the maximum period found under subsection (3A) below, as the court may specify; or".

(3) After subsection (3) of that section insert—

"(3A) The maximum period referred to in subsection (3)(a) and (aa) above is the shorter of—

(a) three months, and

(b) the period beginning with the date of the offender's failure and ending with the last day of the term of the detention and training order.

(3B) For the purposes of subsection (3A) above a failure that is found to have occurred over two or more days is to be taken to have occurred on the first of those days.

(3C) A court may order a period of detention or supervision, or impose a fine, under subsection (3) above before or after the end of the term of the detention and training order.

(3D) A period of detention or supervision ordered under subsection (3) above—

(a) begins on the date the order is made, and

(b) may overlap to any extent with the period of supervision under the detention and training order."

(4) After subsection (4) of that section insert—

"(4A) Where an order under subsection (3)(a) above is made in the case of a person who has attained the age of 18, the order has effect to require the person to be detained in prison for the period specified by the court."

(5) After subsection (5) of that section insert—

"(5A) Sections 104A and 104B below make further provision about the operation of orders under subsection (3) above."

(6) In subsection (6) of that section, after "(a)" insert ", (aa)".

(7) After that section insert—

"104A Application of sections 103 to 105 in relation to orders under section 104(3)(aa)

(1) Subsections (3) to (7) of section 103 above apply in relation to a period of supervision to which an offender is subject by virtue of an order under section 104(3)(aa) above as they apply to the period of supervision under a detention and training order.

(2) In the application of section 103 above by virtue of subsection (1) above, subsection (7)(a) of that section is to be read as requiring a notice to be given to the offender as soon as is reasonably practicable after the order under section 104(3)(aa) above is made.

(3) Section 104 above and section 105 below apply where an offender is subject to a period of supervision under section 104(3)(aa) above as they apply where a detention and training order is in force in respect of an offender.

(4) In the application of section 104 above by virtue of subsection (3) above—

(a) the references in that section to section 103(6)(b) above are to be read as references to that provision as applied by subsection (1) above,

(b) the references in subsections (3A)(b) and (3C) of that section to the term of the detention and training order are to be read as references to the term of the period of supervision under section 104(3)(aa) above, and

(c) the reference in subsection (3D)(b) of that section to the period of supervision under the detention and training order is to be read as including a reference to the period of supervision under section 104(3)(aa) above.

(5) In the application of section 105 below by virtue of subsection (3) above—

(a) paragraph (a) of subsection (1) of that section is to be read as if the words "after his release and" were omitted, and

(b) the reference in that paragraph to the date on which the term of the detention and training order ends is to be read as a reference to the date on which the period of supervision under section 104(3)(aa) ends.

104B Interaction of orders under section 104(3)(a) with other sentences

(1) Where a court makes a detention and training order in the case of an offender who is subject to a period of detention under section 104(3)(a) above, the detention and training order takes effect—

(a) at the beginning of the day on which it is made, or

(b) if the court so orders, at the time when the period of detention under section 104(3)(a) above ends.

(2) Where a court orders an offender who is subject to a detention and training order to be subject to a period of detention under section 104(3)(a) above for a failure to comply with requirements under a different detention and training order, the period of detention takes effect as follows—

(a) if the offender has been released by virtue of subsection (2), (3), (4) or (5) of section 102 above, at the beginning of the day on which the order for the period of detention is made, and

(b) if not, either as mentioned in paragraph (a) above or, if the court so orders, at the time when the offender would otherwise be released by virtue of subsection (2), (3), (4) or (5) of section 102 above.

(3) Subject to subsection (4) below, where at any time an offender is subject concurrently—

(a) to a detention and training order, and

(b) to a period of detention under section 104(3)(a) above,

the offender is to be treated for the purposes of sections 102 to 105 of this Act as if the offender were subject only to the detention and training order.

(4) Nothing in subsection (3) above requires the offender to be released in respect of either the order or the period of detention unless and until the offender is required to be released in respect of each of them.

(5) The Secretary of State may by regulations make provision about the interaction between a period of detention under section 104(3)(a) above and a custodial sentence in a case where—

(a) an offender who is subject to such a period of detention becomes subject to a custodial sentence, or

(b) an offender who is subject to a custodial sentence becomes subject to such a period of detention.

(6) The provision that may be made by regulations under subsection (5) above includes—

(a) provision as to the time at which the period of detention under section 104(3)(a) above or the custodial sentence is to take effect;

(b) provision for the offender to be treated, for the purposes of the enactments specified in the regulations, as subject only to the period of detention or the custodial sentence;

(c) provision about the effect of enactments relating to the person's release from detention or imprisonment in a case where that release is not to take effect immediately by virtue of provision in the regulations.

(7) The power of the Secretary of State to make regulations under subsection (5) above—

(a) is exercisable by statutory instrument;

(b) includes power to make supplementary, incidental, transitional, transitory or saving provision.

(8) A statutory instrument containing regulations under subsection (5) above is subject to annulment in pursuance of a resolution of either House of Parliament."

(8) Before the coming into force of section 61 of the Criminal Justice and Court Services Act 2000 (abolition of sentence of detention in a young offender institution) section 104(4A) of the Powers of Criminal Courts (Sentencing) Act 2000 has effect as if it referred to a person who has attained the age of 21.

(9) In section 213 of the Armed Forces Act 2006 (application of provisions relating to civilian detention and training orders to orders under section 211 of that Act)—

(a) in subsection (2), after "(13)" insert ", 104B(1)", and

(b) after subsection (3) insert—

"(4) Subsection (5) applies where an order under section 104(3) (further period of detention or supervision) of the Sentencing Act is made against an offender for breach of supervision requirements—

(a) during a period of supervision under an order under section 211 of this Act,

(b) during a further period of supervision imposed for breach of supervision requirements during a period within paragraph (a), or

(c) during one of a series of further periods of supervision—

(i) each of which apart from the first was imposed for breach of supervision requirements during the previous further period of supervision, and

(ii) the first of which was imposed for breach of supervision requirements during a period within paragraph (a).

(5) In the application of sections 104A and 104B of the Sentencing Act in relation to the offender, references to section 105 of that Act include section 214 of this Act.

(6) In subsection (4)—

"further period of supervision" means a period of supervision imposed under section 104(3)(aa) of the Sentencing Act;

"supervision requirements" means requirements under section 103(6)(b) of that Act.

(7) In section 104B of the Sentencing Act, references to a custodial sentence within the meaning of that Act include a custodial sentence within the meaning of this Act."

(10) The amendments made by this section apply in relation to a failure to comply with requirements under section 103(6)(b) of the Powers of Criminal Courts (Sentencing) Act 2000 that occurs after this section comes into force.

(11) Where a failure is found to have occurred over two or more days, it is to be taken for the purposes of subsection (10) to have occurred on the first of those days.

81 Youth rehabilitation order: curfew requirement

(1) Paragraph 14 of Schedule 1 to the Criminal Justice and Immigration Act 2008 (youth rehabilitation order: curfew requirement) is amended as follows.

(2) In sub-paragraph (2) (order may not specify curfew period of more than 12 hours) for "12" substitute "16".

(3) In sub-paragraph (3) (order may not specify curfew periods outside period of 6 months from making of order) for "6" substitute "12".

82 Youth rehabilitation order: mental health treatment requirement

(1) Paragraph 20 of Schedule 1 to the Criminal Justice and Immigration Act 2008 (youth rehabilitation order: mental health treatment requirement) is amended as follows.

(2) In sub-paragraph (3)(a) (requirement for court to be satisfied as to offender's mental condition on evidence of registered medical practitioner)—

(a) omit the words from ", on the evidence" to "1983 (c. 20),", and

(b) in sub-paragraph (ii), for "that Act" substitute "the Mental Health Act 1983".

(3) Omit sub-paragraph (5) (application of section 54(2) and (3) of the Mental Health Act 1983 to proof of offender's mental condition).

83 Youth rehabilitation order: duration

(1) In Schedule 1 to the Criminal Justice and Immigration Act 2008 (further provisions about youth rehabilitation orders), in paragraph 32 (requirement for order to specify date by which requirements must have been complied with)—

(a) in sub-paragraph (1), after the first "date" insert "("the end date")",

(b) for sub-paragraph (2) substitute—

"(2) If a youth rehabilitation order imposes two or more different requirements falling within Part 2 of this Schedule, the order may also specify a date by which each of those requirements must have been complied with; and the last of those dates must be the same as the end date.", and

(c) after sub-paragraph (3) insert—

"(4) Subject to paragraph 10(7) (duration of youth rehabilitation order imposing unpaid work requirement), a youth rehabilitation order ceases to be in force on the end date."

(2) In Schedule 2 to that Act (breach, revocation or amendment of youth rehabilitation order), in paragraph 6 (powers of magistrates' court in case of breach of order)—

(a) in sub-paragraph (6), at the beginning insert "Subject to sub-paragraph (6A),", and

(b) after that sub-paragraph insert—

"(6A) When imposing a requirement under sub-paragraph (2)(b), the court may amend the order to substitute a later date for that specified under paragraph 32(1) of Schedule 1.

(6B) A date substituted under sub-paragraph (6A)—

(a) may not fall outside the period of six months beginning with the date previously specified under paragraph 32(1) of Schedule 1;

(b) subject to that, may fall more than three years after the date on which the order took effect.

(6C) The power under sub-paragraph (6A) may not be exercised in relation to an order if that power or the power in paragraph 8(6A) has previously been exercised in relation to that order.

(6D) A date substituted under sub-paragraph (6A) is to be treated as having been specified in relation to the order under paragraph 32(1) of Schedule 1."

(3) In that Schedule, in paragraph 8 (powers of Crown Court in case of breach of order)—

(a) in sub-paragraph (6), at the beginning insert "Subject to sub-paragraph (6A),", and

(b) after that sub-paragraph insert—

"(6A) When imposing a requirement under sub-paragraph (2)(b), the Crown Court may amend the order to substitute a later date for that specified under paragraph 32(1) of Schedule 1.

(6B) A date substituted under sub-paragraph (6A)—

(a) may not fall outside the period of six months beginning with the date previously specified under paragraph 32(1) of Schedule 1;

(b) subject to that, may fall more than three years after the date on which the order took effect.

(6C) The power under sub-paragraph (6A) may not be exercised in relation to an order if that power or the power in paragraph 6(6A) has previously been exercised in relation to that order.

(6D) A date substituted under sub-paragraph (6A) is to be treated as having been specified in relation to the order under paragraph 32(1) of Schedule 1."

(4) In that Schedule, in paragraph 16(1) (exercise of powers to amend order: further provision), at the beginning insert "Subject to paragraph 16A,".

(5) After that paragraph insert—

"Extension of order

16A (1) The appropriate court may, on the application of the offender or the responsible officer, amend a youth rehabilitation order by substituting a later date for that specified under paragraph 32(1) of Schedule 1.

(2) A date substituted under sub-paragraph (1)—

(a) may not fall outside the period of six months beginning with the date previously specified under paragraph 32(1) of Schedule 1;

(b) subject to that, may fall more than three years after the date on which the order took effect.

(3) The power under sub-paragraph (1) may not be exercised in relation to an order if it has previously been exercised in relation to that order.

(4) A date substituted under sub-paragraph (1) is to be treated as having been specified in relation to the order under paragraph 32(1) of Schedule 1.

(5) In this paragraph "the appropriate court" means—

(a) if the order was made by a youth court or other magistrates' court, or was made by the Crown Court and contains a direction under paragraph 36 of Schedule 1, the court determined under sub-paragraph (6), and

(b) if the order was made by the Crown Court and does not contain a direction under paragraph 36 of Schedule 1, the Crown Court.

(6) The court referred to in sub-paragraph (5)(a) is—

(a) if the offender is aged under 18 when the application is made, a youth court acting in the local justice area specified in the youth rehabilitation order, and

(b) if the offender is aged 18 or over at that time, a magistrates' court (other than a youth court) acting in that local justice area."

84 Youth rehabilitation order: fine for breach

(1) Schedule 2 to the Criminal Justice and Immigration Act 2008 (breach of requirement of youth rehabilitation order) is amended as follows.

(2) In paragraph 6 (powers of magistrates' court in case of breach), in sub-paragraph (2)(a), for sub-paragraphs (i) and (ii) substitute "£2,500".

(3) In paragraph 8 (powers of Crown Court in case of breach), in sub-paragraph (2)(a), for sub-paragraphs (i) and (ii) substitute "£2,500".

(4) In paragraph 10 (power to amend amounts of fine)—
   (a) in sub-paragraph (1) omit "(i) or (ii)" in both places, and
   (b) in sub-paragraph (3)—
      (i) in paragraph (a) omit "(i) or (ii)" in both places, and
      (ii) in paragraph (b), for "this Act was passed" substitute "section 84 of the Legal Aid, Sentencing and Punishment of Offenders Act 2012 came into force".

Fines

85 Removal of limit on certain fines on conviction by magistrates' court

(1) Where, on the commencement day, a relevant offence would, apart from this subsection, be punishable on summary conviction by a fine or maximum fine of £5,000 or more (however expressed), the offence is punishable on summary conviction on or after that day by a fine of any amount.

(2) Where, on the commencement day, a relevant power could, apart from this subsection, be exercised to create an offence punishable on summary conviction by a fine or maximum fine of £5,000 or more (however expressed), the power may be exercised on or after that day to create an offence punishable on summary conviction by a fine of any amount.

(3) For the purposes of this section—
   (a) an offence is relevant if, immediately before the commencement day, it is a common law offence or it is contained in an Act or an instrument made under an Act (whether or not the offence is in force at that time), and
   (b) a power is relevant if, immediately before the commencement day, it is contained in an Act or an instrument made under an Act (whether or not the power is in force at that time).

(4) Nothing in subsection (1) affects—
   (a) fines for offences committed before the commencement day,
   (b) the operation of restrictions on fines that may be imposed on a person aged under 18, or
   (c) fines that may be imposed on a person convicted by a magistrates' court who is to be sentenced as if convicted on indictment,

and provision made in exercise of a relevant power in reliance on subsection (2) does not affect such fines or the operation of such restrictions.

(5) The Secretary of State may by regulations make provision disapplying subsection (1) or (2).

(6) The Secretary of State may by regulations make provision—
   (a) for an offence in relation to which subsection (1) is disapplied to be punishable on summary conviction by a fine or maximum fine of an amount specified or described in the regulations, and

(b) for a power in relation to which subsection (2) is disapplied to be exercisable to create an offence punishable on summary conviction by a fine or maximum fine of an amount specified or described in the regulations.

(7) Subsection (8) applies in relation to—

(a) a relevant offence that, immediately before the commencement day, is punishable on summary conviction by a fine or maximum fine expressed as a proportion of an amount of £5,000 or more (however that amount is expressed), and

(b) a relevant power which, immediately before the commencement day, can be exercised to create an offence punishable on summary conviction by such a fine or maximum fine.

(8) The Secretary of State may by regulations make provision—

(a) for the offence to be punishable on summary conviction by a fine or maximum fine of that proportion of an amount specified or described in the regulations, and

(b) for the power to be exercisable to create an offence punishable on summary conviction by such a fine or maximum fine.

(9) Regulations under this section may not include provision affecting—

(a) fines for offences committed before the regulations come into force,

(b) the operation of restrictions on fines that may be imposed on a person aged under 18, or

(c) fines that may be imposed on a person convicted by a magistrates' court who is to be sentenced as if convicted on indictment,

and provision made in exercise of a relevant power in reliance on regulations under this section may not include such provision.

(10) Regulations under this section—

(a) may make different provision for different cases or circumstances,

(b) may make provision generally or only for specified cases or circumstances, and

(c) may make consequential, incidental, supplementary, transitional, transitory or saving provision.

(11) Regulations under this section, and regulations under section 149 making provision in relation to this section, may amend, repeal, revoke or otherwise modify any provision which, immediately before the commencement day, is contained in an Act or an instrument made under an Act (whether or not the provision is in force at that time).

(12) Regulations under this section are to be made by statutory instrument.

(13) A statutory instrument containing regulations under this section may not be made unless a draft of the instrument has been laid before, and approved by a resolution of, each House of Parliament.

(14) If, immediately before the commencement day, the sum specified as level 5 on the standard scale in section 37(2) of the Criminal Justice Act 1982 (standard scale of fines for summary offences) is greater than £5,000, the references in this section to £5,000 have effect as if they were references to that sum.

(15) Powers under this section—

(a) may be exercised from time to time, and

(b) are without prejudice to other powers to modify fines for relevant offences or fines that may be specified or described when exercising a relevant power.

(16) For the purposes of this section, an offence is relevant whether it is a summary offence or an offence triable either way.

(17) In this section—

"Act" includes an Act or Measure of the National Assembly for Wales;

"the commencement day" means the day on which subsection (1) of this section comes into force;

and references to an offence, power or provision contained in an Act or instrument include an offence, power or provision applied by, or extending to England and Wales by virtue of, an Act or instrument.

86 Power to increase certain other fines on conviction by magistrates' court

(1) Subsection (2) applies in relation to a relevant offence which, immediately before the commencement day, is punishable on summary conviction by a fine or maximum fine of a fixed amount of less than £5,000.

(2) The Secretary of State may by regulations make provision for the offence to be punishable on summary conviction by a fine or maximum fine of an amount specified or described in the regulations.

(3) Subsection (4) applies in relation to a relevant power which, immediately before the commencement day, can be exercised to create an offence punishable on summary conviction by a fine or maximum fine of a fixed amount of less than £5,000 but not to create an offence so punishable by a fine or maximum fine of a fixed amount of £5,000 or more.

(4) The Secretary of State may by regulations make provision for the power to be exercisable to create an offence punishable on summary conviction by a fine or maximum fine of an amount specified or described in the regulations.

(5) Regulations under this section may not specify or describe an amount exceeding whichever is the greater of—

(a) £5,000, or

(b) the sum specified for the time being as level 4 on the standard scale.

(6) Regulations under this section may not include provision affecting—

(a) fines for offences committed before the regulations come into force,

(b) the operation of restrictions on fines that may be imposed on a person aged under 18, or

(c) fines that may be imposed on a person convicted by a magistrates' court who is to be sentenced as if convicted on indictment,

and provision made in exercise of a relevant power in reliance on regulations under subsection (4) may not include such provision.

(7) Regulations under this section—

(a) may make different provision for different cases or circumstances,

(b) may make provision generally or only for specified cases or circumstances, and

(c) may make consequential, incidental, supplementary, transitional, transitory or saving provision.

(8) Regulations under this section may amend, repeal, revoke or otherwise modify any provision which, immediately before the commencement day, is contained in an Act or an instrument made under an Act (whether or not the provision is in force at that time).

(9) Regulations under this section are to be made by statutory instrument.

(10) A statutory instrument containing regulations under this section may not be made unless a draft of the instrument has been laid before, and approved by a resolution of, each House of Parliament.

(11) If, immediately before the commencement day, the sum specified as level 5 on the standard scale in section 37(2) of the Criminal Justice Act 1982 (standard scale of fines for summary offences) is greater than £5,000, the references in this section to £5,000 have effect as if they were references to that sum.

(12) Powers under this section—
   (a) may be exercised from time to time, and
   (b) are without prejudice to other powers to modify fines for relevant offences or fines that may be specified or described when exercising a relevant power.

(13) In this section "Act", "the commencement day", "relevant offence" and "relevant power", and references to a provision contained in an Act or instrument, have the same meaning as in section 85.

87 Power to amend standard scale of fines for summary offences

(1) The Secretary of State may by order substitute for the sums for the time being specified as levels 1 to 4 on the standard scale in section 37(2) of the Criminal Justice Act 1982 (standard scale of fines for summary offences) such other sums as the Secretary of State considers appropriate.

(2) The power under subsection (1) may not be exercised so as to alter the ratio of one of those levels to another.

(3) In section 143 of the Magistrates' Courts Act 1980 (power to alter sums including standard scale of fines for summary offences), in subsection (3)(b), after "subsection (1) above" insert "or section 87 of the Legal Aid, Sentencing and Punishment of Offenders Act 2012".

(4) In section 37 of the Criminal Justice Act 1982 (standard scale of fines for summary offences), in subsection (3), at the end insert "or section 87 of the Legal Aid, Sentencing and Punishment of Offenders Act 2012".

(5) An order under this section is to be made by statutory instrument.

(6) A statutory instrument containing an order under this section may not be made unless a draft of the instrument has been laid before, and approved by a resolution of, each House of Parliament.

(7) An order under this section does not affect fines for offences committed before the order comes into force.

88 Withdrawal of warrants of control issued by fines officer

(1) Schedule 5 to the Courts Act 2003 (collection of fines and other sums imposed on conviction) is amended as follows.

(2) In paragraph 7(1) (Part 3 of Schedule does not apply on an appeal against a further steps notice) for "or 37(9)" substitute ", 37(9) or 37A(4)".

(3) In paragraph 37(7) (further steps notice must specify steps that fines officer intends to take) for "intends" substitute "wishes to be able".

(4) After paragraph 37 insert—

"*Issue by fines officer of replacement notice*

37A (1) This paragraph applies if—

(a) the fines officer has delivered to P a notice ("the current notice") that is—

(i) a further steps notice that has not been replaced by a notice under this paragraph, or

(ii) a notice under this paragraph that has not been replaced by a further notice under this paragraph,

(b) P remains liable to pay any part of the sum due, and

(c) the fines officer wishes to be able to take one or more steps listed in paragraph 38 but not specified in the current notice.

(2) The fines officer may deliver to P a notice replacing the current notice.

(3) A notice under this paragraph (a "replacement notice") must—

(a) state that the fines officer intends to take one or more of the steps listed in paragraph 38,

(b) specify the steps that the fines officer wishes to be able to take, and

(c) be in writing and dated.

(4) P may, within 10 working days from the date of a replacement notice, appeal to the magistrates' court against it.

(5) If a step is being taken in reliance on a notice at the time when the notice is replaced by a replacement notice, the taking of the step may continue despite the replacement."

(5) In paragraph 38(1) (list of steps referred to)—

(a) after "37(6)(b)" insert ", 37A(3)(a)", and

(b) in paragraph (a) (steps include issuing warrants that authorise taking control, and sale, of goods) for "levying" substitute "recovering".

(6) In paragraph 39 (powers of court on referrals and appeals)—

(a) in sub-paragraph (1)(c)—

(i) after "37(9)" insert "or 37A(4)", and

(ii) after "further steps notice" insert "or replacement notice", and

(b) in sub-paragraph (4) after "further steps notice" insert "or replacement notice".

(7) In paragraph 40 (implementation of notice)—

(a) after "further steps notice", in both places, insert "or replacement notice", and

(b) after "may be taken" insert "and retaken".

(8) After paragraph 40 insert—

"Withdrawal of warrant of control by fines officer

40A (1) This paragraph applies if, in taking a step specified in a further steps notice or replacement notice, the fines officer has issued a warrant of control for the purpose of recovering the sum due.

(2) The fines officer may withdraw the warrant if—

(a) P remains liable to pay any part of the sum due, and

(b) the fines officer is satisfied that the warrant was issued by mistake, including in particular a mistake made in consequence of the non-disclosure or misrepresentation of a material fact.

Discharge of warrant of control by magistrates' court

40B (1) This paragraph applies if—

(a) in taking a step specified in a further steps notice or replacement notice, the fines officer has issued a warrant of control for the purpose of recovering the sum due, and

(b) the fines officer subsequently refers P's case to the magistrates' court under paragraph 42.

(2) The magistrates' court may discharge the warrant if—

(a) P remains liable to pay any part of the sum due, and

(b) the power conferred by section 142(1) of the Magistrates' Courts Act 1980 (power of magistrates' court to re-open cases to rectify mistakes etc) would have been exercisable by the court if the court had issued the warrant.

Duty of fines officer if warrant of control withdrawn or discharged

40C (1) This paragraph applies if condition A or B is met.

(2) Condition A is that the fines officer has withdrawn a warrant of control under paragraph 40A.

(3) Condition B is that—

(a) in taking a step specified in a further steps notice or replacement notice, the fines officer has issued a warrant of control for the purpose of recovering the sum due,

(b) the fines officer has referred P's case to the magistrates' court under paragraph 42,

(c) the magistrates' court has discharged the warrant of control under paragraph 40B(2), and

(d) the magistrates' court has not discharged the collection order or exercised any of its powers under paragraph 42(2).

(4) If P remains liable to pay any part of the sum due, the fines officer must—

(a) take (or retake) one or more of the steps specified in the further steps notice or replacement notice that was the last notice to be delivered to P under paragraph 37 or 37A before the warrant of control was issued, or

(b) deliver to P a replacement notice and take one or more of the steps specified in that notice, or
(c) refer P's case to, or back to, the magistrates' court under paragraph 42."

Repeal of uncommenced provisions

89 Custody plus orders and intermittent custody orders

(1) In the Criminal Justice Act 2003, omit the following provisions (custody plus and intermittent custody)—
(a) sections 181 to 188;
(b) Schedules 10 and 11.

(2) Schedule 10 (amendments consequential on subsection (1)) has effect.

CHAPTER 2

BAIL

90 Amendment of bail enactments

Schedule 11 (amendment of enactments relating to bail) has effect.

CHAPTER 3

REMANDS OF CHILDREN OTHERWISE THAN ON BAIL

Remands

91 Remands of children otherwise than on bail

(1) This section applies where—
(a) a court deals with a child charged with or convicted of one or more offences by remanding the child, and
(b) the child is not released on bail.

(2) This section also applies where—
(a) a court remands a child in connection with extradition proceedings, and
(b) the child is not released on bail.

(3) Subject to subsection (4), the court must remand the child to local authority accommodation in accordance with section 92.

(4) The court may instead remand the child to youth detention accommodation in accordance with section 102 where—
(a) in the case of a child remanded under subsection (1), the first or second set of conditions for such a remand (see sections 98 and 99) is met in relation to the child, or

(b) in the case of a child remanded under subsection (2), the first or second set of conditions for such a remand in an extradition case (see sections 100 and 101) is met in relation to the child.

(5) This section is subject to section 128(7) of the Magistrates' Courts Act 1980 (remands to police detention for periods of not more than 3 days); but that provision has effect in relation to a child as if for the reference to 3 clear days there were substituted a reference to 24 hours.

(6) In this Chapter, "child" means a person under the age of 18.

(7) References in this Chapter (other than in relation to extradition proceedings) to the remand of a child include a reference to—

(a) the sending of a child for trial, and

(b) the committal of a child for sentence,

and related expressions are to be construed accordingly.

(8) Before the insertion of section 51A of the Crime and Disorder Act 1998 (sending cases to the Crown Court: children and young persons) by Schedule 3 to the Criminal Justice Act 2003 is fully in force, subsection (7) has effect as if it also referred to the committal of a child for trial.

(9) Subsection (7) also applies to any provision of an Act other than this Act that refers (directly or indirectly) to the remand of a child under this section.

Remands to local authority accommodation

92 Remands to local authority accommodation

(1) A remand to local authority accommodation is a remand to accommodation provided by or on behalf of a local authority.

(2) A court that remands a child to local authority accommodation must designate the local authority that is to receive the child.

(3) That authority must be—

(a) in the case of a child who is being looked after by a local authority, that authority, and

(b) in any other case, the local authority in whose area it appears to the court that the child habitually resides or the offence or one of the offences was committed.

(4) The designated authority must—

(a) receive the child, and

(b) provide or arrange for the provision of accommodation for the child whilst the child is remanded to local authority accommodation.

(5) Where a child is remanded to local authority accommodation, it is lawful for any person acting on behalf of the designated authority to detain the child.

93 Conditions etc on remands to local authority accommodation

(1) A court remanding a child to local authority accommodation may require the child to comply with any conditions that could be imposed under section 3(6) of the Bail Act 1976 if the child were then being granted bail.

(2) The court may also require the child to comply with any conditions imposed for the purpose of securing the electronic monitoring of the child's compliance with the conditions imposed under subsection (1) if—

(a) in the case of a child remanded under section 91(1) (proceedings other than extradition proceedings), the requirements in section 94 are met, or

(b) in the case of a child remanded under section 91(2) (extradition proceedings), the requirements in section 95 are met.

(3) A court remanding a child to local authority accommodation may impose on the designated authority—

(a) requirements for securing compliance with any conditions imposed on the child under subsection (1) or (2), or

(b) requirements stipulating that the child must not be placed with a named person.

(4) A court may only impose a condition under subsection (1) or (2), or a requirement under subsection (3), after consultation with the designated authority.

(5) Where a child has been remanded to local authority accommodation, a relevant court—

(a) may, on the application of the designated authority, impose on that child any conditions that could be imposed under subsection (1) or (2) if the court were then remanding the child to local authority accommodation, and

(b) where it does so, may impose on the authority requirements for securing compliance with the conditions imposed under paragraph (a).

(6) Where a child has been remanded to local authority accommodation, a relevant court may, on the application of the designated authority or that child, vary or revoke any conditions or requirements imposed under this section (including as previously varied under this subsection).

(7) A court that imposes conditions on a child under this section or varies conditions so imposed—

(a) must explain to the child in open court and in ordinary language why it is imposing or varying those conditions, and

(b) if the court is a magistrates' court, must cause a reason given under paragraph (a) to be specified in the warrant of commitment and entered in the register.

(8) In this section "relevant court"—

(a) in relation to a child remanded to local authority accommodation by virtue of section 91(1) (proceedings other than extradition proceedings), means—

(i) the court by which the child was so remanded, or

(ii) any magistrates' court that has jurisdiction in the place where the child is for the time being;

(b) in relation to a child remanded to local authority accommodation by virtue of section 91(2) (extradition proceedings), means the court by which the child was so remanded.

(9) References in this section to consultation are to such consultation (if any) as is reasonably practicable in all the circumstances of the case.

94 Requirements for electronic monitoring

(1) The requirements referred to in section 93(2)(a) (requirements for imposing electronic monitoring condition: non-extradition cases) are those set out in subsections (2) to (6).

(2) The first requirement is that the child has reached the age of twelve.

(3) The second requirement is that the offence mentioned in section 91(1), or one or more of those offences, is an imprisonable offence.

(4) The third requirement is that—

(a) the offence mentioned in section 91(1), or one or more of those offences, is a violent or sexual offence or an offence punishable in the case of an adult with imprisonment for a term of 14 years or more, or

(b) the offence or offences mentioned in section 91(1), together with any other imprisonable offences of which the child has been convicted in any proceedings, amount or would, if the child were convicted of that offence or those offences, amount to a recent history of committing imprisonable offences while on bail or subject to a custodial remand.

(5) The fourth requirement is that the court is satisfied that the necessary provision for electronic monitoring can be made under arrangements currently available in each local justice area which is a relevant area.

(6) The fifth requirement is that a youth offending team has informed the court that, in its opinion, the imposition of an electronic monitoring condition will be suitable in the child's case.

(7) For the purposes of this section, a local justice area is a relevant area in relation to a proposed electronic monitoring condition if the court considers that it will not be practicable to secure the electronic monitoring in question unless electronic monitoring arrangements are available in that area.

(8) In this Chapter—

"electronic monitoring condition" means a condition imposed on a child remanded to local authority accommodation for the purpose of securing the electronic monitoring of the child's compliance with conditions imposed under section 93(1) or (5);

"imprisonable offence" means—

(a) an offence punishable in the case of an adult with imprisonment, or

(b) in relation to an offence of which a child has been accused or convicted outside England and Wales, an offence equivalent to an offence that, in England and Wales, is punishable in the case of an adult with imprisonment;

"sexual offence" means an offence specified in Part 2 of Schedule 15 to the Criminal Justice Act 2003;

"violent offence" means murder or an offence specified in Part 1 of Schedule 15 to the Criminal Justice Act 2003;

"youth offending team" means a team established under section 39 of the Crime and Disorder Act 1998.

(9) References in this Chapter to a child being subject to a custodial remand are to the child being—

(a) remanded to local authority accommodation or youth detention accommodation, or

(b) subject to a form of custodial detention in a country or territory outside England and Wales while awaiting trial or sentence in that country or territory or during a trial in that country or territory.

(10) The reference in subsection (9) to a child being remanded to local authority accommodation or youth detention accommodation includes—

(a) a child being remanded to local authority accommodation under section 23 of the Children and Young Persons Act 1969, and

(b) a child being remanded to prison under that section as modified by section 98 of the Crime and Disorder Act 1998 or under section 27 of the Criminal Justice Act 1948.

95 Requirements for electronic monitoring: extradition cases

(1) The requirements referred to in section 93(2)(b) (requirements for imposing electronic monitoring condition: extradition cases) are those set out in subsections (2) to (6).

(2) The first requirement is that the child has reached the age of twelve.

(3) The second requirement is that the offence to which the extradition proceedings relate, or one or more of those offences, is an imprisonable offence.

(4) The third requirement is that—

(a) the conduct constituting the offence to which the extradition proceedings relate, or one or more of those offences, would, if committed in England and Wales, constitute a violent or sexual offence or an offence punishable in the case of an adult with imprisonment for a term of 14 years or more, or

(b) the offence or offences to which the extradition proceedings relate, together with any other imprisonable offences of which the child has been convicted, amount or would, if the child were convicted of that offence or those offences, amount to a recent history of committing imprisonable offences while on bail or subject to a custodial remand.

(5) The fourth requirement is that the court is satisfied that the necessary provision for electronic monitoring can be made under arrangements currently available in each local justice area which is a relevant area.

(6) The fifth requirement is that a youth offending team has informed the court that, in its opinion, the imposition of an electronic monitoring condition will be suitable in the child's case.

(7) For the purposes of this section, a local justice area is a relevant area in relation to a proposed electronic monitoring condition if the court considers that it will not be practicable to secure the electronic monitoring in question unless electronic monitoring arrangements are available in that area.

96 Further provisions about electronic monitoring

(1) Where a court imposes an electronic monitoring condition, the condition must include provision making a person responsible for the monitoring.

(2) A person who is made responsible by virtue of subsection (1) must be of a description specified in an order made by the Secretary of State.

(3) The Secretary of State may make rules for regulating—
   (a) the electronic monitoring of compliance with conditions imposed under section 93(1) or (5), and
   (b) in particular, the functions of persons made responsible by virtue of subsection (1) of this section.

(4) Rules under this section may make different provision for different cases.

(5) Any power of the Secretary of State to make an order or rules under this section is exercisable by statutory instrument.

(6) A statutory instrument containing rules under this section is subject to annulment in pursuance of a resolution of either House of Parliament.

97 Liability to arrest for breaking conditions of remand

(1) A child may be arrested without warrant by a constable if—
   (a) the child has been remanded to local authority accommodation,
   (b) conditions under section 93 have been imposed in respect of the child, and
   (c) the constable has reasonable grounds for suspecting that the child has broken any of those conditions.

(2) Subject to subsection (3), a child arrested under subsection (1) must be brought before a justice of the peace—
   (a) as soon as practicable, and
   (b) in any event within the period of 24 hours beginning with the child's arrest.

(3) If the child was arrested during the period of 24 hours ending with the time appointed for the child to appear before the court in pursuance of the remand, the child must be brought before the court before which the child was to have appeared.

(4) In reckoning a period of 24 hours for the purposes of subsection (2) or (3), no account is to be taken of Christmas Day, Good Friday or any Sunday.

(5) If a justice of the peace before whom a child is brought under subsection (2) is of the opinion that the child has broken any condition imposed in respect of the child under section 93, the justice of the peace must remand the child.

(6) Section 91 applies to a child in relation to whom subsection (5) applies as if—
   (a) except in a case within paragraph (b), the child was then charged with or convicted of the offence for which the child had been remanded, or
   (b) in the case of a child remanded in connection with extradition proceedings, the child was then appearing before the justice of the peace in connection with those proceedings.

(7) If a justice of the peace before whom a child is brought under subsection (2) is not of the opinion mentioned in subsection (5), the justice of the peace must remand the child to the place to which the child had been remanded at the time of the child's arrest subject to the same conditions as those which had been imposed on the child at that time.

Remands to youth detention accommodation

98 First set of conditions for a remand to youth detention accommodation

(1) For the purposes of section 91(4)(a), the first set of conditions for a remand to youth detention accommodation is met in relation to a child if each of the following is met in relation to the child—

(a) the age condition (see subsection (2)),

(b) the offence condition (see subsection (3)),

(c) the necessity condition (see subsection (4)), and

(d) the first or second legal representation condition (see subsections (5) and (6)).

(2) The age condition is that the child has reached the age of twelve.

(3) The offence condition is that the offence mentioned in section 91(1), or one or more of those offences—

(a) is a violent or sexual offence, or

(b) is an offence punishable in the case of an adult with imprisonment for a term of 14 years or more.

(4) The necessity condition is that the court is of the opinion, after considering all the options for the remand of the child, that only remanding the child to youth detention accommodation would be adequate—

(a) to protect the public from death or serious personal injury (whether physical or psychological) occasioned by further offences committed by the child, or

(b) to prevent the commission by the child of imprisonable offences.

(5) The first legal representation condition is that the child is legally represented before the court.

(6) The second legal representation condition is that the child is not legally represented before the court and—

(a) representation was provided to the child under Part 1 of this Act for the purposes of the proceedings, but was withdrawn—

(i) because of the child's conduct, or

(ii) because it appeared that the child's financial resources were such that the child was not eligible for such representation,

(b) the child applied for such representation and the application was refused because it appeared that the child's financial resources were such that the child was not eligible for such representation, or

(c) having been informed of the right to apply for such representation and having had the opportunity to do so, the child refused or failed to apply.

99 Second set of conditions for a remand to youth detention accommodation

(1) For the purposes of section 91(4)(a), the second set of conditions for a remand to youth detention accommodation is met in relation to a child if each of the following is met in relation to the child—

(a) the age condition (see subsection (2)),

(b) the sentencing condition (see subsection (3)),

(c) the offence condition (see subsection (4)),

(d) the first or second history condition or both (see subsections (5) and (6)),

(e) the necessity condition (see subsection (7)), and

(f) the first or second legal representation condition (see subsections (8) and (9)).

(2) The age condition is that the child has reached the age of twelve.

(3) The sentencing condition is that it appears to the court that there is a real prospect that the child will be sentenced to a custodial sentence for the offence mentioned in section 91(1) or one or more of those offences.

(4) The offence condition is that the offence mentioned in section 91(1), or one or more of those offences, is an imprisonable offence.

(5) The first history condition is that—

(a) the child has a recent history of absconding while subject to a custodial remand, and

(b) the offence mentioned in section 91(1), or one or more of those offences, is alleged to be or has been found to have been committed while the child was remanded to local authority accommodation or youth detention accommodation.

(6) The second history condition is that the offence or offences mentioned in section 91(1), together with any other imprisonable offences of which the child has been convicted in any proceedings, amount or would, if the child were convicted of that offence or those offences, amount to a recent history of committing imprisonable offences while on bail or subject to a custodial remand.

(7) The necessity condition is that the court is of the opinion, after considering all the options for the remand of the child, that only remanding the child to youth detention accommodation would be adequate—

(a) to protect the public from death or serious personal injury (whether physical or psychological) occasioned by further offences committed by the child, or

(b) to prevent the commission by the child of imprisonable offences.

(8) The first legal representation condition is that the child is legally represented before the court.

(9) The second legal representation condition is that the child is not legally represented before the court and—

(a) representation was provided to the child under Part 1 of this Act for the purposes of the proceedings, but was withdrawn—

(i) because of the child's conduct, or

(ii) because it appeared that the child's financial resources were such that the child was not eligible for such representation,

(b) the child applied for such representation and the application was refused because it appeared that the child's financial resources were such that the child was not eligible for such representation, or

(c) having been informed of the right to apply for such representation and having had the opportunity to do so, the child refused or failed to apply.

(10) In this Chapter "custodial sentence" means a sentence or order mentioned in section 76(1) of the Powers of Criminal Courts (Sentencing) Act 2000.

(11) The reference in subsection (5)(b) to a child being remanded to local authority accommodation or youth detention accommodation includes—

(a) a child being remanded to local authority accommodation under section 23 of the Children and Young Persons Act 1969, and

(b) a child being remanded to prison under that section as modified by section 98 of the Crime and Disorder Act 1998 or under section 27 of the Criminal Justice Act 1948.

100 First set of conditions for a remand to youth detention accommodation: extradition cases

(1) For the purposes of section 91(4)(b), the first set of conditions for a remand to youth detention accommodation in an extradition case is met in relation to a child if each of the following is met in relation to the child—

(a) the age condition (see subsection (2)),

(b) the offence condition (see subsection (3)),

(c) the necessity condition (see subsection (4)), and

(d) the first or second legal representation condition (see subsections (5) and (6)).

(2) The age condition is that the child has reached the age of twelve.

(3) The offence condition is that the conduct constituting the offence to which the extradition proceedings relate, or one or more of those offences, would, if committed in England and Wales, constitute—

(a) a violent or sexual offence, or

(b) an offence punishable in the case of an adult with imprisonment for a term of 14 years or more.

(4) The necessity condition is that the court is of the opinion, after considering all the options for the remand of the child, that only remanding the child to youth detention accommodation would be adequate—

(a) to protect the public from death or serious personal injury (whether physical or psychological) occasioned by further offences committed by the child, or

(b) to prevent the commission by the child of imprisonable offences.

(5) The first legal representation condition is that the child is legally represented before the court.

(6) The second legal representation condition is that the child is not legally represented before the court and—

(a) representation was provided to the child under Part 1 of this Act for the purposes of the proceedings, but was withdrawn—

(i) because of the child's conduct, or

(ii) because it appeared that the child's financial resources were such that the child was not eligible for such representation,

(b) the child applied for such representation and the application was refused because it appeared that the child's financial resources were such that the child was not eligible for such representation, or

(c) having been informed of the right to apply for such representation and having had the opportunity to do so, the child refused or failed to apply.

101 Second set of conditions for a remand to youth detention accommodation: extradition cases

(1) For the purposes of section 91(4)(b), the second set of conditions for a remand to youth detention accommodation in an extradition case is met in relation to a child if each of the following is met in relation to the child—
   (a) the age condition (see subsection (2)),
   (b) the sentencing condition (see subsection (3)),
   (c) the offence condition (see subsection (4)),
   (d) the first or second history condition or both (see subsections (5) and (6)),
   (e) the necessity condition (see subsection (7)), and
   (f) the first or second legal representation condition (see subsections (8) and (9)).

(2) The age condition is that the child has reached the age of twelve.

(3) The sentencing condition is that it appears to the court that, if the child were convicted in England and Wales of an offence equivalent to the offence to which the extradition proceedings relate or one or more of those offences, there would be a real prospect that the child would be sentenced to a custodial sentence for that offence or those offences.

(4) The offence condition is that the offence to which the extradition proceedings relate, or one or more of those offences, is an imprisonable offence.

(5) The first history condition is that—
   (a) the child has a recent history of absconding while subject to a custodial remand, and
   (b) the offence to which the extradition proceedings relate, or one or more of those offences, is alleged to be or has been found to have been committed while the child was subject to a custodial remand.

(6) The second history condition is that the offence or offences to which the extradition proceedings relate, together with any other imprisonable offences of which the child has been convicted, amount or would, if the child were convicted of that offence or those offences, amount to a recent history of committing imprisonable offences while on bail or subject to a custodial remand.

(7) The necessity condition is that the court is of the opinion, after considering all the options for the remand of the child, that only remanding the child to youth detention accommodation would be adequate—
   (a) to protect the public from death or serious personal injury (whether physical or psychological) occasioned by further offences committed by the child, or
   (b) to prevent the commission by the child of imprisonable offences.

(8) The first legal representation condition is that the child is legally represented before the court.

(9) The second legal representation condition is that the child is not legally represented before the court and—
   (a) representation was provided to the child under Part 1 of this Act for the purposes of the proceedings, but was withdrawn—
      (i) because of the child's conduct, or
      (ii) because it appeared that the child's financial resources were such that the child was not eligible for such representation,
   (b) the child applied for such representation and the application was refused because it appeared that the child's financial resources were such that the child was not eligible for such representation, or
   (c) having been informed of the right to apply for such representation and having had the opportunity to do so, the child refused or failed to apply.

102 Remands to youth detention accommodation

(1) A remand to youth detention accommodation is a remand to such accommodation of a kind listed in subsection (2) as the Secretary of State directs in the child's case.

(2) Those kinds of accommodation are—
   (a) a secure children's home,
   (b) a secure training centre,
   (c) a young offender institution, and
   (d) accommodation, or accommodation of a description, for the time being specified by order under section 107(1)(e) of the Powers of Criminal Courts (Sentencing) Act 2000 (youth detention accommodation for purposes of detention and training order provisions).

(3) A child's detention in one of those kinds of accommodation pursuant to a remand to youth detention accommodation is lawful.

(4) Where a court remands a child to youth detention accommodation, the court must—
   (a) state in open court that it is of the opinion mentioned in section 98(4), 99(7), 100(4) or 101(7) (as the case may be), and
   (b) explain to the child in open court and in ordinary language why it is of that opinion.

(5) A magistrates' court must ensure a reason that it gives under subsection (4)(b)—
   (a) is specified in the warrant of commitment, and
   (b) is entered in the register.

(6) Where a court remands a child to youth detention accommodation, the court must designate a local authority as the designated authority for the child for the purposes of—
   (a) subsection (8),
   (b) regulations under section 103 (arrangements for remands), and
   (c) section 104 (looked after child status).

(7) That authority must be—
   (a) in the case of a child who is being looked after by a local authority, that authority, and

(b) in any other case, the local authority in whose area it appears to the court that the child habitually resides or the offence or one of the offences was committed.

(8) Before giving a direction under subsection (1), the Secretary of State must consult the designated authority.

(9) A function of the Secretary of State under this section (other than the function of making regulations) is exercisable by the Youth Justice Board for England and Wales concurrently with the Secretary of State.

(10) The Secretary of State may by regulations provide that subsection (9) is not to apply, either generally or in relation to a particular description of case.

(11) In this Chapter "secure children's home" means accommodation which is provided in a children's home, within the meaning of the Care Standards Act 2000—

(a) which provides accommodation for the purposes of restricting liberty, and

(b) in respect of which a person is registered under Part 2 of that Act.

(12) Before the coming into force in relation to England of section 107(2) of the Health and Social Care (Community Health and Standards) Act 2003, subsection (11) has effect as if it defined "secure children's home" in relation to England as accommodation which—

(a) is provided in a children's home, within the meaning of the Care Standards Act 2000, in respect of which a person is registered under Part 2 of that Act, and

(b) is approved by the Secretary of State for the purpose of restricting the liberty of children.

Supplementary

103 Arrangements for remands

(1) The Secretary of State may make arrangements for or in connection with the accommodation in secure children's homes, or accommodation within section 102(2)(d), of children remanded to youth detention accommodation.

(2) The Secretary of State may by regulations make provision about the recovery from the designated authority by a person mentioned in subsection (3) of the costs of—

(a) a child being subject to a remand to youth detention accommodation;

(b) the exercise of functions of the kind mentioned in—

(i) section 80(1)(a) to (e) of the Criminal Justice Act 1991 (escort functions) read with section 92(3) of that Act, or

(ii) paragraph 1(1)(a) to (d) of Schedule 1 to the Criminal Justice and Public Order Act 1994 (escort functions),

in relation to a child subject to such a remand.

(3) Those persons are—

(a) the Secretary of State;

(b) a person other than the Secretary of State by whom the accommodation pursuant to the remand to youth detention accommodation is provided or the functions are exercised (as the case may be).

(4) The Secretary of State may make payments to a local authority for the purpose of enabling the authority—
   (a) to exercise functions under section 92(4) (duty to receive and accommodate child remanded to local authority accommodation);
   (b) to make payments pursuant to regulations under this section.

(5) A function of the Secretary of State under this section (other than the function of making regulations) is exercisable by the Youth Justice Board for England and Wales concurrently with the Secretary of State.

(6) The power to make regulations under subsection (2) includes power to make provision about the recovery of costs by the Youth Justice Board for England and Wales.

(7) The Secretary of State may by regulations provide that subsection (5), or provision made by virtue of subsection (6), is not to apply, either generally or in relation to a particular description of case.

104 Looked after child status

(1) A child who is remanded to youth detention accommodation is to be treated as a child who is looked after by the designated authority.

(2) The Secretary of State may by regulations provide for any Act or instrument made under an Act that applies to a child looked after by a local authority to apply with modifications, or not to apply, in relation to a child who is to be treated as looked after by a designated authority by virtue of this Chapter.

(3) In this section "Act" includes an Act or Measure of the National Assembly for Wales.

105 Minor and consequential amendments

Schedule 12 (remands of children otherwise than on bail: minor and consequential amendments) has effect.

106 Regulations under this Chapter

(1) Regulations under this Chapter are to be made by statutory instrument.

(2) Regulations under this Chapter may—
   (a) make different provision for different cases;
   (b) include supplementary, incidental, transitional, transitory or saving provision.

(3) A statutory instrument containing regulations under this Chapter is subject to annulment in pursuance of a resolution of either House of Parliament, subject to subsection (4).

(4) A statutory instrument containing regulations under section 102(10) or 103(7) (whether alone or with any other provision) may not be made unless a draft of the instrument has been laid before, and approved by a resolution of, each House of Parliament.

107 Interpretation of Chapter

(1) In this Chapter—

"child" has the meaning given by section 91(6);

"court" and "magistrates' court" include a justice of the peace;

"custodial sentence" has the meaning given by section 99(10);

"the designated authority"—

(a) in relation to a child remanded to local authority accommodation, means the local authority that is designated by the court under section 92(2) to receive the child;

(b) in relation to a child remanded to youth detention accommodation, means the local authority that is designated by the court under section 102(6) as the designated authority for the child;

"electronic monitoring condition" has the meaning given by section 94(8);

"extradition proceedings" means proceedings under the Extradition Act 2003;

"imprisonable offence" has the meaning given by section 94(8);

"local authority" means—

(a) a county council;

(b) a county borough council;

(c) a district council for an area for which there is no county council;

(d) a London borough council;

(e) the Common Council of the City of London;

(f) the Council of the Isles of Scilly;

"secure children's home" has the meaning given by section 102(11);

"sexual offence" has the meaning given by section 94(8);

"violent offence" has the meaning given by section 94(8);

"youth offending team" has the meaning given by section 94(8).

(2) In this Chapter, references to the remand of a child, and related expressions, are to be construed in accordance with section 91(7) and (8).

(3) In this Chapter, references to a remand to local authority accommodation, and related expressions, are to be construed in accordance with section 92(1).

(4) In this Chapter, references to a child being subject to a custodial remand are to be construed in accordance with section 94(9).

(5) In this Chapter, references to a remand to youth detention accommodation, and related expressions, are to be construed in accordance with section 102(1).

(6) In this Chapter, references to a child who is looked after by a local authority are to be construed in accordance with section 22 of the Children Act 1989.

(7) Subsections (3) and (5) are subject to sections 94(10) and 99(11) (references to remand to local authority accommodation or youth detention accommodation to include such a remand under section 23 of the Children and Young Persons Act 1969 or a remand to prison).

CHAPTER 4

RELEASE ON LICENCE ETC

Calculation of days to be served

108 Crediting of periods of remand in custody

(1) Omit section 240 of the Criminal Justice Act 2003 (court to direct that remand time be credited towards time served).

(2) Before section 240A of that Act insert—

"240ZA Time remanded in custody to count as time served: terms of imprisonment and detention

(1) This section applies where—

(a) an offender is serving a term of imprisonment in respect of an offence, and

(b) the offender has been remanded in custody (within the meaning given by section 242) in connection with the offence or a related offence.

(2) It is immaterial for that purpose whether, for all or part of the period during which the offender was remanded in custody, the offender was also remanded in custody in connection with other offences (but see subsection (5)).

(3) The number of days for which the offender was remanded in custody in connection with the offence or a related offence is to count as time served by the offender as part of the sentence.
But this is subject to subsections (4) to (6).

(4) If, on any day on which the offender was remanded in custody, the offender was also detained in connection with any other matter, that day is not to count as time served.

(5) A day counts as time served—

(a) in relation to only one sentence, and

(b) only once in relation to that sentence.

(6) A day is not to count as time served as part of any period of 28 days served by the offender before automatic release (see section 255B(1)).

(7) For the purposes of this section a suspended sentence—

(a) is to be treated as a sentence of imprisonment when it takes effect under paragraph 8(2)(a) or (b) of Schedule 12, and

(b) is to be treated as being imposed by the order under which it takes effect.

(8) In this section "related offence" means an offence, other than the offence for which the sentence is imposed ("offence A"), with which the offender was charged and the charge for which was founded on the same facts or evidence as offence A.

(9) For the purposes of the references in subsections (3) and (5) to the term of imprisonment to which a person has been sentenced (that is to say,

the reference to the offender's "sentence"), consecutive terms and terms which are wholly or partly concurrent are to be treated as a single term if—

(a) the sentences were passed on the same occasion, or

(b) where they were passed on different occasions, the person has not been released at any time during the period beginning with the first and ending with the last of those occasions.

(10) The reference in subsection (4) to detention in connection with any other matter does not include remand in custody in connection with another offence but includes—

(a) detention pursuant to any custodial sentence;

(b) committal in default of payment of any sum of money;

(c) committal for want of sufficient distress to satisfy any sum of money;

(d) committal for failure to do or abstain from doing anything required to be done or left undone.

(11) This section applies to a determinate sentence of detention under section 91 or 96 of the Sentencing Act or section 227 or 228 of this Act as it applies to an equivalent sentence of imprisonment."

109 Crediting of periods of remand on bail

(1) Section 240A of the Criminal Justice Act 2003 (crediting periods of remand on bail: terms of imprisonment and detention) is amended as follows.

(2) In subsection (2), for "subsection (4)" substitute "subsections (3A) and (3B)".

(3) For subsections (3) to (7) substitute—

"(3) The credit period is calculated by taking the following steps.

Step 1

Add—

(a) the day on which the offender's bail was first subject to the relevant conditions (and for this purpose a condition is not prevented from being a relevant condition by the fact that it does not apply for the whole of the day in question), and

(b) the number of other days on which the offender's bail was subject to those conditions (but exclude the last of those days if the offender spends the last part of it in custody).

Step 2

Deduct the number of days on which the offender, whilst on bail subject to the relevant conditions, was also—

(a) subject to any requirement imposed for the purpose of securing the electronic monitoring of the offender's compliance with a curfew requirement, or

(b) on temporary release under rules made under section 47 of the Prison Act 1952.

Step 3

From the remainder, deduct the number of days during that remainder on which the offender has broken either or both of the relevant conditions.

Step 4

Divide the result by 2.

Step 5

If necessary, round up to the nearest whole number.

(3A) A day of the credit period counts as time served—

(a) in relation to only one sentence, and

(b) only once in relation to that sentence.

(3B) A day of the credit period is not to count as time served as part of any period of 28 days served by the offender before automatic release (see section 255B(1))."

(4) In subsection (8)—

(a) omit "or (5)";

(b) for paragraph (b) substitute—

"(b) the number of days (if any) which it deducted under each of steps 2 and 3."

(5) Omit subsections (9) and (10).

(6) In subsection (11)—

(a) for "Subsections (7) to (10) of section 240" substitute "Subsections (7) to (9) and (11) of section 240ZA";

(b) in paragraph (b), for "in subsection (8) the reference to subsection (3) of section 240 is" substitute "in subsection (9) the references to subsections (3) and (5) of section 240ZA are".

(7) In subsection (12)—

(a) before the definition of "electronic monitoring condition" insert—

""curfew requirement" means a requirement (however described) to remain at one or more specified places for a specified number of hours in any given day, provided that the requirement is imposed by a court or the Secretary of State and arises as a result of a conviction;";

(b) omit the definition of "related offence" and the "and" preceding it.

(8) In the heading of the section, for "Crediting periods of remand on bail" substitute "Time remanded on bail to count towards time served".

110 Amendments consequential on sections 108 and 109

(1) The Criminal Justice Act 2003 is amended as follows.

(2) In section 237(1C) (meaning of "fixed-term prisoner")—

(a) for "section 240" substitute "section 240ZA";

(b) after "Armed Forces Act 2006)" insert "or section 240A".

(3) Section 241 (effect of direction under section 240 or 240A) is amended as follows.

(4) In subsection (1)—

(a) for "to whom a direction under section 240 or 240A relates" substitute "to whom section 240ZA applies or a direction under section 240A relates";

(b) for "specified in the direction" substitute "specified in section 240ZA or in the direction under section 240A".

(5) In subsection (1A), for "a direction under section 240 or 240A includes a direction under" substitute "section 240ZA includes".

(6) In the heading, for "direction under section 240 or 240A" substitute "section 240ZA or direction under section 240A".

(7) In section 242 (interpretation of sections 240 to 241), in subsections (1) and (2) and in the heading, for "sections 240" substitute "sections 240ZA".

(8) For section 243(2) (persons extradited to the United Kingdom) substitute—

"(2) In the case of an extradited prisoner, the court must specify in open court the number of days for which the prisoner was kept in custody while awaiting extradition.

(2A) Section 240ZA applies to days specified under subsection (2) as if they were days for which the prisoner was remanded in custody in connection with the offence or a related offence."

(9) In section 246 (power to release prisoners early)—

(a) in subsection (4)(i), for "to whom a direction under section 240 or 240A relates" substitute "to whom section 240ZA applies or a direction under section 240A relates";

(b) in subsection (4A)(b), for "a direction under section 240 includes a direction under" substitute "section 240ZA includes".

(10) In section 269 (determination of minimum term in relation to mandatory life sentence)—

(a) in subsection (3)(b), for the words from "any direction which it would have given" to "certain types of condition)" substitute "section 240ZA (crediting periods of remand in custody) or of any direction which it would have given under section 240A (crediting periods of remand on certain types of bail)";

(b) after that subsection insert—

"(3A) The reference in subsection (3)(b) to section 240ZA includes section 246 of the Armed Forces Act 2006 (crediting periods in service custody)."

(11) In section 305(1A) (modification of reference to want of sufficient distress), inserted by paragraph 155 of Schedule 13 to the Tribunals, Courts and Enforcement Act 2007, for "In the definition of "sentence of imprisonment" in subsection (1) the reference" substitute "In this Part any reference".

(12) In section 330(5) (rules to be subject to affirmative resolution)—

(a) after paragraph (b) insert "or", and

(b) omit paragraph (d) and the "or" preceding it.

(13) Schedule 13 (crediting of time in custody) has effect.

(14) In consequence of the amendments made by this section, in the Criminal Justice and Immigration Act 2008 omit—

(a) section 21(2), (5) and (7);

(b) section 22(2) and (3);

(c) section 23 and Schedule 6.

Release

111 Prisoners serving less than 12 months

(1) After section 243 of the Criminal Justice Act 2003 insert—

"*Unconditional release*

243A Duty to release prisoners serving less than 12 months

(1) This section applies to a fixed-term prisoner who is serving a sentence which is for a term of less than twelve months.

(2) As soon as a prisoner to whom this section applies has served the requisite custodial period for the purposes of this section, it is the duty of the Secretary of State to release that person unconditionally.

(3) For the purposes of this section "the requisite custodial period" is—

(a) in relation to a person serving a sentence of imprisonment for a term of less than twelve months or a determinate sentence of detention under section 91 or 96 of the Sentencing Act for such a term, one-half of the sentence, and

(b) in relation to a person serving two or more concurrent or consecutive sentences, the period determined under sections 263(2) and 264(2).

(4) This section is subject to—

(a) section 256B (supervision of young offenders after release), and

(b) paragraph 8 of Schedule 20B (transitional cases)."

(2) Schedule 14 (amendments consequential on subsection (1)) has effect.

112 Restrictions on early release subject to curfew

(1) In section 246 of the Criminal Justice Act 2003 (power to release prisoners on licence), subsection (4) is amended as follows.

(2) After paragraph (a) insert—

"(aa) the sentence is for a term of 4 years or more,".

(3) In paragraph (g)—

(a) for "during the currency of the sentence" substitute "at any time", and

(b) at the end insert "(and the revocation has not been cancelled under section 255(3))".

(4) Omit the "or" at the end of paragraph (h) and after that paragraph insert—

"(ha) the prisoner has at any time been returned to prison under section 40 of the Criminal Justice Act 1991 or section 116 of the Sentencing Act, or".

(5) After subsection (4) of that section insert—

"(4ZA) Where subsection (4)(aa) applies to a prisoner who is serving two or more terms of imprisonment, the reference to the term of the sentence is—

(a) if the terms are partly concurrent, a reference to the period which begins when the first term begins and ends when the last term ends;

(b) if the terms are to be served consecutively, a reference to the aggregate of the terms."

(6) In subsection (6) of that section, at the end insert—

""term of imprisonment" includes a determinate sentence of detention under section 91 or 96 of the Sentencing Act or under section 227 or 228 of this Act."

Further release after recall

113 Cancellation of revocation of licence

(1) After section 254(2) of the Criminal Justice Act 2003 (representations by person recalled) insert—

"(2A) The Secretary of State, after considering any representations under subsection (2)(a) or any other matters, may cancel a revocation under this section.

(2B) The Secretary of State may cancel a revocation under subsection (2A) only if satisfied that the person recalled has complied with all the conditions specified in the licence.

(2C) Where the revocation of a person's licence is cancelled under subsection (2A), the person is to be treated as if the recall under subsection (1) had not happened."

(2) In section 255(3) of that Act (cancellation of revocation under section 255), for "subsection (2)(b)" substitute "subsection (2)(a)".

114 Further release after recall

(1) For sections 255A to 255D of the Criminal Justice Act 2003 (further release after recall) substitute—

"Further release after recall

255A Further release after recall: introductory

(1) This section applies for the purpose of identifying which of sections 255B and 255C governs the further release of a person who has been recalled under section 254.

(2) The Secretary of State must, on recalling a person other than an extended sentence prisoner, consider whether the person is suitable for automatic release.

(3) For this purpose "automatic release" means release at the end of the period of 28 days beginning with the date on which the person returns to custody.

(4) A person is suitable for automatic release only if the Secretary of State is satisfied that the person will not present a risk of serious harm to members of the public if released at the end of that period.

(5) The person must be dealt with—
(a) in accordance with section 255B if suitable for automatic release;
(b) in accordance with section 255C otherwise.

(6) For the purposes of this section, a person returns to custody when that person, having been recalled, is detained (whether or not in prison) in pursuance of the sentence.

(7) An "extended sentence prisoner" is a prisoner serving an extended sentence imposed under—
(a) section 227 or 228 of this Act, or
(b) section 85 of the Sentencing Act;

and paragraph (b) includes (in accordance with paragraph 1(3) of Schedule 11 to the Sentencing Act) a reference to section 58 of the Crime and Disorder Act 1998.

255B Automatic release

(1) A prisoner who is suitable for automatic release ("P") must—
(a) on return to prison, be informed that he or she will be released under this section (subject to subsections (8) and (9)), and
(b) at the end of the 28 day period mentioned in section 255A(3), be released by the Secretary of State on licence under this Chapter (unless P is released before that date under subsection (2) or (5)).

(2) The Secretary of State may, at any time after P is returned to prison, release P again on licence under this Chapter.

(3) The Secretary of State must not release P under subsection (2) unless the Secretary of State is satisfied that it is not necessary for the protection of the public that P should remain in prison until the end of the period mentioned in subsection (1)(b).

(4) If P makes representations under section 254(2) before the end of that period, the Secretary of State must refer P's case to the Board on the making of those representations.

(5) Where on a reference under subsection (4) the Board directs P's immediate release on licence under this Chapter, the Secretary of State must give effect to the direction.

(6) Subsection (7) applies if P is recalled before the date on which P would (but for the earlier release) have served the requisite custodial period for the purposes of section 243A or (as the case may be) section 244.

(7) Where this subsection applies—
(a) if P is released under this section before that date, P's licence must include a curfew condition complying with section 253, and
(b) P is not to be so released (despite subsections (1)(b) and (5)) unless the Secretary of State is satisfied that arrangements are in place to enable that condition to be complied with.

(8) Subsection (9) applies if, after P has been informed that he or she will be released under this section, the Secretary of State receives further information about P (whether or not relating to any time before P was recalled).

(9) If the Secretary of State determines, having regard to that and any other relevant information, that P is not suitable for automatic release—

(a) the Secretary of State must inform P that he or she will not be released under this section, and

(b) section 255C applies to P as if the Secretary of State had determined, on P's recall, that P was not suitable for automatic release.

255C Extended sentence prisoners and those not suitable for automatic release

(1) This section applies to a prisoner ("P") who—

(a) is an extended sentence prisoner, or

(b) is not considered to be suitable for automatic release.

(2) The Secretary of State may, at any time after P is returned to prison, release P again on licence under this Chapter.

(3) The Secretary of State must not release P under subsection (2) unless the Secretary of State is satisfied that it is not necessary for the protection of the public that P should remain in prison.

(4) The Secretary of State must refer P's case to the Board—

(a) if P makes representations under section 254(2) before the end of the period of 28 days beginning with the date on which P returns to custody, on the making of those representations, or

(b) if, at the end of that period, P has not been released under subsection (2) and has not made such representations, at that time.

(5) Where on a reference under subsection (4) the Board directs P's immediate release on licence under this Chapter, the Secretary of State must give effect to the direction.

(6) Subsection (7) applies if P is recalled before the date on which P would (but for the earlier release) have served the requisite custodial period for the purposes of section 243A or (as the case may be) section 244.

(7) Where this subsection applies—

(a) if P is released under this section before that date, P's licence must include a curfew condition complying with section 253, and

(b) P is not to be so released (despite subsection (5)) unless the Secretary of State is satisfied that arrangements are in place to enable that condition to be complied with.

(8) For the purposes of this section, P returns to custody when P, having been recalled, is detained (whether or not in prison) in pursuance of the sentence."

(2) After section 244(1) of that Act (duty to release certain prisoners on licence at half-way point) insert—

"(1A) Subsection (1) does not apply if the prisoner has been released on licence under section 246 and recalled under section 254 (provision for the release of such persons being made by sections 255B and 255C)."

(3) In the heading of section 253 of that Act (curfew conditions) after "section 246" insert ", 255B or 255C".

(4) In section 256(1) of that Act (review by the Board), for "section 255B(4), 255C(4) or 255D(1)" substitute "section 255B(4) or 255C(4)".

(5) In consequence of the amendments made by this section, omit section 29(2) and (3) of the Criminal Justice and Immigration Act 2008.

Other provisions about release

115 Supervision of young offenders after release

After section 256A of the Criminal Justice Act 2003 insert—

"Supervision of young offenders after release

256B Supervision of young offenders after release

(1) This section applies where a person ("the offender") is released under this Chapter from one of the following terms if the term is for less than 12 months—

(a) a term of detention in a young offender institution;

(b) a term of detention under section 91 of the Sentencing Act;

(c) a term of detention under section 209 of the Armed Forces Act 2006.

(2) The offender is to be under the supervision of—

(a) an officer of a provider of probation services,

(b) a social worker of a local authority, or

(c) if the offender is under the age of 18 years at the date of release, a member of the youth offending team.

(3) Where the supervision is to be provided by an officer of a provider of probation services, the officer must be an officer acting in the local justice area in which the offender resides for the time being.

(4) Where the supervision is to be provided by—

(a) a social worker of a local authority, or

(b) a member of a youth offending team,

the social worker or member must be a social worker of, or a member of a youth offending team established by, the local authority within whose area the offender resides for the time being.

(5) The supervision period begins on the offender's release and ends three months later (whether or not the offender is detained under section 256C or otherwise during that period).

(6) During the supervision period, the offender must comply with such requirements, if any, as may for the time being be specified in a notice from the Secretary of State.

(7) The requirements that may be specified in a notice under subsection (6) include—

(a) requirements for securing the electronic monitoring of the offender's compliance with any other requirements specified in the notice;

(b) requirements for securing the electronic monitoring of the offender's whereabouts (otherwise than for the purpose of securing compliance with requirements specified in the notice);

(c) in the circumstances mentioned in subsection (8), requirements to provide, when instructed to do so by an officer of a provider of probation services or a person authorised by the Secretary of State, any sample mentioned in the instruction for the purpose of ascertaining whether the offender has any specified Class A drug in his or her body.

(8) The circumstances referred to in subsection (7)(c) are that—

(a) the offender has attained the age of 18 years;

(b) the offender's term of detention was imposed for a trigger offence; and

(c) the requirements to provide samples are being imposed for the purpose of determining whether the offender is complying with any other requirements specified in the notice.

(9) The function of giving such an instruction as is mentioned in subsection (7)(c) must be exercised in accordance with guidance given from time to time by the Secretary of State; and the Secretary of State may make rules about the requirements that may be imposed by virtue of subsection (7) and the provision of samples in pursuance of such an instruction.

(10) In this section—

"specified Class A drug" has the same meaning as in Part 3 of the Criminal Justice and Court Services Act 2000;

"trigger offence"—

(a) has the same meaning as in that Part, unless paragraph (b) applies;

(b) if the offender's term of detention was imposed for an offence under section 42 of the Armed Forces Act 2006 (criminal conduct), means such an offence as respects which the corresponding offence under the law of England and Wales is a trigger offence within the meaning of that Part.

256C Breach of supervision requirements

(1) Where an offender is under supervision under section 256B and it appears on information to a justice of the peace that the offender has failed to comply with requirements under section 256B(6), the justice may—

(a) issue a summons requiring the offender to appear at the place and time specified in the summons, or

(b) if the information is in writing and on oath, issue a warrant for the offender's arrest.

(2) Any summons or warrant issued under this section must direct the offender to appear or be brought—

(a) before a court acting for the local justice area in which the offender resides, or
(b) if it is not known where the offender resides, before a court acting for same local justice area as the justice who issued the summons or warrant.

(3) Where the offender does not appear in answer to a summons issued under subsection (1)(a), the court may issue a warrant for the offender's arrest.

(4) If it is proved to the satisfaction of the court that the offender has failed to comply with requirements under section 256B(6), the court may—
(a) order the offender to be detained, in prison or such youth detention accommodation as the Secretary of State may determine, for such period, not exceeding 30 days, as the court may specify, or
(b) impose on the offender a fine not exceeding level 3 on the standard scale.

(5) An offender detained in pursuance of an order under subsection (4)(a) is to be regarded as being in legal custody.

(6) A fine imposed under subsection (4)(b) is to be treated, for the purposes of any enactment, as being a sum adjudged to be paid by a conviction.

(7) An offender may appeal to the Crown Court against any order made under subsection (4)(a) or (b).

(8) In this section "court" means—
(a) if the offender has attained the age of 18 years at the date of release, a magistrates' court other than a youth court;
(b) if the offender is under the age of 18 years at the date of release, a youth court."

116 Miscellaneous amendments relating to release and recall

(1) The Criminal Justice Act 2003 is amended as follows.

(2) Omit section 248(2) (Secretary of State to consult Board before releasing extended sentence prisoner on compassionate grounds).

(3) In section 256(1) (review by the Board)—
(a) for "recommend" substitute "direct";
(b) for "recommendation" substitute "direction".

(4) In section 256A (further review)—
(a) in subsection (4)(a), for "recommending" substitute "directing";
(b) in subsection (4)(c), for "recommendation" substitute "direction";
(c) in subsection (5), for "recommendation" (in both places) substitute "direction".

(5) In section 260(5) (duties and powers remaining exercisable in relation to persons removed from prison), after "244" insert ", 247".

(6) In section 261(5) (re-entry to UK of offender removed early: re-release), after

"sentence expiry date," insert "—

(a) if the person is serving an extended sentence imposed under section 227 or 228, section 247 has effect in relation to that person as if the reference to one-half of the appropriate custodial term were a reference to the further custodial period;

(b) in any other case,".

(7) In section 261(6) (re-entry to UK of offender removed early: definitions), in the definition of "requisite custodial period", after the words "requisite custodial period" insert "—

(a) in relation to a prisoner serving an extended sentence imposed under section 227 or 228, means one-half of the appropriate custodial term (determined by the court under that section);

(b) in any other case,".

(8) In section 263(2)(b) (concurrent terms: authority to release), for "section 244" substitute "section 246".

(9) In section 263(2)(c) (concurrent terms: licence period), for the words "for so long, and subject to such conditions, as is" substitute "—

(i) until the last date on which the offender is required to be on licence in respect of any of the terms, and

(ii) subject to such conditions as are".

117 Replacement of transitory provisions

(1) Chapter 6 of Part 12 of the Criminal Justice Act 2003 (release on licence) is amended as follows.

(2) In section 237(1)(b) ("fixed-term prisoner" includes those serving sentence of detention)—

(a) after "91" insert "or 96";

(b) before "228" insert "227 or".

(3) At the end of that section insert—

"(3) In this Chapter, references to a sentence of detention under section 96 of the Sentencing Act or section 227 of this Act are references to a sentence of detention in a young offender institution."

(4) In section 244(3)(a) (duty to release prisoners: requisite custodial period), after "91" insert "or 96".

(5) In section 250(4) (licence conditions)—

(a) after "91" insert "or 96";

(b) before "228" insert "227 or".

(6) In section 258 (early release of fine defaulters and contemnors), after subsection (3) insert—

"(3A) The reference in subsection (3) to sentences of imprisonment includes sentences of detention under section 91 or 96 of the Sentencing Act or under section 227 or 228 of this Act."

(7) In section 263(4) (concurrent terms)—

(a) after "91" insert "or 96";

(b) before "228" insert "227 or".

(8) In section 264(7) (consecutive terms)—

(a) after "91" insert "or 96";

(b) before "228" insert "227 or".

(9) In section 265(2) (restriction on consecutive sentences)—

(a) after "91" insert "or 96";

(b) before "228" insert "227 or".

(10) In Part 2 of the Crime (Sentences) Act 1997 (life sentences: release on licence)—

(a) in section 31A(5) (termination of licences), in the definition of "preventive sentence", after "a sentence of imprisonment" insert "or detention in a young offender institution";

(b) in section 34(2)(d) (interpretation), after "a sentence of imprisonment" insert "or detention in a young offender institution".

(11) In the Criminal Justice Act 2003 (Sentencing) (Transitory Provisions) Order 2005 (S.I. 2005/643), article 3(7), (10), (11), (12), (13), (14), (15) and (17)(a) and (b) (transitory provision replaced by this section) are revoked.

118 Repeal of uncommenced provisions

(1) This section repeals certain provisions which have not been commenced.

(2) Omit section 266 of the Criminal Justice Act 2003 (which amends section 64 of the Criminal Justice and Court Services Act 2000 in relation to drug testing requirements).

(3) Omit section 34 of the Police and Justice Act 2006 (which makes amendments of Part 12 of the Criminal Justice Act 2003 relating to imprisonment for bail offences).

(4) Omit the following provisions of the Criminal Justice and Immigration Act 2008 (which relate to the early release of persons with a settled intention of residing permanently outside the UK)—

(a) section 33(2), (4), (7) and (8) (amendments of the Criminal Justice Act 1991);

(b) section 34(2), (4)(b), (7) and (10) (amendments of the Criminal Justice Act 2003).

(5) In Schedule 8 to the Crime and Disorder Act 1998 (minor and consequential amendments) omit—

(a) paragraph 86 (amendments of section 41 of the Criminal Justice Act 1991);

(b) paragraph 90 (amendment of section 47 of that Act).

Life sentence prisoners

119 Removal of prisoners from the United Kingdom

After section 32 of the Crime (Sentences) Act 1997 insert—

"Persons liable to removal from the United Kingdom

32A Removal of prisoners liable to removal from United Kingdom

(1) Where P—

(a) is a life prisoner in respect of whom a minimum term order has been made, and

(b) is liable to removal from the United Kingdom,

the Secretary of State may remove P from prison under this section at any time after P has served the relevant part of the sentence (whether or not the Parole Board has directed P's release under section 28).

(2) But if P is serving two or more life sentences—

(a) this section does not apply to P unless a minimum term order has been made in respect of each of those sentences; and

(b) the Secretary of State may not remove P from prison under this section until P has served the relevant part of each of them.

(3) If P is removed from prison under this section—

(a) P is so removed only for the purpose of enabling the Secretary of State to remove P from the United Kingdom under powers conferred by—

(i) Schedule 2 or 3 to the Immigration Act 1971, or

(ii) section 10 of the Immigration and Asylum Act 1999, and

(b) so long as remaining in the United Kingdom, P remains liable to be detained in pursuance of the sentence.

(4) So long as P, having been removed from prison under this section, remains in the United Kingdom but has not been returned to prison, any duty or power of the Secretary of State under section 28 or 30 is exercisable in relation to P as if P were in prison.

(5) In this section—

"liable to removal from the United Kingdom" has the meaning given by section 259 of the Criminal Justice Act 2003;

"the relevant part" has the meaning given by section 28.

32B Re-entry into United Kingdom of offender removed from prison

(1) This section applies if P, having been removed from prison under section 32A, is removed from the United Kingdom.

(2) If P enters the United Kingdom—

(a) P is liable to be detained in pursuance of the sentence from the time of P's entry into the United Kingdom;

(b) if no direction was given by the Parole Board under subsection (5) of section 28 before P's removal from prison, that section applies to P;

(c) if such a direction was given before that removal, P is to be treated as if P had been recalled to prison under section 32.

(3) A person who is liable to be detained by virtue of subsection (2)(a) is, if at large, to be taken for the purposes of section 49 of the Prison Act 1952 (persons unlawfully at large) to be unlawfully at large.

(4) Subsection (2)(a) does not prevent P's further removal from the United Kingdom."

Application and transitional provision

120 Application and transitional etc provision

Schedule 15 (application of sections 108 to 119 and transitional and transitory provision) has effect.

Simplification of existing transitional provisions

121 Simplification of existing transitional provisions

(1) Chapter 6 of Part 12 of the Criminal Justice Act 2003 ("the 2003 Act") is to apply to any person serving a sentence for an offence committed before 4 April 2005 (whenever that sentence was or is imposed).

(2) Section 258 of the 2003 Act (release of fine defaulters and contemnors) is to apply to any person who was, before 4 April 2005, committed to prison or to be detained under section 108 of the Powers of Criminal Courts (Sentencing) Act 2000—

(a) in default of payment of a sum adjudged to be paid by a conviction, or
(b) for contempt of court or any kindred offence.

(3) In accordance with subsections (1) and (2)—

(a) the repeal of Part 2 of the Criminal Justice Act 1991 which is made by section 303(a) of the 2003 Act has effect in relation to any person mentioned in those subsections;
(b) paragraphs 15 to 18, 19(a), (c) and (d), 20, 22 to 28 and 30 to 34 of Schedule 2 to the Criminal Justice Act 2003 (Commencement No. 8 and Transitional and Saving Provisions) Order 2008 (S.I. 2005/950) (which relate to the coming into force of provisions of Chapter 6 of Part 12 of the 2003 Act) are revoked.

(4) Section 86 of the Powers of Criminal Courts (Sentencing) Act 2000 (extension of periods in custody and on licence in the case of certain sexual offences) is repealed.

(5) Schedule 16 (transitional and other provision consequential on this section) has effect.

(6) Schedule 17 (amendments to the 2003 Act restating the effect of certain transitional and other provision relating to the release and recall of prisoners) has effect.

CHAPTER 5

DANGEROUS OFFENDERS

122 Life sentence for second listed offence

(1) In Chapter 5 of Part 12 of the Criminal Justice Act 2003 (sentencing: dangerous offenders), after section 224 insert—

"224A Life sentence for second listed offence

(1) This section applies where—

(a) a person aged 18 or over is convicted of an offence listed in Part 1 of Schedule 15B,

(b) the offence was committed after this section comes into force, and

(c) the sentence condition and the previous offence condition are met.

(2) The court must impose a sentence of imprisonment for life unless the court is of the opinion that there are particular circumstances which—

(a) relate to the offence, to the previous offence referred to in subsection (4) or to the offender, and

(b) would make it unjust to do so in all the circumstances.

(3) The sentence condition is that, but for this section, the court would, in compliance with sections 152(2) and 153(2), impose a sentence of imprisonment for 10 years or more, disregarding any extension period imposed under section 226A.

(4) The previous offence condition is that —

(a) at the time the offence was committed, the offender had been convicted of an offence listed in Schedule 15B ("the previous offence"), and

(b) a relevant life sentence or a relevant sentence of imprisonment or detention for a determinate period was imposed on the offender for the previous offence.

(5) A life sentence is relevant for the purposes of subsection (4)(b) if—

(a) the offender was not eligible for release during the first 5 years of the sentence, or

(b) the offender would not have been eligible for release during that period but for the reduction of the period of ineligibility to take account of a relevant pre-sentence period.

(6) An extended sentence imposed under this Act (including one imposed as a result of the Armed Forces Act 2006) is relevant for the purposes of subsection (4)(b) if the appropriate custodial term imposed was 10 years or more.

(7) Any other extended sentence is relevant for the purposes of subsection (4)(b) if the custodial term imposed was 10 years or more.

(8) Any other sentence of imprisonment or detention for a determinate period is relevant for the purposes of subsection (4)(b) if it was for a period of 10 years or more.

(9) An extended sentence or other sentence of imprisonment or detention is also relevant if it would have been relevant under subsection (7) or (8) but for the reduction of the sentence, or any part of the sentence, to take account of a relevant pre-sentence period.

(10) For the purposes of subsections (4) to (9)—

"extended sentence" means—

(a) a sentence imposed under section 85 of the Sentencing Act or under section 226A, 226B, 227 or 228 of this Act (including one imposed as a result of section 219A, 220, 221A or 222 of the Armed Forces Act 2006), or

(b) an equivalent sentence imposed under the law of Scotland, Northern Ireland or a member State (other than the United Kingdom);

"life sentence" means—

(a) a life sentence as defined in section 34 of the Crime (Sentences) Act 1997, or

(b) an equivalent sentence imposed under the law of Scotland, Northern Ireland or a member State (other than the United Kingdom);

"relevant pre-sentence period", in relation to the previous offence referred to in subsection (4), means any period which the offender spent in custody or on bail before the sentence for that offence was imposed;

"sentence of imprisonment or detention" includes any sentence of a period in custody (however expressed).

(11) An offence the sentence for which is imposed under this section is not to be regarded as an offence the sentence for which is fixed by law."

(2) Schedule 18 (new Schedule 15B to the Criminal Justice Act 2003) has effect.

(3) Schedule 19 (life sentence for second listed offence: consequential and transitory provision) has effect.

123 Abolition of certain sentences for dangerous offenders

In Chapter 5 of Part 12 of the Criminal Justice Act 2003 (sentencing: dangerous offenders) omit—

(a) section 225(3) to (4) (imprisonment for public protection for serious offences),

(b) section 226(3) to (4) (detention for public protection for serious offences),

(c) section 227 (extended sentence for certain violent or sexual offences: persons 18 or over), and

(d) section 228 (extended sentence for certain violent or sexual offences: persons under 18).

124 New extended sentences

In Chapter 5 of Part 12 of the Criminal Justice Act 2003 (sentencing: dangerous offenders), after section 226 and the italic heading "Extended sentences" insert—

"226A Extended sentence for certain violent or sexual offences: persons 18 or over

(1) This section applies where—

(a) a person aged 18 or over is convicted of a specified offence (whether the offence was committed before or after this section comes into force),

(b) the court considers that there is a significant risk to members of the public of serious harm occasioned by the commission by the offender of further specified offences,

(c) the court is not required by section 224A or 225(2) to impose a sentence of imprisonment for life, and

(d) condition A or B is met.

(2) Condition A is that, at the time the offence was committed, the offender had been convicted of an offence listed in Schedule 15B.

(3) Condition B is that, if the court were to impose an extended sentence of imprisonment, the term that it would specify as the appropriate custodial term would be at least 4 years.

(4) The court may impose an extended sentence of imprisonment on the offender.

(5) An extended sentence of imprisonment is a sentence of imprisonment the term of which is equal to the aggregate of—

(a) the appropriate custodial term, and

(b) a further period (the "extension period") for which the offender is to be subject to a licence.

(6) The appropriate custodial term is the term of imprisonment that would (apart from this section) be imposed in compliance with section 153(2).

(7) The extension period must be a period of such length as the court considers necessary for the purpose of protecting members of the public from serious harm occasioned by the commission by the offender of further specified offences, subject to subsections (8) and (9).

(8) The extension period must not exceed—

(a) 5 years in the case of a specified violent offence, and

(b) 8 years in the case of a specified sexual offence.

(9) The term of an extended sentence of imprisonment imposed under this section in respect of an offence must not exceed the term that, at the time the offence was committed, was the maximum term permitted for the offence.

(10) In subsections (1)(a) and (8), references to a specified offence, a specified violent offence and a specified sexual offence include an offence that—

(a) was abolished before 4 April 2005, and

(b) would have constituted such an offence if committed on the day on which the offender was convicted of the offence.

(11) Where the offence mentioned in subsection (1)(a) was committed before 4 April 2005—

(a) subsection (1)(c) has effect as if the words "by section 224A or 225(2)" were omitted, and

(b) subsection (6) has effect as if the words "in compliance with section 153(2)" were omitted.

226B Extended sentence for certain violent or sexual offences: persons under 18

(1) This section applies where—

(a) a person aged under 18 is convicted of a specified offence (whether the offence was committed before or after this section comes into force),

(b) the court considers that there is a significant risk to members of the public of serious harm occasioned by the commission by the offender of further specified offences,

(c) the court is not required by section 226(2) to impose a sentence of detention for life under section 91 of the Sentencing Act, and

(d) if the court were to impose an extended sentence of detention, the term that it would specify as the appropriate custodial term would be at least 4 years.

(2) The court may impose an extended sentence of detention on the offender.

(3) An extended sentence of detention is a sentence of detention the term of which is equal to the aggregate of—

(a) the appropriate custodial term, and

(b) a further period (the "extension period") for which the offender is to be subject to a licence.

(4) The appropriate custodial term is the term of detention that would (apart from this section) be imposed in compliance with section 153(2).

(5) The extension period must be a period of such length as the court considers necessary for the purpose of protecting members of the public from serious harm occasioned by the commission by the offender of further specified offences, subject to subsections (6) and (7).

(6) The extension period must not exceed—

(a) 5 years in the case of a specified violent offence, and

(b) 8 years in the case of a specified sexual offence.

(7) The term of an extended sentence of detention imposed under this section in respect of an offence may not exceed the term that, at the time the offence was committed, was the maximum term of imprisonment permitted for the offence in the case of a person aged 18 or over.

(8) In subsections (1)(a) and (6), references to a specified offence, a specified violent offence and a specified sexual offence include an offence that—

(a) was abolished before 4 April 2005, and

(b) would have constituted such an offence if committed on the day on which the offender was convicted of the offence.

(9) Where the offence mentioned in subsection (1)(a) was committed before 4 April 2005—
(a) subsection (1) has effect as if paragraph (c) were omitted, and
(b) subsection (4) has effect as if the words "in compliance with section 153(2)" were omitted."

125 New extended sentences: release on licence etc

(1) Chapter 6 of Part 12 of the Criminal Justice Act 2003 (sentencing: release and recall) is amended as follows.

(2) In section 244(1) (duty to release prisoners on licence) (as amended by Schedule 14 to this Act) after "243A" insert ", 246A".

(3) After section 246 insert—

"246A Release on licence of prisoners serving extended sentence under section 226A or 226B

(1) This section applies to a prisoner ("P") who is serving an extended sentence imposed under section 226A or 226B.

(2) It is the duty of the Secretary of State to release P on licence under this section as soon as P has served the requisite custodial period for the purposes of this section unless either or both of the following conditions are met—
(a) the appropriate custodial term is 10 years or more;
(b) the sentence was imposed in respect of an offence listed in Parts 1 to 3 of Schedule 15B or in respect of offences that include one or more offences listed in those Parts of that Schedule.

(3) If either or both of those conditions are met, it is the duty of the Secretary of State to release P on licence in accordance with subsections (4) to (7).

(4) The Secretary of State must refer P's case to the Board—
(a) as soon as P has served the requisite custodial period, and
(b) where there has been a previous reference of P's case to the Board under this subsection and the Board did not direct P's release, not later than the second anniversary of the disposal of that reference.

(5) It is the duty of the Secretary of State to release P on licence under this section as soon as—
(a) P has served the requisite custodial period, and
(b) the Board has directed P's release under this section.

(6) The Board must not give a direction under subsection (5) unless—
(a) the Secretary of State has referred P's case to the Board, and
(b) the Board is satisfied that it is no longer necessary for the protection of the public that P should be confined.

(7) It is the duty of the Secretary of State to release P on licence under this section as soon as P has served the appropriate custodial term, unless P has previously been released on licence under this section and recalled under section 254 (provision for the release of such persons being made by section 255C).

(8) For the purposes of this section—

"appropriate custodial term" means the term determined as such by the court under section 226A or 226B (as appropriate);

"the requisite custodial period" means—

(a) in relation to a person serving one sentence, two-thirds of the appropriate custodial term, and

(b) in relation to a person serving two or more concurrent or consecutive sentences, the period determined under sections 263(2) and 264(2)."

(4) Schedule 20 (release of new extended sentence prisoners: consequential amendments of Chapter 6 of Part 12 of the Criminal Justice Act 2003) has effect.

126 Sections 123 to 125: consequential and transitory provision

Schedule 21 (abolition of certain sentences for dangerous offenders and new extended sentences: consequential and transitory provision) has effect.

127 Dangerous offenders subject to service law etc

Schedule 22 (dangerous offenders subject to service law etc) has effect.

128 Power to change test for release on licence of certain prisoners

(1) The Secretary of State may by order provide that, following a referral by the Secretary of State of the case of a discretionary release prisoner, the Parole Board—

(a) must direct the prisoner's release if it is satisfied that conditions specified in the order are met, or

(b) must do so unless it is satisfied that conditions specified in the order are met.

(2) "Discretionary release prisoner" means—

(a) an IPP prisoner,

(b) an extended sentence prisoner, or

(c) a person to whom paragraph 4, 15, 24 or 27 of Schedule 20B to the Criminal Justice Act 2003 (determinate sentence prisoners subject to transitional provisions) applies.

(3) An order under this section may—

(a) amend section 28 of the Crime (Sentences) Act 1997 (duty to release IPP prisoners and others),

(b) amend section 246A of the Criminal Justice Act 2003 (release on licence of extended sentence prisoners),

(c) amend paragraph 6, 15, 25 or 28 of Schedule 20B to the Criminal Justice Act 2003 (release on licence of determinate sentence prisoners subject to transitional provisions),

(d) make provision in relation to any person whose case is disposed of by the Parole Board on or after the day on which the regulations come into force (even if the Secretary of State referred that person's case to the Board before that day),

(e) make different provision in relation to each of the categories of discretionary release prisoner mentioned in subsection (2), and

(f) include consequential provision.

(4) An order under this section is to be made by statutory instrument.

(5) A statutory instrument containing an order under this section may not be made unless a draft of the instrument has been laid before, and approved by a resolution of, each House of Parliament.

(6) In this section—

"extended sentence prisoner" means a prisoner who is serving a sentence under section 226A or 226B of the Criminal Justice Act 2003 (including one imposed as a result of section 219A or 221A of the Armed Forces Act 2006);

"IPP prisoner" means a prisoner who is serving one or more of the following sentences and is not serving any other life sentence—

(a) a sentence of imprisonment for public protection or detention in a young offender institution for public protection under section 225 of the Criminal Justice Act 2003 (including one imposed as a result of section 219 of the Armed Forces Act 2006);

(b) a sentence of detention for public protection under section 226 of the Criminal Justice Act 2003 (including one imposed as a result of section 221 of the Armed Forces Act 2006);

"life sentence" has the same meaning as in section 34 of the Crime (Sentences) Act 1997.

CHAPTER 6

PRISONERS ETC

129 Employment in prisons: deductions etc from payments to prisoners

(1) In section 47 of the Prison Act 1952 (power of Secretary of State to make rules for the regulation and management of prisons etc), in subsection (1) omit "employment,".

(2) After that subsection insert—

"(1A) The Secretary of State may make rules about—

(a) the employment of persons who are required to be detained in secure training centres or young offender institutions;

(b) the making of payments to such persons in respect of work or other activities undertaken by them, or in respect of their unemployment."

(3) In that section, after subsection (5) insert—

"(6) Rules made under this section may—

(a) make different provision for different cases;

(b) contain supplementary, incidental, transitional, transitory or saving provision."

(4) After that section insert—

"47A Rules about employment in prisons etc

(1) The Secretary of State may make rules about—

(a) the employment of prisoners;

(b) the making of payments to prisoners in respect of work or other activities undertaken by them, or in respect of their unemployment.

(2) The Secretary of State may make rules about the making, by the governor of the prison in which a prisoner is detained or the Secretary of State, of reductions in payments to the prisoner in respect of—

(a) work undertaken by the prisoner,

(b) other activities undertaken by the prisoner, or

(c) the prisoner's unemployment,

where those payments are made by or on behalf of the Secretary of State.

(3) Rules under subsection (2) may make provision, in a case where reductions are made by the governor, for amounts generated by the reductions to be used by the governor—

(a) for making payments for the benefit of victims or communities;

(b) for making payments for the purposes of the rehabilitation of offenders;

(c) for other prescribed purposes.

(4) Rules under subsection (2) may make provision, in a case where reductions are made by the governor—

(a) for amounts generated by the reductions to be used by the governor for making payments into an account of a prescribed kind;

(b) for the administration of the account;

(c) for the making of payments out of the account to a prisoner before or after the prisoner's release on fulfilment by the prisoner of prescribed conditions.

(5) Rules under subsection (2) that make provision for amounts generated by reductions to be used to make payments may provide for such payments to be made after the deduction of amounts of a prescribed description.

(6) The Secretary of State may make rules about the making of deductions from, or the imposition of levies on, payments to a prisoner in respect of—

(a) work undertaken by the prisoner,

(b) other activities undertaken by the prisoner, or

(c) the prisoner's unemployment,

where those payments are made otherwise than by or on behalf of the Secretary of State.

(7) Rules under subsection (6)—

(a) may provide for deductions to be made, or levies to be imposed, by the governor of the prison or by the Secretary of State;

(b) must provide that, if the governor makes the deductions or imposes the levies, the governor must pay amounts generated to the Secretary of State.

(8) The Secretary of State may make rules providing—

(a) for the making of payments by the Secretary of State into an account of a prescribed kind;

(b) for the administration of the account;

(c) for the making of payments out of the account to a prisoner before or after the prisoner's release on fulfilment by the prisoner of prescribed conditions.

(9) Rules under this section may—

(a) make different provision for different cases;

(b) contain supplementary, incidental, transitional, transitory or saving provision.

(10) In this section references to the governor of a prison include—

(a) the director of a contracted out prison within the meaning of Part 4 of the Criminal Justice Act 1991, and

(b) an officer of a prison who may exercise the functions of a governor in accordance with rules under section 47 or this section.

(11) In this section—

"prescribed" means prescribed by rules under this section;

"prisoner" includes a prisoner on temporary release."

(5) In section 66(4) of the Criminal Justice Act 1967 (procedure applying to rules under section 47 of the Prison Act 1952), for "of the said Act of 1952" substitute "or section 47A of the Prison Act 1952".

(6) In section 127(6) of the Criminal Justice and Public Order Act 1994 (inducements to prison officers to contravene prison rules: meaning of "prison rules"), after "section 47" insert "or 47A".

(7) In section 4 of the Prisoners' Earnings Act 1996 (interpretation)—

(a) omit subsection (2) (application of the Act to England and Wales), and

(b) in subsection (3) (application of the Act to Scotland), for "In the application of this Act to Scotland" substitute "In this Act".

(8) In section 5 of that Act (short title, commencement and extent), for subsection (3) substitute—

"(3) This Act extends to Scotland only."

(9) In section 45(2) of the National Minimum Wage Act 1998 (exclusion for prisoners doing work in pursuance of prison rules: interpretation), in paragraph (a) of the definition of "prison rules", after "section 47" insert "or 47A".

(10) Before the coming into force of section 59 of the Criminal Justice and Court Services Act 2000 (abolition of power to provide remand centres), section 47(1A) of the Prison Act 1952 has effect as if it referred also to persons required to be detained in remand centres.

(11) Before the coming into force of section 61 of the Criminal Justice and Court Services Act 2000 (abolition of sentences of detention in a young offender institution, custody for life etc)—

(a) section 47(1A) of the Prison Act 1952 has effect as if the references to persons required to be detained in young offender institutions were to persons aged under 18 required to be so detained, and

(b) section 47A of that Act has effect as if—
(i) "prison" included a young offender institution, and
(ii) "prisoner" included a person aged 18 or over who is required to be detained in a young offender institution.

(12) The Secretary of State may make such payments to such persons as the Secretary of State considers appropriate in connection with measures that appear to the Secretary of State to be intended to—
(a) rehabilitate offenders,
(b) prevent re-offending, or
(c) limit the impact of crime.

(13) In making payments under subsection (12), the Secretary of State must have regard to the sums that have been made available to, or received by, the Secretary of State by virtue of rules under section 47A of the Prison Act 1952 (reductions, deductions and levies in respect of payments to prisoners etc.).

130 Transfer of prisoners: prosecution of other offences

In the Repatriation of Prisoners Act 1984, after section 3 insert—

"3A Prosecution of other offences

(1) This section applies where—
(a) a person has been transferred into Great Britain under a warrant under section 1, and
(b) the international arrangements in accordance with which the person has been transferred contain a speciality provision.

(2) The person must not, unless a condition in subsection (3) is met—
(a) be prosecuted for any offence committed before the departure of that person from the country or territory from which that person has been transferred, or
(b) be detained or otherwise subjected to any restriction of liberty for any offence committed before the departure of that person from the country or territory from which that person has been transferred, other than the offence in respect of which the person has been transferred.

(3) For the purposes of subsection (2), the conditions are as follows—
(a) the person has consented to the transfer;
(b) the offence is an offence which is not punishable with imprisonment or another form of detention;
(c) the offence is an offence in respect of which the person will not be detained in connection with the person's trial, sentence or appeal;
(d) the person is given an opportunity to leave Great Britain and—
(i) the person does not do so before the end of the permitted period, or
(ii) if the person does so before the end of the permitted period, the person subsequently returns to Great Britain;
(e) after the transfer has taken place, the person has made a renunciation of the application of subsection (2) to the offence;

(f) the appropriate authority of the country or territory from which the person has been transferred consents to the prosecution of the offence.

(4) For the purpose of subsection (3)(d) the "permitted period" is 45 days starting with the day on which the person's sentence ends.

(5) For the purpose of subsection (3)(e) a renunciation must be made before a court before which the person may be prosecuted for that offence.

(6) In this section a "speciality provision" means a provision preventing or limiting the prosecution, detention or other restriction of liberty of the person ("P") for any offence committed before the departure of P from the country or territory from which P has been transferred, other than for the offence in respect of which P has been transferred."

131 Transit of prisoners

(1) In the Repatriation of Prisoners Act 1984, after section 6 insert—

"6A Transit

(1) The relevant Minister may issue a transit order where—
  (a) the United Kingdom is a party to international arrangements providing for the transfer between the United Kingdom and a country or territory outside the British Islands of persons to whom subsection (2) applies; and
  (b) the relevant Minister has received a request from the appropriate authority of that country or territory in accordance with those arrangements for the transit of a person to whom subsection (2) applies through a part of Great Britain.

(2) A person falls within this subsection if—
  (a) that person is for the time being required to be detained in a prison, a hospital or any other institution either—
    (i) by virtue of an order made in the course of the exercise by a court or tribunal in a country or territory outside the British Islands of its criminal jurisdiction; or
    (ii) by virtue of any provisions of the law of such a country or territory which are similar to any of the provisions of this Act; and
  (b) except in a case where a transit request is made in the circumstances described in section 6D(1), that person is present in a country or territory outside the British Islands.

(3) The relevant Minister may issue a transit order where—
  (a) international arrangements apply to any of the Channel Islands or the Isle of Man which provide for the transfer between that island and a country or territory outside the British Islands of persons to whom subsection (4) applies; and
  (b) the relevant Minister has received a request from the appropriate authority of that island for the transit of a person to whom subsection (4) applies through a part of Great Britain.

(4) A person falls within this subsection if—

(a) that person is for the time being required to be detained in a prison, a hospital or any other institution either—
   (i) by virtue of an order made in the course of the exercise of its criminal jurisdiction by a court or tribunal in the island from which the transit request is made; or
   (ii) by virtue of any provisions of the law of that island which are similar to any of the provisions of this Act; and
(b) except in a case where a transit request is made in the circumstances described in section 6D(1), that person is present in that island.

(5) Terms used in subsection (2)(a) or (4)(a) have the same meaning as in section 1(7).

(6) In this section and sections 6B, 6C and 6D "transit order" means an order issued by the relevant Minister, in respect of a person who has been the subject of a request within subsection (1)(b) or (3)(b), which authorises the detention of that person in any part of Great Britain at any time when that person is in transit.

(7) In subsection (6) "detention" includes detention while the person is being taken from one place to another place within Great Britain.

(8) A person may be detained pursuant to a transit order only for as long as is reasonable and necessary to allow the transit to take place.

(9) In this section and section 6B "relevant Minister" means—
(a) the Scottish Ministers, in a case where it is proposed that the person who is the subject of a request under subsection (1)(b) or (3)(b) will, whilst in transit—
   (i) be present only in Scotland, or
   (ii) arrive in Scotland before being taken to another part of Great Britain;
(b) the Secretary of State, in any other case.

(10) For the purposes of this section and sections 6B and 6C a person who is the subject of a transit order is "in transit" at any time during the period beginning with the arrival of that person in Great Britain and ending with the removal of that person from Great Britain.

6B Transit: supplementary

(1) A person who is the subject of a transit order is deemed to be in the legal custody of the relevant Minister at any time when that person is in transit.

(2) A constable may for the purposes of a transit order detain a person who is the subject of that order.

(3) The relevant Minister may, from time to time, designate any person as a person who is for the time being authorised for the purposes of a transit order to detain a person under the order.

(4) A person authorised under subsection (3) has all the powers, authority, protection and privileges of a constable in any part of Great Britain in which the person who is the subject of the transit order is for the time being.

(5) If a person who is the subject of a transit order escapes or is unlawfully at large, that person may be arrested without warrant by a constable.

(6) A constable may search a person who is the subject of a transit order, and any item in the possession of that person, for any item which that person might use—
   (a) to cause physical injury to that person or to any other person; or
   (b) to assist that person to escape from detention.

(7) The power conferred by subsection (6) does not authorise a constable to require a person to remove any clothing other than an outer coat, jacket, headgear or gloves.

(8) The power conferred by subsection (6) includes power to use reasonable force where necessary.

(9) A constable searching a person in the exercise of the power conferred by subsection (6) may seize any item found if the constable has reasonable grounds for believing that the person searched might use the item —
   (a) to cause physical injury to that person or to any other person; or
   (b) to assist that person to escape from detention.

(10) Any item seized from a person under subsection (9) may be retained while that person is in transit.

(11) In this section "constable" means—
   (a) any person who is a constable in any part of Great Britain or who has, under any enactment (including subsection (4) above), the powers of a constable in any part of Great Britain, or
   (b) any person who is a prison officer within the meaning of section 117(1) of the Criminal Justice and Public Order Act 1994.

(12) A person who is a constable by virtue of subsection (11)(a) has, for the purposes of section 6A, this section and section 6C, all the powers, authority, protection and privileges of a constable in any part of Great Britain in which a person who is the subject of a transit order is for the time being.

6C Transit through different parts of Great Britain

(1) Where the Scottish Ministers issue a transit order and it is proposed that the person who is the subject of the order will be taken to a part of Great Britain other than Scotland whilst in transit, they must notify the Secretary of State.

(2) The Scottish Ministers need not notify the Secretary of State where the Secretary of State has agreed in writing to the transit order.

(3) Unless the Secretary of State agrees in writing to the transit order, that order authorises the detention of the person subject to it in Scotland only.

(4) But where the person escapes or is unlawfully at large, the order also authorises—
   (a) the arrest of the person under section 6B(5) in a part of Great Britain other than Scotland, and

(b) the detention of the person in that part by a constable (within the meaning of that section) for the purpose of taking the person to Scotland.

(5) Where the Secretary of State issues a transit order and it is proposed that the person who is the subject of the order will be taken to Scotland whilst in transit, the Secretary of State must notify the Scottish Ministers.

(6) The Secretary of State need not notify the Scottish Ministers where the Scottish Ministers have agreed in writing to the transit order.

(7) Unless the Scottish Ministers agree in writing to the transit order, that order authorises the detention of the person subject to it only in a part of Great Britain other than Scotland.

(8) But where the person escapes or is unlawfully at large, the order also authorises—

(a) the arrest of the person under section 6B(5) in Scotland, and

(b) the detention of the person in Scotland by a constable (within the meaning of that section) for the purpose of taking the person to a part of Great Britain other than Scotland.

6D Transit: unscheduled arrivals

(1) This section applies where—

(a) a person is being transferred between two countries or territories outside the United Kingdom in accordance with international arrangements between those two countries or territories providing for the transfer of persons within section 6A(2)(a) or (4)(a),

(b) the United Kingdom is a party to international arrangements of the kind mentioned in section 6A(1)(a) with at least one of those countries or territories such that the country or territory can make a request under section 6A(1)(b), and

(c) the person makes an unscheduled arrival in Great Britain.

(2) A constable may detain a person to whom subsection (1) applies until the expiry of the period of 72 hours beginning with the person's arrival in Great Britain or until a transit order is issued under section 6A in respect of that person, whichever is the sooner.

(3) In this section "constable" means any person who is a constable in any part of Great Britain or who has, under any enactment (including section 6B(4) above), the powers of a constable in any part of Great Britain.

(4) A person who is a constable by virtue of subsection (3) has for the purposes of this section all the powers, authority, protection and privileges of a constable in the part of Great Britain in which the person mentioned in subsection (2) is for the time being."

(2) In section 9 of the Repatriation of Prisoners Act 1984 (short title, commencement and extent)—

(a) at the beginning of subsection (3) insert "Subject to subsection (3A),", and

(b) after that subsection insert—

"(3A) Sections 3A and 6A to 6D extend to England and Wales and Scotland only."

CHAPTER 7

OUT OF COURT DISPOSALS

Penalty notices

132 Penalty notices for disorderly behaviour

Schedule 23 (penalty notices for disorderly behaviour) has effect.

Cautions

133 Conditional cautions: involvement of prosecutors

(1) The Criminal Justice Act 2003 is amended as follows.

(2) In section 22(3A) (conditions that may be attached to a conditional caution) for "by a relevant prosecutor" substitute "in the condition".

(3) In section 23(2) (relevant prosecutor must decide there is sufficient evidence to prosecute and that a conditional caution should be given) after "a relevant prosecutor" insert "or the authorised person".

(4) In section 23A(5) (relevant prosecutor must specify amount of financial penalty and how it is to be paid etc) for "a relevant prosecutor must also" substitute "the condition must".

(5) In section 23B (variation of conditions by relevant prosecutor) after "A relevant prosecutor" insert "or an authorised person".

(6) In section 25 (code of practice) in subsection (2)(ga) (Secretary of State's code of practice may include provision about what a relevant prosecutor may provide under section 23A(5)(b)) for "by a relevant prosecutor" substitute "in a condition".

134 Conditional cautions: removal etc of certain foreign offenders

In section 22 of the Criminal Justice Act 2003 (conditional cautions)—

(a) in subsection (3) (both as originally enacted and as substituted by section 17 of the Police and Justice Act 2006) (conditions attached to conditional cautions to have certain objects) for "such a caution" substitute "any conditional caution", and

(b) after subsection (3C) insert—

"(3D) A conditional caution given to a relevant foreign offender may have conditions attached to it that have one or more of the objects mentioned in subsection (3E) (whether or not in addition to conditions with one or more of the objects mentioned in subsection (3)).

(3E) The objects are—
(a) bringing about the departure of the relevant foreign offender from the United Kingdom;
(b) ensuring that the relevant foreign offender does not return to the United Kingdom for a period of time.

(3F) If a relevant foreign offender is given a conditional caution with a condition attached to it with the object of ensuring that the offender does not return to the United Kingdom for a period of time, the expiry of that period does not of itself give rise to any right on the part of the offender to return to the United Kingdom.

(3G) In this section "relevant foreign offender" means—
(a) an offender directions for whose removal from the United Kingdom have been, or may be, given under—
(i) Schedule 2 to the Immigration Act 1971, or
(ii) section 10 of the Immigration and Asylum Act 1999, or
(b) an offender against whom a deportation order under section 5 of the Immigration Act 1971 is in force."

Youth cautions

135 Youth cautions

(1) Omit sections 65 (reprimands and warning) and 66 (effect of reprimands and warnings) of the Crime and Disorder Act 1998.

(2) Before section 66A of that Act insert—

"Young offenders: youth cautions

66ZA Youth cautions

(1) A constable may give a child or young person ("Y") a caution under this section (a "youth caution") if—
(a) the constable decides that there is sufficient evidence to charge Y with an offence,
(b) Y admits to the constable that Y committed the offence, and
(c) the constable does not consider that Y should be prosecuted or given a youth conditional caution in respect of the offence.

(2) A youth caution given to a person under the age of 17 must be given in the presence of an appropriate adult.

(3) If a constable gives a youth caution to a person, the constable must explain the matters referred to in subsection (4) in ordinary language to—
(a) that person, and
(b) where that person is under the age of 17, the appropriate adult.

(4) Those matters are—
(a) the effect of subsections (1) to (3) and (5) to (7) of section 66ZB, and

(b) any guidance issued under subsection (4) of that section.

(5) The Secretary of State must publish, in such manner as the Secretary of State considers appropriate, guidance as to—

(a) the circumstances in which it is appropriate to give youth cautions,

(b) the places where youth cautions may be given,

(c) the category of constable by whom youth cautions may be given, and

(d) the form which youth cautions are to take and the manner in which they are to be given and recorded.

(6) No caution other than a youth caution or a youth conditional caution may be given to a child or young person.

(7) In this Chapter "appropriate adult", in relation to a child or young person, means—

(a) a parent or guardian of the child or young person,

(b) if the child or young person is in the care of a local authority or voluntary organisation, a person representing that authority or organisation,

(c) a social worker of a local authority, or

(d) if no person falling within paragraph (a), (b) or (c) is available, any responsible person aged 18 or over who is not a police officer or a person employed by the police.

66ZB Effect of youth cautions

(1) If a constable gives a youth caution to a person, the constable must as soon as practicable refer the person to a youth offending team.

(2) Subject to subsection (3), on a referral of a person under subsection (1), the youth offending team—

(a) must assess the person, and

(b) unless they consider it inappropriate to do so, must arrange for the person to participate in a rehabilitation programme.

(3) If the person has not previously been referred under subsection (1) and has not previously been given a youth conditional caution, the youth offending team—

(a) may assess the person, and

(b) may arrange for the person to participate in a rehabilitation programme.

(4) The Secretary of State must publish, in such manner as the Secretary of State considers appropriate, guidance as to—

(a) what should be included in a rehabilitation programme arranged for a person under subsection (2) or (3),

(b) the manner in which any failure by a person to participate in a programme is to be recorded, and

(c) the persons to whom any such failure must be notified.

(5) Subsection (6) applies if—

(a) a person who has received two or more youth cautions is convicted of an offence committed within two years beginning with the date of the last of those cautions, or

(b) a person who has received a youth conditional caution followed by a youth caution is convicted of an offence committed within two years beginning with the date of the youth caution.

(6) The court by or before which the person is convicted—

(a) must not make an order under section 12(1)(b) of the Powers of Criminal Courts (Sentencing) Act 2000 (conditional discharge) in respect of the offence unless it is of the opinion that there are exceptional circumstances relating to the offence or the person that justify it doing so, and

(b) where it does so, must state in open court that it is of that opinion and its reasons for that opinion.

(7) There may be cited in criminal proceedings—

(a) a youth caution given to a person, and

(b) a report on a failure by a person to participate in a rehabilitation programme arranged for the person under subsection (2) or (3),

in the same circumstances as a conviction of the person may be cited.

(8) In this section "rehabilitation programme" means a programme with the purpose of rehabilitating participants and preventing them from re-offending."

(3) Schedule 24 (youth cautions: consequential amendments) has effect.

(4) The amendments made by this section and that Schedule do not apply in relation to an offence committed before they come into force.

(5) A reprimand or warning of a person under section 65 of the Crime and Disorder Act 1998, or any caution treated as such by virtue of paragraph 5 of Schedule 9 to that Act, is to be treated for the purposes of any enactment or instrument (whenever passed or made) as a youth caution given to that person under section 66ZA(1) of that Act.

(6) A referral of a person to a youth offending team under section 66(1) of the Crime and Disorder Act 1998 is to be treated for the purposes of section 66ZB of that Act as a referral under that section.

(7) A rehabilitation programme provided under section 66 of the Crime and Disorder Act 1998 is to be treated for the purposes of any enactment or instrument (whenever passed or made) as provided under section 66ZB of that Act.

136 Youth conditional cautions: previous convictions

In section 66A(1) of the Crime and Disorder Act 1998 (requirements to be met before youth conditional caution may be given) omit paragraph (a) and the "and" at the end of that paragraph (requirement of no previous convictions).

137 Youth conditional cautions: references to youth offending teams

In section 66A of the Crime and Disorder Act 1998 (youth conditional cautions) after subsection (6) insert—

"(6A) If an authorised person gives a youth conditional caution to an offender, the authorised person must as soon as practicable refer the offender to a youth offending team."

138 Youth conditional cautions: involvement of prosecutors

(1) The Crime and Disorder Act 1998 is amended as follows.

(2) In section 66A(4) (conditions that may be attached to a youth conditional caution) for "by a relevant prosecutor" substitute "in the condition".

(3) In section 66B(2) (relevant prosecutor must decide that there is sufficient evidence to prosecute and that a conditional caution should be given) after "a relevant prosecutor" insert "or the authorised person".

(4) In section 66C(5) (relevant prosecutor must specify amount of financial penalty and how it must be paid etc) for "a relevant prosecutor must also" substitute "the condition must".

(5) In section 66D (variation of conditions by relevant prosecutor) after "A relevant prosecutor" insert "or an authorised person".

(6) In section 66G (code of practice) in subsection (2)(h) (Secretary of State's code of practice may include provision about what a relevant prosecutor may provide under section 66C(5)(b)) for "by a relevant prosecutor" substitute "in a condition".

CHAPTER 8

REHABILITATION OF OFFENDERS

139 Establishment or alteration of rehabilitation periods

(1) The Rehabilitation of Offenders Act 1974 is amended as follows.

(2) In section 5(1)(b) and (d) (sentences excluded from rehabilitation) for "thirty months" substitute "forty eight months".

(3) In the opening words of section 5(1A) (references to provisions of the Armed Forces Act 2006) for "subsection (1)(d)" substitute "this section".

(4) For section 5(2) to (11) (rehabilitation periods) substitute—

"(2) For the purposes of this Act and subject to subsections (3) and (4), the rehabilitation period for a sentence is the period—

(a) beginning with the date of the conviction in respect of which the sentence is imposed, and

(b) ending at the time listed in the following Table in relation to that sentence:

Sentence	*End of rehabilitation period for adult offenders*	*End of rehabilitation period for offenders under 18 at date of conviction*
A custodial sentence of more than 30 months and up to, or consisting of, 48 months	The end of the period of 7 years beginning with the day on which the sentence (including any licence period) is completed	The end of the period of 42 months beginning with the day on which the sentence (including any licence period) is completed
A custodial sentence of more than 6 months and up to, or consisting of, 30 months	The end of the period of 48 months beginning with the day on which the sentence (including any licence period) is completed	The end of the period of 24 months beginning with the day on which the sentence (including any licence period) is completed
A custodial sentence of 6 months or less	The end of the period of 24 months beginning with the day on which the sentence (including any licence period) is completed	The end of the period of 18 months beginning with the day on which the sentence (including any licence period) is completed
Removal from Her Majesty's service	The end of the period of 12 months beginning with the date of the conviction in respect of which the sentence is imposed	The end of the period of 6 months beginning with the date of the conviction in respect of which the sentence is imposed
A sentence of service detention	The end of the period of 12 months beginning with the day on which the sentence is completed	The end of the period of 6 months beginning with the day on which the sentence is completed

Sentence	*End of rehabilitation period for adult offenders*	*End of rehabilitation period for offenders under 18 at date of conviction*
A fine	The end of the period of 12 months beginning with the date of the conviction in respect of which the sentence is imposed	The end of the period of 6 months beginning with the date of the conviction in respect of which the sentence is imposed
A compensation order	The date on which the payment is made in full	The date on which the payment is made in full
A community or youth rehabilitation order	The end of the period of 12 months beginning with the day provided for by or under the order as the last day on which the order is to have effect	The end of the period of 6 months beginning with the day provided for by or under the order as the last day on which the order is to have effect
A relevant order	The day provided for by or under the order as the last day on which the order is to have effect	The day provided for by or under the order as the last day on which the order is to have effect

(3) Where no provision is made by or under a community or youth rehabilitation order or a relevant order for the last day on which the order is to have effect, the rehabilitation period for the order is to be the period of 24 months beginning with the date of conviction.

(4) There is no rehabilitation period for—

(a) an order discharging a person absolutely for an offence, or

(b) any other sentence in respect of a conviction where the sentence is not dealt with in the Table or under subsection (3),

and, in such cases, references in this Act to any rehabilitation period are to be read as if the period of time were nil.

(5) See also—

(a) section 8AA (protection afforded to spent alternatives to prosecution), and

(b) Schedule 2 (protection for spent cautions).

(6) The Secretary of State may by order amend column 2 or 3 of the Table or the number of months for the time being specified in subsection (3).

(7) For the purposes of this section—
   (a) consecutive terms of imprisonment or other custodial sentences are to be treated as a single term,
   (b) terms of imprisonment or other custodial sentences which are wholly or partly concurrent (that is terms of imprisonment or other custodial sentences imposed in respect of offences of which a person was convicted in the same proceedings) are to be treated as a single term,
   (c) no account is to be taken of any subsequent variation, made by a court dealing with a person in respect of a suspended sentence of imprisonment, of the term originally imposed,
   (d) no account is to be taken of any subsequent variation of the day originally provided for by or under an order as the last day on which the order is to have effect,
   (e) no account is to be taken of any detention or supervision ordered by a court under section 104(3) of the Powers of Criminal Courts (Sentencing) Act 2000,
   (f) a sentence imposed by a court outside England and Wales is to be treated as the sentence mentioned in this section to which it most closely corresponds.

(8) In this section—

"community or youth rehabilitation order" means—
   (a) a community order under section 177 of the Criminal Justice Act 2003,
   (b) a service community order or overseas community order under the Armed Forces Act 2006,
   (c) a youth rehabilitation order under Part 1 of the Criminal Justice and Immigration Act 2008, or
   (d) any order of a kind superseded (whether directly or indirectly) by an order mentioned in paragraph (a), (b) or (c),

"custodial sentence" means—
   (a) a sentence of imprisonment,
   (b) a sentence of detention in a young offender institution,
   (c) a sentence of Borstal training,
   (d) a sentence of youth custody,
   (e) a sentence of corrective training,
   (f) a sentence of detention under section 91 of the Powers of Criminal Courts (Sentencing) Act 2000 or section 209 of the Armed Forces Act 2006,
   (g) a detention and training order under section 100 of the Powers of Criminal Courts (Sentencing) Act 2000 or an order under section 211 of the Armed Forces Act 2006,
   (h) any sentence of a kind superseded (whether directly or indirectly) by a sentence mentioned in paragraph (f) or (g),

"earlier statutory order" means—
   (a) an order under section 54 of the Children and Young Persons Act 1933 committing the person convicted to custody in a remand home,

(b) an approved school order under section 57 of that Act, or

(c) any order of a kind superseded (whether directly or indirectly) by an order mentioned in any of paragraphs (c) to (e) of the definition of "relevant order" or in paragraph (a) or (b) above,

"relevant order" means—

(a) an order discharging a person conditionally for an offence,

(b) an order binding a person over to keep the peace or be of good behaviour,

(c) an order under section 1(2A) of the Street Offences Act 1959,

(d) a hospital order under Part 3 of the Mental Health Act 1983 (with or without a restriction order),

(e) a referral order under section 16 of the Powers of Criminal Courts (Sentencing) Act 2000,

(f) an earlier statutory order, or

(g) any order which imposes a disqualification, disability, prohibition or other penalty and is not otherwise dealt with in the Table or under subsection (3),

but does not include a reparation order under section 73 of the Powers of Criminal Courts (Sentencing) Act 2000,

"removal from Her Majesty's service" means a sentence of dismissal with disgrace from Her Majesty's service, a sentence of dismissal from Her Majesty's service or a sentence of cashiering or discharge with ignominy,

"sentence of imprisonment" includes a sentence of penal servitude (and "term of imprisonment" is to be read accordingly),

"sentence of service detention" means—

(a) a sentence of service detention (within the meaning given by section 374 of the Armed Forces Act 2006), or a sentence of detention corresponding to such a sentence, in respect of a conviction in service disciplinary proceedings, or

(b) any sentence of a kind superseded (whether directly or indirectly) by a sentence mentioned in paragraph (a)."

(5) In section 6 (subsequent convictions to extend the rehabilitation period applicable to a conviction)—

(a) in subsection (5) (exception to rule for certain orders imposing disqualifications etc) for "in accordance with section 5(8) above" substitute "by virtue of paragraph (g) of the definition of "relevant order" in section 5(8) above", and

(b) omit subsection (6) (other exceptions to the rule).

(6) After section 8A (protection afforded to spent cautions) insert—

"8AA Protection afforded to spent alternatives to prosecution

(1) The following provisions of this Act apply, with the modifications specified in subsection (3), to a spent alternative to prosecution as they apply to a spent caution—

(a) section 9A (unauthorised disclosure of spent cautions), and

(b) paragraphs 2 to 6 of Schedule 2 (protection relating to spent cautions and ancillary circumstances).

(2) An alternative to prosecution becomes spent for the purposes of this Act when it becomes spent under the law of Scotland.

(3) The modifications mentioned in subsection (1) are—

(a) references to cautions are to be read as references to alternatives to prosecution (and references to cautioned are to be read accordingly),

(b) references to the offence which was the subject of the caution are to be read as references to the offence in respect of which the alternative to prosecution was given,

(c) paragraphs (e) and (f) of paragraph 2(1) of Schedule 2 are to be read as if they were—

"(e) anything done or undergone in pursuance of the terms of the alternative to prosecution,",

(d) references to cautions for an offence are to be read as references to alternatives to prosecution in respect of an offence, and

(e) the reference in paragraph 5 of Schedule 2 to the rehabilitation period applicable to the caution is to be read as a reference to the time at which the alternative to prosecution becomes spent.

(4) In this section "alternative to prosecution" has the same meaning as in section 8B as that section has effect in the law of Scotland but disregarding subsection (1)(f) of that section."

(7) In paragraph 1 of Schedule 2 (protection for spent cautions)—

(a) in sub-paragraph (1)(a) (when conditional cautions to be regarded as spent cautions) for ", at the end of the relevant period for the caution;" substitute "—

(i) at the end of the period of three months from the date on which the caution is given, or

(ii) if earlier, when the caution ceases to have effect; and", and

(b) omit sub-paragraphs (2) and (3) (meaning of "the relevant period for the caution").

140 No rehabilitation for certain immigration or nationality purposes

Before section 57 of the UK Borders Act 2007 (and after the italic cross-heading before that section) insert—

"56A No rehabilitation for certain immigration or nationality purposes

(1) Section 4(1), (2) and (3) of the Rehabilitation of Offenders Act 1974 (effect of rehabilitation) do not apply—

(a) in relation to any proceedings in respect of a relevant immigration decision or a relevant nationality decision, or

(b) otherwise for the purposes of, or in connection with, any such decision.

(2) In this section—

"immigration officer" means a person appointed by the Secretary of State as an immigration officer under paragraph 1 of Schedule 2 to the Immigration Act 1971,

"relevant immigration decision" means any decision, or proposed decision, of the Secretary of State or an immigration officer under or by virtue of the Immigration Acts, or rules made under section 3 of the Immigration Act 1971 (immigration rules), in relation to the entitlement of a person to enter or remain in the United Kingdom (including, in particular, the removal of a person from the United Kingdom, whether by deportation or otherwise),

"relevant nationality decision" means any decision, or proposed decision, of the Secretary of State under or by virtue of—

(a) the British Nationality Act 1981,

(b) the British Nationality (Hong Kong) Act 1990, or

(c) the Hong Kong (War Wives and Widows) Act 1996,

in relation to the good character of a person.

(3) The references in subsection (2) to the Immigration Acts and to the Acts listed in the definition of "relevant nationality decision" include references to any provision made under section 2(2) of the European Communities Act 1972, or of EU law, which relates to the subject matter of the Act concerned."

141 Transitional and consequential provision

(1) Section 139 applies in relation to convictions or (as the case may be) cautions before the commencement date (as well as in relation to convictions or cautions on or after that date).

(2) The Rehabilitation of Offenders Act 1974 ("the 1974 Act") applies in relation to convictions or cautions before the commencement date as if the amendments and repeals made by section 139 had always had effect.

(3) Where by virtue of subsection (2)—

(a) a person would, before the commencement date, have been treated for the purposes of the 1974 Act as a rehabilitated person in respect of a conviction, or

(b) a conviction would, before that date, have been treated for the purposes of that Act as spent,

the person or conviction concerned is (subject to any order made by virtue of section 4(4) or 7(4) of that Act) to be so treated on and after that date.

(4) Where by virtue of subsection (2)—

(a) a person would, before the commencement date, have been treated as mentioned in paragraph 3(1) of Schedule 2 to the 1974 Act in respect of a caution, or

(b) a caution would, before that date, have been treated for the purposes of that Act as spent,

the person or caution concerned is (subject to any order made by virtue of paragraph 4 or 6(1) and (4) of that Schedule to that Act) to be so treated on and after that date.

(5) But—

(a) no person who, immediately before the commencement date—
(i) is treated as a rehabilitated person for the purposes of the 1974 Act in respect of a conviction, or
(ii) is treated as mentioned in paragraph 3(1) of Schedule 2 to that Act in respect of a caution, and
(b) no conviction or caution which, immediately before the commencement date, is treated for the purposes of that Act as spent,

is to cease to be so treated merely because of section 139.

(6) Section 139 does not apply in relation to alternatives to prosecution given before the commencement date.

(7) Section 140 applies in relation to convictions before the commencement date (as well as in relation to convictions on or after that date).

(8) Section 140 applies as mentioned in subsection (7) above whether or not, immediately before the commencement date—
(a) the person concerned is treated as a rehabilitated person for the purposes of the 1974 Act in respect of the conviction, or
(b) the conviction is treated for the purposes of that Act as spent.

(9) But section 140 does not affect—
(a) any proceedings begun, but not completed, before the commencement date,
(b) any applications for immigration or nationality decisions made, but not finally determined, before the commencement date, or
(c) the validity of any proceedings, or any relevant immigration or nationality decision (within the meaning of section 56A of the UK Borders Act 2007) which is made, before the commencement date.

(10) Schedule 25 (consequential provision) has effect.

(11) Any reference in this section to section 139 is to be read as including a reference to Schedule 25.

(12) In this section "the commencement date" means such day as may be specified by order of the Secretary of State made by statutory instrument; and different days may be specified for different purposes.

CHAPTER 9

OFFENCES

142 Offences of threatening with article with blade or point or offensive weapon in public or on school premises

(1) In the Prevention of Crime Act 1953, after section 1 (prohibition of the carrying of offensive weapons without lawful authority or reasonable excuse) insert—

"1A Offence of threatening with offensive weapon in public

(1) A person is guilty of an offence if that person—
(a) has an offensive weapon with him or her in a public place,
(b) unlawfully and intentionally threatens another person with the weapon, and

(c) does so in such a way that there is an immediate risk of serious physical harm to that other person.

(2) For the purposes of this section physical harm is serious if it amounts to grievous bodily harm for the purposes of the Offences against the Person Act 1861.

(3) In this section "public place" and "offensive weapon" have the same meaning as in section 1.

(4) A person guilty of an offence under this section is liable—

(a) on summary conviction, to imprisonment for a term not exceeding 12 months or to a fine not exceeding the statutory maximum, or to both;

(b) on conviction on indictment, to imprisonment for a term not exceeding 4 years or to a fine, or to both.

(5) Where a person aged 16 or over is convicted of an offence under this section, the court must impose an appropriate custodial sentence (with or without a fine) unless the court is of the opinion that there are particular circumstances which—

(a) relate to the offence or to the offender, and

(b) would make it unjust to do so in all the circumstances.

(6) In this section "appropriate custodial sentence" means—

(a) in the case of a person who is aged 18 or over when convicted, a sentence of imprisonment for a term of at least 6 months;

(b) in the case of a person who is aged at least 16 but under 18 when convicted, a detention and training order of at least 4 months.

(7) In considering whether it is of the opinion mentioned in subsection (5) in the case of a person aged under 18, the court must have regard to its duty under section 44 of the Children and Young Persons Act 1933.

(8) In relation to an offence committed before the commencement of section 154(1) of the Criminal Justice Act 2003, the reference in subsection (4)(a) to 12 months is to be read as a reference to 6 months.

(9) In relation to times before the coming into force of paragraph 180 of Schedule 7 to the Criminal Justice and Court Services Act 2000, the reference in subsection (6)(a) to a sentence of imprisonment, in relation to an offender aged under 21 at the time of conviction, is to be read as a reference to a sentence of detention in a young offender institution.

(10) If on a person's trial for an offence under this section (whether on indictment or not) the person is found not guilty of that offence but it is proved that the person committed an offence under section 1, the person may be convicted of the offence under that section."

(2) In the Criminal Justice Act 1988 after section 139A (offence of having article with blade or point or offensive weapon on school premises) insert—

"139AA Offence of threatening with article with blade or point or offensive weapon

(1) A person is guilty of an offence if that person—

(a) has an article to which this section applies with him or her in a public place or on school premises,

(b) unlawfully and intentionally threatens another person with the article, and

(c) does so in such a way that there is an immediate risk of serious physical harm to that other person.

(2) In relation to a public place this section applies to an article to which section 139 applies.

(3) In relation to school premises this section applies to each of these—

(a) an article to which section 139 applies;

(b) an offensive weapon within the meaning of section 1 of the Prevention of Crime Act 1953.

(4) For the purposes of this section physical harm is serious if it amounts to grievous bodily harm for the purposes of the Offences against the Person Act 1861.

(5) In this section—

"public place" has the same meaning as in section 139;

"school premises" has the same meaning as in section 139A.

(6) A person guilty of an offence under this section is liable—

(a) on summary conviction, to imprisonment for a term not exceeding 12 months or to a fine not exceeding the statutory maximum, or to both;

(b) on conviction on indictment, to imprisonment for a term not exceeding 4 years or to a fine, or to both.

(7) Where a person aged 16 or over is convicted of an offence under this section, the court must impose an appropriate custodial sentence (with or without a fine) unless the court is of the opinion that there are particular circumstances which—

(a) relate to the offence or to the offender, and

(b) would make it unjust to do so in all the circumstances.

(8) In this section "appropriate custodial sentence" means—

(a) in the case of a person who is aged 18 or over when convicted, a sentence of imprisonment for a term of at least 6 months;

(b) in the case of a person who is aged at least 16 but under 18 when convicted, a detention and training order of at least 4 months.

(9) In considering whether it is of the opinion mentioned in subsection (7) in the case of a person aged under 18, the court must have regard to its duty under section 44 of the Children and Young Persons Act 1933.

(10) In relation to an offence committed before the commencement of section 154(1) of the Criminal Justice Act 2003, the reference in subsection (6)(a) to 12 months is to be read as a reference to 6 months.

(11) In relation to times before the coming into force of paragraph 180 of Schedule 7 to the Criminal Justice and Court Services Act 2000, the reference in subsection (8)(a) to a sentence of imprisonment, in relation to an offender aged under 21 at the time of conviction, is to be read as a reference to a sentence of detention in a young offender institution.

(12) If on a person's trial for an offence under this section (whether on indictment or not) the person is found not guilty of that offence but it is

proved that the person committed an offence under section 139 or 139A, the person may be convicted of the offence under that section."

(3) Schedule 26 (knives and offensive weapons: minor and consequential amendments) has effect.

143 Offence of causing serious injury by dangerous driving

(1) The Road Traffic Act 1988 is amended as follows.

(2) After section 1 insert—

"1A Causing serious injury by dangerous driving

(1) A person who causes serious injury to another person by driving a mechanically propelled vehicle dangerously on a road or other public place is guilty of an offence.

(2) In this section "serious injury" means—

(a) in England and Wales, physical harm which amounts to grievous bodily harm for the purposes of the Offences against the Person Act 1861, and

(b) in Scotland, severe physical injury."

(3) In section 2A (meaning of dangerous driving) in subsections (1) and (2) after "sections 1" insert ", 1A".

(4) Section 1A inserted by subsection (2) has effect only in relation to driving occurring after that subsection comes into force.

(5) In Part 1 of Schedule 2 to the Road Traffic Offenders Act 1988 (prosecution and punishment of offences under the Traffic Acts) in the appropriate place insert—

"RTA section 1A	Causing serious injury by dangerous driving.	(a) Summarily.	(a) 12 months or the statutory maximum or both.	Obligatory.	Obligatory.	3-11."
		(b) On indictment.	(b) 5 years or a fine or both.			

(6) In the entry inserted by subsection (5), in relation to an offence committed before the commencement of section 154(1) of the Criminal Justice Act 2003 "12 months" is to be read as "6 months (in England and Wales) or 12 months (in Scotland)".

(7) Schedule 27 (causing serious injury by dangerous driving: minor and consequential amendments) has effect.

144 Offence of squatting in a residential building

(1) A person commits an offence if—

(a) the person is in a residential building as a trespasser having entered it as a trespasser,

(b) the person knows or ought to know that he or she is a trespasser, and

(c) the person is living in the building or intends to live there for any period.

(2) The offence is not committed by a person holding over after the end of a lease or licence (even if the person leaves and re-enters the building).

(3) For the purposes of this section—

(a) "building" includes any structure or part of a structure (including a temporary or moveable structure), and

(b) a building is "residential" if it is designed or adapted, before the time of entry, for use as a place to live.

(4) For the purposes of this section the fact that a person derives title from a trespasser, or has the permission of a trespasser, does not prevent the person from being a trespasser.

(5) A person convicted of an offence under this section is liable on summary conviction to imprisonment for a term not exceeding 51 weeks or a fine not exceeding level 5 on the standard scale (or both).

(6) In relation to an offence committed before the commencement of section 281(5) of the Criminal Justice Act 2003, the reference in subsection (5) to 51 weeks is to be read as a reference to 6 months.

(7) For the purposes of subsection (1)(a) it is irrelevant whether the person entered the building as a trespasser before or after the commencement of this section.

(8) In section 17 of the Police and Criminal Evidence Act 1984 (entry for purpose of arrest etc)—

(a) in subsection (1)(c), after sub-paragraph (v) insert—

"(vi) section 144 of the Legal Aid, Sentencing and Punishment of Offenders Act 2012 (squatting in a residential building);";

(b) in subsection (3), for "or (iv)" substitute ", (iv) or (vi)".

(9) In Schedule 10 to the Criminal Justice and Public Order Act 1994 (consequential amendments), omit paragraph 53(b).

145 Scrap metal dealing: increase in penalties for existing offences

(1) The Scrap Metal Dealers Act 1964 is amended as follows.

(2) For the following words (which have effect as references to a fine not exceeding level 3 on the standard scale) substitute in each case "a fine not exceeding level 5 on the standard scale"—

(a) in section 1(7) (dealer failing to register) the words from "a fine" to the end;

(b) in section 2(6) (dealer failing to record dealings) the words from "a fine" to the end;

(c) in section 3(4) (itinerant collector failing to keep receipts) the words from "a fine" to the end;

(d) in section 4(4) (convicted dealer failing to meet additional requirements) the same words before "and the court".

(3) For the following words (which have effect as references to a fine not exceeding level 1 on the standard scale) substitute in each case "a fine not exceeding level 3 on the standard scale"—

(a) in section 1(8) (dealer failing to give notice of cessation of business) the words from "a fine" to the end;

(b) in section 5(1) (dealer acquiring metal from a person under 16) the same words before the proviso;

(c) in section 5(2) (selling metal to a dealer under a false name or address) the words from "a fine" to the end;

(d) in section 6(5) (obstructing entry and inspection) the words from "a fine" to the end.

146 Offence of buying scrap metal for cash etc

(1) The Scrap Metal Dealers Act 1964 is amended as follows.

(2) After section 3 insert—

"3A Offence of buying scrap metal for cash etc

(1) A scrap metal dealer must not pay for scrap metal except—

(a) by a cheque which under section 81A of the Bills of Exchange Act 1882 is not transferable, or

(b) by an electronic transfer of funds (authorised by credit or debit card or otherwise).

(2) The Secretary of State may by order amend subsection (1) to permit other methods of payment.

(3) In this section paying includes paying in kind (with goods or services).

(4) If a scrap metal dealer pays for scrap metal in breach of subsection (1), each of the following is guilty of an offence—

(a) the scrap metal dealer;

(b) a person who makes the payment acting for the dealer;

(c) a manager who fails to take reasonable steps to prevent the payment being made in breach of subsection (1).

(5) In subsection (4)(c) "manager" means a person who works in the carrying on of the dealer's business as a scrap metal dealer in a capacity, whether paid or unpaid, which authorises the person to prevent the payment being made in breach of subsection (1).

(6) Subsection (1) does not apply if—

(a) the payment is made in the carrying on of the dealer's business as a scrap metal dealer as part of the business of an itinerant collector, and

(b) at the time of the payment an order under section 3(1) is in force in relation to the dealer.

(7) A person guilty of an offence under this section is liable on summary conviction to a fine not exceeding level 5 on the standard scale.

(8) An order under subsection (2) is to be made by statutory instrument.

(9) A statutory instrument containing an order under subsection (2) may not be made unless a draft of the instrument has been laid before and approved by a resolution of each House of Parliament."

(3) Section 2 (records of dealings) is amended as follows.

(4) After subsection (2)(d) insert—

"(da) where paragraph (d) applies, any part of the price that is unpaid at the time when the entry is to be made;".

(5) In subsection (2)(e) for "the last preceding paragraph" substitute "paragraph (d)".

(6) After subsection (4) insert—

"(4A) If a scrap metal dealer pays at any time for scrap metal falling within subsection (1)(a)—

(a) the dealer must keep, with the book containing the entry relating to receipt of the scrap metal, a copy of the cheque (if the payment was by cheque), or any receipt identifying the transfer (if the payment was by electronic transfer and such a receipt was obtained), and

(b) the particulars required by this section to be entered include those listed in subsection (4B).

(4B) The particulars are—

(a) the full name and address of any person who makes the payment acting for the dealer;

(b) the full name and address of the person to whom the payment is made;

(c) in the case of an electronic transfer where no receipt identifying the transfer was obtained, particulars identifying the transfer.

(4C) Anything kept by virtue of subsection (4A)(a) must be marked so as to identify the scrap metal by reference to the entry relating to receipt of the metal.

(4D) An entry in pursuance of subsection (4A)(b)—

(a) must be made immediately after the payment is made, and

(b) if not made at the same time as the entry relating to receipt of the scrap metal, must identify the metal by reference to that entry."

(7) In subsection (5), after "this section and" insert "the book and anything required by subsection (4A)(a) to be kept with it".

(8) Section 3 (special provisions as to records in certain cases) is amended as follows.

(9) In subsection (5)(d), for "subsection (4)" substitute "subsections (4) and (4D)(a)".

(10) In subsection (6)(a)—

(a) after "books" insert ", and the obligation imposed by subsection (4A)(a) of that section to keep anything with a book,";

(b) after "the like particulars" insert ", and to keeping the same things,";

(c) for "and (3)" substitute ", (3) and (4A) to (4D)".

(11) In subsection (6)(c), for "subsection (4)" substitute "subsections (4) and (4D)(a)".

(12) In section 4(1) (power for court to impose additional requirements on convicted dealers)—

(a) omit "or" at the end of paragraph (a), and

(b) after that paragraph insert—

"(aa) is convicted of an offence under section 3A, or".

(13) Section 6 (rights of entry and inspection) is amended as follows.

(14) After subsection (3) insert—

"(3A) Whether or not a place is one to which a constable has a right of entry in accordance with subsection (1), a justice of the peace may issue a warrant described in subsection (3B) if satisfied by information on oath that there are reasonable grounds for believing that the place—

(a) is a scrap metal store where scrap metal paid for contrary to section 3A is or has been received or kept, or

(b) is a place to which admission is reasonably required in order to ascertain whether that section is being complied with.

(3B) The warrant is a warrant signed by the justice issuing it which specifies the place concerned and authorises a constable to enter the place, if need be by force, at any time within one month from the date of the warrant.

(3C) A constable authorised to enter a place by a warrant granted under subsection (3A) has a right—

(a) to inspect that place;

(b) to require production of, and to inspect, any scrap metal kept at that place;

(c) to require production of and to inspect any book which the dealer is required by this Act to keep at that place and any copy or receipt required to be kept with the book, or, as the case may be, any receipt which the dealer is required to keep as mentioned in section 3(1)(b), and to take copies of the book, copy or receipt;

(d) to require production of and to inspect any other record kept at that place relating to payment for scrap metal, and to take copies of the record."

(15) In subsection (4) for "the last preceding subsection" substitute "subsection (3) or (3A)".

147 Review of offence of buying scrap metal for cash etc

(1) Before the end of 5 years beginning with the day on which section 146(2) comes into force, the Secretary of State must—

(a) carry out a review of the offence created by that subsection, and

(b) publish a report of the conclusions of the review.

(2) The report must in particular—

(a) set out the objectives intended to be achieved by creating the offence,

(b) assess the extent to which those objectives have been achieved, and

(c) assess whether it is appropriate to retain the offence to achieve those objectives.

148 Reasonable force for the purposes of self-defence etc

(1) Section 76 of the Criminal Justice and Immigration Act 2008 (reasonable force for the purposes of self-defence etc) is amended as follows.

(2) In subsection (2) after paragraph (a) omit "and" and insert—

"(aa) the common law defence of defence of property; and".

(3) After subsection (6) insert—

"(6A) In deciding the question mentioned in subsection (3), a possibility that D could have retreated is to be considered (so far as relevant) as a factor to be taken into account, rather than as giving rise to a duty to retreat."

(4) In subsection (8) for "Subsection (7) is" substitute "Subsections (6A) and (7) are".

(5) In subsection (10)(a) after sub-paragraph (i) omit "or" and insert—

"(ia) the purpose of defence of property under the common law, or".

(6) Paragraph 27 of Schedule 27 to the Criminal Justice and Immigration Act 2008 (which provides for section 76 of that Act to apply whenever the alleged offence took place, but not in relation to certain proceedings if they began, or the arraignment took place, before that section comes into force) applies to any amendment made by this section to section 76 of that Act as it applies to that section, but as if references to the date on which that section comes into force were references to the date on which the amendment comes into force.

PART 4

FINAL PROVISIONS

149 Power to make consequential and supplementary provision etc

(1) The Lord Chancellor or the Secretary of State may by regulations make consequential, supplementary, incidental, transitional, transitory or saving provision in relation to any provision of this Act.

(2) The regulations may, in particular amend, repeal, revoke or otherwise modify legislation.

(3) Regulations under this section are to be made by statutory instrument.

(4) A statutory instrument containing regulations under this section is subject to annulment in pursuance of a resolution of either House of Parliament, subject to subsection (5).

(5) A statutory instrument containing regulations under this section that amend or repeal an Act (whether alone or with other provision) may not be made unless a draft of the instrument has been laid before, and approved by a resolution of, each House of Parliament.

(6) In this section—

"Act" includes an Act or Measure of the National Assembly for Wales;

"legislation", in relation to regulations made in relation to a provision of this Act, means—

(a) this Act or an Act passed before or in the same Session as this Act, or

(b) an instrument made under an Act before the provision comes into force.

150 Financial provision

There is to be paid out of money provided by Parliament—

(a) any expenditure incurred by a Minister of the Crown by virtue of this Act, and

(b) any increase attributable to this Act in the sums payable under any other Act out of money so provided.

151 Commencement

(1) The provisions of this Act come into force on such day as the Lord Chancellor or the Secretary of State may appoint by order, subject to subsections (2) and (3).

(2) The following provisions come into force on the day on which this Act is passed—

(a) section 77,

(b) section 119, and

(c) this Part.

(3) This section does not apply to section 76 (but see section 77).

(4) An order under this section is to be made by statutory instrument.

(5) An order under this section may—

(a) appoint different days for different purposes, and

(b) make transitional, transitory or saving provision.

(6) An order under this section bringing into force section 133, 134, 136, 137 or 138 may appoint different days for different areas.

152 Extent

(1) Parts 1 to 3 of this Act extend to England and Wales only, subject to subsections (2) to (8).

(2) Sections 130 and 131(1) extend to England and Wales and Scotland.

(3) The following provisions extend to England and Wales and Northern Ireland—

(a) section 22,

(b) section 33,

(c) section 40 and Schedule 6, and

(d) sections 41 to 43.

(4) Section 77 extends to England and Wales, Scotland and Northern Ireland, subject to subsection (11).

(5) In Chapter 8 of Part 3—
(a) section 139 extends to England and Wales only,
(b) sections 140 and 141 extend to England and Wales, Scotland and Northern Ireland,
(c) paragraphs 1 to 11 of Schedule 25 extend to England and Wales only,
(d) paragraphs 12 to 17 of that Schedule extend to Scotland only, and
(e) Part 2 of that Schedule extends to England and Wales only.

(6) An amendment, repeal or revocation made by this Act has the same extent as the relevant part of the Act or instrument amended, repealed or revoked (ignoring extent by virtue of an Order in Council), subject to subsections (2), (5), (7) and (8).

(7) Subsection (6) applies to section 148(1) to (5) only so far as the provisions amended extend to England and Wales or apply in relation to service offences.

(8) Subsection (6) does not apply to paragraphs 15 and 18 of Schedule 7, which extend to England and Wales only.

(9) The following have the same extent as the amendments, modifications, enactments, instruments or provisions to which they relate—
(a) section 68(7),
(b) section 80(10) and (11),
(c) section 135(4), (5) and (7),
(d) section 148(6),
(e) Part 4 of Schedule 7 and Part 3 of Schedule 8, and
(f) Schedule 15.

(10) Sections 149, 150, 151, this section and section 154 extend to England and Wales, Scotland and Northern Ireland.

(11) But, in so far as sections 77, 149 and 151 confer power to make provision modifying or otherwise relating to a provision of, or made under or applied by, the Armed Forces Act 2006, they have the same extent as that Act (ignoring extent by virtue of an Order in Council).

153 Channel Islands, Isle of Man and British overseas territories

(1) The power conferred by section 9(4) of the Repatriation of Prisoners Act 1984 (power to extend to Channel Islands, Isle of Man and British overseas territories) is exercisable in relation to any amendment of that Act that is made by or under this Act.

(2) The powers conferred by sections 177, 178 and 222 of the Extradition Act 2003 (powers to apply provisions to extradition to or from British overseas territories and to extend to Channel Islands and Isle of Man) are exercisable in relation to any amendment of that Act that is made by or under this Act.

(3) The power conferred by section 338 of the Criminal Justice Act 2003 (power to extend to Channel Islands and Isle of Man) is exercisable in relation to any amendment of that Act that is made by or under this Act.

(4) In section 384 of the Armed Forces Act 2006 (extent to Channel Islands, Isle of Man and British overseas territories) references to that Act include that Act as amended by or under this Act.

154 Short title

This Act may be cited as the Legal Aid, Sentencing and Punishment of Offenders Act 2012.

SCHEDULES

SCHEDULE 1

Section 9

CIVIL LEGAL SERVICES

PART 1

SERVICES

Care, supervision and protection of children

1 (1) Civil legal services provided in relation to—
  (a) orders under section 25 of the Children Act 1989 ("the 1989 Act") (secure accommodation);
  (b) orders under Part 4 of the 1989 Act (care and supervision);
  (c) orders under Part 5 of the 1989 Act (protection of children);
  (d) approval by a court under paragraph 19 of Schedule 2 to the 1989 Act (arrangements to assist children to live abroad);
  (e) parenting orders under section 8 of the Crime and Disorder Act 1998 ("the 1998 Act");
  (f) child safety orders under section 11 of the 1998 Act;
  (g) orders for contact under section 26 of the Adoption and Children Act 2002 ("the 2002 Act");
  (h) applications for leave of the court to remove a child from a person's custody under section 36 of the 2002 Act;
  (i) placement orders, recovery orders or adoption orders under Chapter 3 of Part 1 of the 2002 Act (see sections 21, 41 and 46 of that Act);
  (j) orders under section 84 of the 2002 Act (parental responsibility prior to adoption abroad).

(2) Civil legal services provided in relation to an order under an enactment made—
  (a) as an alternative to an order mentioned in sub-paragraph (1), or
  (b) in proceedings heard together with proceedings relating to such an order.

Exclusions

(3) Sub-paragraphs (1) and (2) are subject to the exclusions in Parts 2 and 3 of this Schedule.

Definitions

(4) In this paragraph "children" means persons under the age of 18.

Special educational needs

2 (1) Civil legal services provided in relation to—
(a) matters arising under Part 4 of the Education Act 1996 (special educational needs);
(b) assessments relating to learning difficulties under sections 139A and 140 of the Learning and Skills Act 2000.

Exclusions

(2) Sub-paragraph (1) is subject to the exclusions in Parts 2 and 3 of this Schedule.

Abuse of child or vulnerable adult

3 (1) Civil legal services provided in relation to abuse of an individual that took place at a time when the individual was a child or vulnerable adult, but only where—
(a) the services are provided to the individual, or
(b) the individual has died and the services are provided—
(i) to the individual's personal representative, or
(ii) for the purposes of a claim under the Fatal Accidents Act 1976 for the benefit of the individual's dependants.

General exclusions

(2) Sub-paragraph (1) is subject to—
(a) the exclusions in Part 2 of this Schedule, with the exception of paragraphs 1, 2, 3, 8 and 12 of that Part, and
(b) the exclusion in Part 3 of this Schedule.

Specific exclusions

(3) The services described in sub-paragraph (1) do not include services provided in relation to clinical negligence.

(4) The services described in sub-paragraph (1) do not include services provided in relation to a matter arising under a family enactment.

Definitions

(5) In this paragraph—
"abuse" means physical or mental abuse, including—
(a) sexual abuse, and
(b) abuse in the form of violence, neglect, maltreatment and exploitation;
"child" means a person under the age of 18;
"clinical negligence" means breach of a duty of care or trespass to the person committed in the course of the provision of clinical or medical services (including dental or nursing services);
"family enactment" has the meaning given in paragraph 12;
"personal representative", in relation to an individual who has died, means—
(a) a person responsible for administering the individual's estate under the law of England and Wales, Scotland or Northern Ireland, or

(b) a person who, under the law of another country or territory, has functions equivalent to those of administering the individual's estate;

"vulnerable adult" means a person aged 18 or over whose ability to protect himself or herself from abuse is significantly impaired through physical or mental disability or illness, through old age or otherwise.

Working with children and vulnerable adults

4 (1) Civil legal services provided in relation to—

(a) the inclusion of a person in a barred list or the removal of a person from a barred list;

(b) a disqualification order under section 28, 29 or 29A of the Criminal Justice and Court Services Act 2000 (disqualification from working with children);

(c) a direction under section 142 of the Education Act 2002 (prohibition from teaching etc).

Exclusions

(2) Sub-paragraph (1) is subject to the exclusions in Parts 2 and 3 of this Schedule.

Definitions

(3) In this paragraph "barred list" means a list maintained under—

(a) section 2 of the Safeguarding Vulnerable Groups Act 2006 (persons barred from regulated activities relating to children or vulnerable adults);

(b) section 81 of the Care Standards Act 2000;

(c) section 1 of the Protection of Children Act 1999.

Mental health and mental capacity

5 (1) Civil legal services provided in relation to matters arising under—

(a) the Mental Health Act 1983;

(b) paragraph 5(2) of the Schedule to the Repatriation of Prisoners Act 1984;

(c) the Mental Capacity Act 2005.

General exclusions

(2) Sub-paragraph (1) is subject to the exclusions in Parts 2 and 3 of this Schedule.

Specific exclusion

(3) The services described in sub-paragraph (1) do not include services provided in relation to—

(a) the creation of lasting powers of attorney under the Mental Capacity Act 2005, or

(b) the making of advance decisions under that Act.

(4) Sub-paragraph (3) does not exclude services provided in relation to determinations and declarations by a court under the Mental Capacity Act 2005 as to the validity, meaning, effect or applicability of—

(a) a lasting power of attorney that has been created, or

(b) an advance decision that has been made.

Community care

6 (1) Civil legal services provided in relation to community care services.

Exclusions

(2) Sub-paragraph (1) is subject to the exclusions in Parts 2 and 3 of this Schedule.

Definitions

(3) In this paragraph—

"community care services" means services which a relevant person may provide or arrange to be provided under—

(a) Part 3 of the National Assistance Act 1948 ("the 1948 Act") (local authority support for children and families);
(b) section 47 of the 1948 Act (removal to suitable premises of persons in need of care and attention);
(c) section 48 of the 1948 Act (temporary protection for property of persons admitted to hospital);
(d) section 45 of the Health Services and Public Health Act 1968 (arrangements for promoting welfare of old people);
(e) section 117 of the Mental Health Act 1983 (after-care);
(f) section 17 of the Children Act 1989 ("the 1989 Act") (provision of services for children in need);
(g) section 20 of the 1989 Act (provision of accommodation for children);
(h) sections 22A, 22B, 22C and 23 of the 1989 Act (accommodation and maintenance for children in care and looked after children);
(i) sections 23B and 23C of the 1989 Act (local authority functions in respect of relevant children);
(j) sections 24, 24A and 24B of the 1989 Act (provision of services for persons qualifying for advice and assistance);
(k) section 2 of the Carers and Disabled Children Act 2000 (services for carers);
(l) section 254 of, and Schedule 20 to, the National Health Service Act 2006 (functions of local social service authorities);
(m) section 192 of, and Schedule 15 to, the National Health Service (Wales) Act 2006 (functions of local social service authorities);

"relevant person" means—

(a) a district council;
(b) a county council;
(c) a county borough council;
(d) a London borough council;
(e) the Common Council of the City of London;
(f) a Primary Care Trust established under section 18 of the National Health Service Act 2006;
(g) a Local Health Board established under section 11 of the National Health Service (Wales) Act 2006;

(h) any other person prescribed for the purposes of this paragraph.

Facilities for disabled persons

7 (1) Civil legal services provided in relation to grants under Part 1 of the Housing Grants, Construction and Regeneration Act 1996 for the provision of facilities for disabled persons.

Exclusions

(2) Sub-paragraph (1) is subject to the exclusions in Parts 2 and 3 of this Schedule.

Definitions

(3) In this paragraph "disabled person" has the meaning given in section 100 of the Housing Grants, Construction and Regeneration Act 1996.

Appeals relating to welfare benefits

8 (1) Civil legal services provided in relation to an appeal on a point of law to the Upper Tribunal, the Court of Appeal or the Supreme Court relating to a benefit, allowance, payment, credit or pension under—

(a) a social security enactment,

(b) the Vaccine Damage Payments Act 1979, or

(c) Part 4 of the Child Maintenance and Other Payments Act 2008.

Exclusions

(2) Sub-paragraph (1) is subject to—

(a) the exclusions in Part 2 of this Schedule, with the exception of paragraphs 1 and 15 of that Part, and

(b) the exclusion in Part 3 of this Schedule.

Definitions

(3) In this paragraph "social security enactment" means—

(a) the Social Security Contributions and Benefits Act 1992,

(b) the Jobseekers Act 1995,

(c) the State Pension Credit Act 2002,

(d) the Tax Credits Act 2002,

(e) the Welfare Reform Act 2007,

(f) the Welfare Reform Act 2012, or

(g) any other enactment relating to social security.

Inherent jurisdiction of High Court in relation to children and vulnerable adults

9 (1) Civil legal services provided in relation to the inherent jurisdiction of the High Court in relation to children and vulnerable adults.

Exclusions

(2) Sub-paragraph (1) is subject to the exclusions in Parts 2 and 3 of this Schedule.

Definitions

(3) In this paragraph—

"adults" means persons aged 18 or over;

"children" means persons under the age of 18.

Unlawful removal of children

10 (1) Civil legal services provided to an individual in relation to the following orders and requirements where the individual is seeking to prevent the unlawful removal of a related child from the United Kingdom or to secure the return of a related child who has been unlawfully removed from the United Kingdom—

(a) a prohibited steps order or specific issue order (as defined in section 8(1) of the Children Act 1989);

(b) an order under section 33 of the Family Law Act 1986 for disclosure of the child's whereabouts;

(c) an order under section 34 of that Act for the child's return;

(d) a requirement under section 37 of that Act to surrender a passport issued to, or containing particulars of, the child.

(2) Civil legal services provided to an individual in relation to the following orders and applications where the individual is seeking to secure the return of a related child who has been unlawfully removed to a place in the United Kingdom—

(a) a prohibited steps order or specific issue order (as defined in section 8(1) of the Children Act 1989);

(b) an application under section 27 of the Family Law Act 1986 for registration of an order relating to the child;

(c) an order under section 33 of that Act for disclosure of the child's whereabouts;

(d) an order under section 34 of that Act for the child's return.

Exclusions

(3) Sub-paragraphs (1) and (2) are subject to the exclusions in Parts 2 and 3 of this Schedule.

Definitions

(4) For the purposes of this paragraph, a child is related to an individual if the individual is the child's parent or has parental responsibility for the child.

(5) In this paragraph "child" means a person under the age of 18.

Family homes and domestic violence

11 (1) Civil legal services provided in relation to home rights, occupation orders and non-molestation orders under Part 4 of the Family Law Act 1996.

(2) Civil legal services provided in relation to the following in circumstances arising out of a family relationship—

(a) an injunction following assault, battery or false imprisonment;

(b) the inherent jurisdiction of the High Court to protect an adult.

Exclusions

(3) Sub-paragraphs (1) and (2) are subject to—

(a) the exclusions in Part 2 of this Schedule, with the exception of paragraphs 3 and 11 of that Part, and

(b) the exclusion in Part 3 of this Schedule.

Definitions

(4) For the purposes of this paragraph—

(a) there is a family relationship between two people if they are associated with each other, and

(b) "associated" has the same meaning as in Part 4 of the Family Law Act 1996 (see section 62 of that Act).

(5) For the purposes of this paragraph, the Lord Chancellor may by regulations make provision about when circumstances arise out of a family relationship.

Victims of domestic violence and family matters

12 (1) Civil legal services provided to an adult ("A") in relation to a matter arising out of a family relationship between A and another individual ("B") where—

(a) there has been, or is a risk of, domestic violence between A and B, and

(b) A was, or is at risk of being, the victim of that domestic violence.

General exclusions

(2) Sub-paragraph (1) is subject to the exclusions in Part 2 of this Schedule, with the exception of paragraph 11 of that Part.

(3) But the exclusions described in sub-paragraph (2) are subject to the exception in sub-paragraph (4).

(4) The services described in sub-paragraph (1) include services provided in relation to conveyancing, but only where—

(a) the services in relation to conveyancing are provided in the course of giving effect to a court order made in proceedings, and

(b) services described in that sub-paragraph (other than services in relation to conveyancing) are being or have been provided in relation to those proceedings under arrangements made for the purposes of this Part of this Act.

(5) Sub-paragraph (1) is subject to the exclusion in Part 3 of this Schedule.

Specific exclusion

(6) The services described in sub-paragraph (1) do not include services provided in relation to a claim in tort in respect of the domestic violence.

Definitions

(7) For the purposes of this paragraph—

(a) there is a family relationship between two people if they are associated with each other, and

(b) "associated" has the same meaning as in Part 4 of the Family Law Act 1996 (see section 62 of that Act).

(8) For the purposes of this paragraph—

(a) matters arising out of a family relationship include matters arising under a family enactment, and

(b) (subject to paragraph (a)) the Lord Chancellor may by regulations make provision about when matters arise out of a family relationship.

(9) In this paragraph—

"adult" means a person aged 18 or over;

"domestic violence" means any incident of threatening behaviour, violence or abuse (whether psychological, physical, sexual, financial or emotional) between individuals who are associated with each other;

"family enactment" means—

(a) section 17 of the Married Women's Property Act 1882 (questions between husband and wife as to property);

(b) the Maintenance Orders (Facilities for Enforcement) Act 1920;

(c) the Maintenance Orders Act 1950;

(d) the Maintenance Orders Act 1958;

(e) the Maintenance Orders (Reciprocal Enforcement) Act 1972;

(f) Schedule 1 to the Domicile and Matrimonial Proceedings Act 1973 (staying of matrimonial proceedings) and corresponding provision in relation to civil partnerships made by rules of court under section 223 of the Civil Partnership Act 2004;

(g) the Matrimonial Causes Act 1973;

(h) the Inheritance (Provision for Family Dependants) Act 1975;

(i) the Domestic Proceedings and Magistrates' Courts Act 1978;

(j) Part 3 of the Matrimonial and Family Proceedings Act 1984 (financial relief after overseas divorce etc);

(k) Parts 1 and 3 of the Family Law Act 1986 (child custody and declarations of status);

(l) Parts 1 and 2 of the Children Act 1989 (orders with respect to children in family proceedings);

(m) section 53 of, and Schedule 7 to, the Family Law Act 1996 (transfer of tenancies on divorce etc or separation of cohabitants);

(n) Chapters 2 and 3 of Part 2 of the Civil Partnership Act 2004 (dissolution, nullity and other proceedings and property and financial arrangements);

(o) section 54 of the Human Fertilisation and Embryology Act 2008 (applications for parental orders).

Protection of children and family matters

13 (1) Civil legal services provided to an adult ("A") in relation to the following orders and procedures where the child who is or would be the subject of the order is at risk of abuse from an individual other than A—

(a) orders under section 4(2A) of the Children Act 1989 ("the 1989 Act") (removal of father's parental responsibility);

(b) orders under section 6(7) of the 1989 Act (termination of appointment of guardian);

(c) orders mentioned in section 8(1) of the 1989 Act (residence, contact and other orders);

(d) special guardianship orders under Part 2 of the 1989 Act;

(e) orders under section 33 of the Family Law Act 1986 ("the 1986 Act") (disclosure of child's whereabouts);

(f) orders under section 34 of the 1986 Act (return of child).

Exclusions

(2) Sub-paragraph (1) is subject to the exclusions in Parts 2 and 3 of this Schedule.

Definitions

(3) In this paragraph—

"abuse" means physical or mental abuse, including—

(a) sexual abuse, and

(b) abuse in the form of violence, neglect, maltreatment and exploitation;

"adult" means a person aged 18 or over;

"child" means a person under the age of 18.

Mediation in family disputes

14 (1) Mediation provided in relation to family disputes.

(2) Civil legal services provided in connection with the mediation of family disputes.

Exclusions

(3) Sub-paragraphs (1) and (2) are subject to the exclusions in Part 2 of this Schedule, with the exception of paragraph 11 of that Part.

(4) But the exclusions described in sub-paragraph (3) are subject to the exception in sub-paragraph (5).

(5) The services described in sub-paragraph (2) include services provided in relation to conveyancing, but only where—

(a) the services in relation to conveyancing are provided in the course of giving effect to arrangements for the resolution of a family dispute, and

(b) services described in that sub-paragraph or sub-paragraph (1) (other than services in relation to conveyancing) are being or have been provided in relation to the dispute under arrangements made for the purposes of this Part of this Act.

(6) Sub-paragraphs (1) and (2) are subject to the exclusion in Part 3 of this Schedule.

Definitions

(7) For the purposes of this paragraph—

(a) a dispute is a family dispute if it is a dispute between individuals about a matter arising out of a family relationship between the individuals,

(b) there is a family relationship between two individuals if they are associated with each other, and

(c) "associated" has the same meaning as in Part 4 of the Family Law Act 1996 (see section 62 of that Act).

(8) For the purposes of this paragraph—

(a) matters arising out of a family relationship include matters arising under a family enactment, and

(b) (subject to paragraph (a)) the Lord Chancellor may by regulations make provision about when matters arise out of a family relationship.

(9) In this paragraph—

"child" means a person under the age of 18;

"family enactment" has the meaning given in paragraph 12.

Children who are parties to family proceedings

15 (1) Civil legal services provided to a child in relation to family proceedings—

(a) where the child is, or proposes to be, the applicant or respondent;

(b) where the child is made a party to the proceedings by a court under rule 16.2 of the Family Procedure Rules;

(c) where the child is a party to the proceedings and is conducting, or proposes to conduct, the proceedings without a children's guardian or litigation friend in accordance with rule 16.6 of the Family Procedure Rules.

Exclusions

(2) Sub-paragraph (1) is subject to the exclusions in Parts 2 and 3 of this Schedule.

Definitions

(3) For the purposes of this paragraph—

(a) proceedings are family proceedings if they relate to a matter arising out of a family relationship,

(b) there is a family relationship between two individuals if they are associated with each other, and

(c) "associated" has the same meaning as in Part 4 of the Family Law Act 1996 (see section 62 of that Act).

(4) For the purposes of this paragraph—

(a) matters arising out of a family relationship include matters arising under a family enactment, and

(b) (subject to paragraph (a)) the Lord Chancellor may by regulations make provision about when matters arise out of a family relationship.

(5) In this paragraph—

"child" means a person under the age of 18;

"family enactment" has the meaning given in paragraph 12.

Forced marriage

16 (1) Civil legal services provided in relation to forced marriage protection orders under Part 4A of the Family Law Act 1996.

Exclusions

(2) Sub-paragraph (1) is subject to the exclusions in Parts 2 and 3 of this Schedule.

EU and international agreements concerning children

17 (1) Civil legal services provided in relation to—

(a) an application made to the Lord Chancellor under the 1980 European Convention on Child Custody for the recognition or enforcement in England and Wales of a decision relating to the custody of a child;

(b) an application made to the Lord Chancellor under the 1980 Hague Convention in respect of a child who is, or is believed to be, in England and Wales;

(c) the recognition or enforcement of a judgment in England and Wales in accordance with Article 21, 28, 41, 42 or 48 of the 2003 Brussels Regulation.

Exclusions

(2) Sub-paragraph (1) is subject to the exclusions in Parts 2 and 3 of this Schedule.

Definitions

(3) In this paragraph—

"the 1980 European Convention on Child Custody" means the European Convention on Recognition and Enforcement of Decisions concerning Custody of Children and on the Restoration of Custody of Children which was signed in Luxembourg on 20 May 1980;

"the 1980 Hague Convention" means the Convention on the Civil Aspects of International Child Abduction which was signed at The Hague on 25 October 1980;

"the 2003 Brussels Regulation" means Council Regulation (EC) No. 2001/2003 of 27 November 2003 concerning jurisdiction and the recognition and enforcement of judgments in matrimonial matters and the matters of parental responsibility.

(4) For the purposes of this paragraph, an application is made to the Lord Chancellor if it is addressed to the Lord Chancellor or transmitted to the Lord Chancellor in accordance with section 3 or 14 of the Child Abduction and Custody Act 1985.

EU and international agreements concerning maintenance

18 (1) Civil legal services provided in relation to an application under the following for the recognition or enforcement in England and Wales of a maintenance order—

(a) the 1968 Brussels Convention;

(b) the 1973 Hague Convention;

(c) the 1989 Lugano Convention;

(d) the 2000 Brussels Regulation;

(e) the 2007 Lugano Convention.

(2) Civil legal services provided in relation to an application under Article 56 of the EU Maintenance Regulation (applications relating to maintenance decisions).

(3) Civil legal services provided to an individual in relation to proceedings in England and Wales relating to the recognition, enforceability or enforcement of a maintenance decision in circumstances in which the individual falls within Article 47(2) or (3) of the EU Maintenance Regulation (parties who benefited from free legal aid etc in Member State of origin).

Exclusions

(4) Sub-paragraphs (1) to (3) are subject to—

(a) the exclusions in Part 2 of this Schedule, with the exception of paragraph 11 of that Part, and

(b) the exclusion in Part 3 of this Schedule.

Definitions

(5) In this paragraph—

"the 1968 Brussels Convention" means the Convention on jurisdiction and the enforcement of judgments in civil and commercial matters (including the Protocol annexed to that Convention) signed at Brussels on 27 September 1968;

"the 1973 Hague Convention" means the Convention on the recognition and enforcement of decisions relating to maintenance obligations concluded at The Hague on 2 October 1973;

"the 1989 Lugano Convention" means the Convention on jurisdiction and the enforcement of judgments in civil and commercial matters (including the Protocols annexed to that Convention) opened for signature at Lugano on 16 September 1988 and signed by the United Kingdom on 18 September 1989;

"the 2000 Brussels Regulation" means Council Regulation (EC) No. 44/2001 of 22 December 2000 on jurisdiction and the recognition and enforcement of judgments in civil and commercial matters;

"the 2007 Lugano Convention" means the Convention on jurisdiction and enforcement of judgments in civil and commercial matters, between the European Community and the Republic of Iceland, the Kingdom of Norway, the Swiss Confederation and the Kingdom of Denmark signed on behalf of the European Community on 30 October 2007;

"the EU Maintenance Regulation" means Council Regulation (EC) No. 4/2009 of 18 December 2008 on jurisdiction, applicable law, recognition and enforcement of decisions and co-operation in matters relating to maintenance obligations;

"maintenance order", in relation to a convention or regulation listed in this paragraph, means a maintenance judgment within the meaning of that convention or regulation.

Judicial review

19 (1) Civil legal services provided in relation to judicial review of an enactment, decision, act or omission.

General exclusions

(2) Sub-paragraph (1) is subject to—

(a) the exclusions in Part 2 of this Schedule, with the exception of paragraphs 1, 2, 3, 4, 5, 6, 8, 12, 15 and 16 of that Part, and

(b) the exclusion in Part 3 of this Schedule.

Specific exclusion: benefit to individual

(3) The services described in sub-paragraph (1) do not include services provided to an individual in relation to judicial review that does not have the potential to produce a benefit for the individual, a member of the individual's family or the environment.

(4) Sub-paragraph (3) does not exclude services provided in relation to a judicial review where the judicial review ceases to have the potential to produce such a benefit after civil legal services have been provided in relation to the judicial review under arrangements made for the purposes of this Part of this Act.

Specific exclusions: immigration cases

(5) The services described in sub-paragraph (1) do not include services provided in relation to judicial review in respect of an issue relating to immigration where—
- (a) the same issue, or substantially the same issue, was the subject of a previous judicial review or an appeal to a court or tribunal,
- (b) on the determination of the previous judicial review or appeal (or, if there was more than one, the latest one), the court, tribunal or other person hearing the case found against the applicant or appellant on that issue, and
- (c) the services in relation to the new judicial review are provided before the end of the period of 1 year beginning with the day of that determination.

(6) The services described in sub-paragraph (1) do not include services provided in relation to judicial review of removal directions in respect of an individual where the directions were given not more than 1 year after the latest of the following—
- (a) the making of the decision (or, if there was more than one, the latest decision) to remove the individual from the United Kingdom by way of removal directions;
- (b) the refusal of leave to appeal against that decision;
- (c) the determination or withdrawal of an appeal against that decision.

(7) Sub-paragraphs (5) and (6) do not exclude services provided to an individual in relation to—
- (a) judicial review of a negative decision in relation to an asylum application (within the meaning of the EU Procedures Directive) where there is no right of appeal to the First-tier Tribunal against the decision;
- (b) judicial review of certification under section 94 or 96 of the Nationality, Immigration and Asylum Act 2002 (certificate preventing or restricting appeal of immigration decision).

(8) Sub-paragraphs (5) and (6) do not exclude services provided in relation to judicial review of removal directions in respect of an individual where prescribed conditions relating to either or both of the following are met—
- (a) the period between the individual being given notice of the removal directions and the proposed time for his or her removal;
- (b) the reasons for proposing that period.

Definitions

(9) For the purposes of this paragraph an individual is a member of another individual's family if—
- (a) they are relatives (whether of the full blood or half blood or by marriage or civil partnership),
- (b) they are cohabitants (as defined in Part 4 of the Family Law Act 1996), or

(c) one has parental responsibility for the other.

(10) In this paragraph—

"EU Procedures Directive" means Council Directive 2005/85/EC of 1 December 2005 on minimum standards on procedures in Member States for granting and withdrawing refugee status;

"an issue relating to immigration" includes an issue relating to rights described in paragraph 30 of this Part of this Schedule;

"judicial review" means—

(a) the procedure on an application for judicial review (see section 31 of the Senior Courts Act 1981), but not including the procedure after the application is treated under rules of court as if it were not such an application, and

(b) any procedure in which a court, tribunal or other person mentioned in Part 3 of this Schedule is required by an enactment to make a decision applying the principles that are applied by the court on an application for judicial review;

"removal directions" means directions under—

(a) paragraphs 8 to 10A of Schedule 2 to the Immigration Act 1971 (removal of persons refused leave to enter and illegal entrants);

(b) paragraphs 12 to 14 of Schedule 2 to that Act (removal of seamen and aircrew);

(c) paragraph 1 of Schedule 3 to that Act (removal of persons liable to deportation);

(d) section 10 of the Immigration and Asylum Act 1999 (removal of certain persons unlawfully in the United Kingdom);

(e) section 47 of the Immigration, Asylum and Nationality Act 2006 (removal of persons with statutorily extended leave).

Habeas corpus

20 (1) Civil legal services provided in relation to a writ of habeas corpus ad subjiciendum.

Exclusions

(2) Sub-paragraph (1) is subject to the exclusions in Parts 2 and 3 of this Schedule.

Abuse of position or powers by public authority

21 (1) Civil legal services provided in relation to abuse by a public authority of its position or powers.

General exclusions

(2) Sub-paragraph (1) is subject to—

(a) the exclusions in Part 2 of this Schedule, with the exception of paragraphs 1, 2, 3, 4, 5, 6, 8 and 12 of that Part, and

(b) the exclusion in Part 3 of this Schedule.

Specific exclusion

(3) The services described in sub-paragraph (1) do not include services provided in relation to clinical negligence.

Definitions

(4) For the purposes of this paragraph, an act or omission by a public authority does not constitute an abuse of its position or powers unless the act or omission—
   (a) is deliberate or dishonest, and
   (b) results in harm to a person or property that was reasonably foreseeable.

(5) In this paragraph—
   "clinical negligence" means breach of a duty of care or trespass to the person committed in the course of the provision of clinical or medical services (including dental or nursing services);
   "public authority" has the same meaning as in section 6 of the Human Rights Act 1998.

Breach of Convention rights by public authority

22 (1) Civil legal services provided in relation to—
   (a) a claim in tort, or
   (b) a claim for damages (other than a claim in tort),

   in respect of an act or omission by a public authority that involves a significant breach of Convention rights by the authority.

   General exclusions

(2) Sub-paragraph (1) is subject to—
   (a) the exclusions in Part 2 of this Schedule, with the exception of paragraphs 1, 2, 3, 4, 5, 6, 8 and 12 of that Part, and
   (b) the exclusion in Part 3 of this Schedule.

   Specific exclusion

(3) The services described in sub-paragraph (1) do not include services provided in relation to clinical negligence.

   Definitions

(4) In this paragraph—
   "clinical negligence" means breach of a duty of care or trespass to the person committed in the course of the provision of clinical or medical services (including dental or nursing services);
   "Convention rights" has the same meaning as in the Human Rights Act 1998;
   "public authority" has the same meaning as in section 6 of that Act.

Clinical negligence and severely disabled infants

23 (1) Civil legal services provided in relation to a claim for damages in respect of clinical negligence which caused a neurological injury to an individual ("V") as a result of which V is severely disabled, but only where the first and second conditions are met.

(2) The first condition is that the clinical negligence occurred—
   (a) while V was in his or her mother's womb, or
   (b) during or after V's birth but before the end of the following period—
      (i) if V was born before the beginning of the 37th week of pregnancy, the period of 8 weeks beginning with the first day of what would have been that week;

(ii) if V was born during or after the 37th week of pregnancy, the period of 8 weeks beginning with the day of V's birth.

(3) The second condition is that—

(a) the services are provided to V, or

(b) V has died and the services are provided to V's personal representative.

General exclusions

(4) Sub-paragraph (1) is subject to—

(a) the exclusions in Part 2 of this Schedule, with the exception of paragraphs 1, 2, 3 and 8 of that Part, and

(b) the exclusion in Part 3 of this Schedule.

Definitions

(5) In this paragraph—

"birth" means the moment when an individual first has a life separate from his or her mother and references to an individual being born are to be interpreted accordingly;

"clinical negligence" means breach of a duty of care or trespass to the person committed in the course of the provision of clinical or medical services (including dental or nursing services);

"disabled" means physically or mentally disabled;

"personal representative", in relation to an individual who has died, means—

(a) a person responsible for administering the individual's estate under the law of England and Wales, Scotland or Northern Ireland, or

(b) a person who, under the law of another country or territory, has functions equivalent to those of administering the individual's estate.

Special Immigration Appeals Commission

24 (1) Civil legal services provided in relation to proceedings before the Special Immigration Appeals Commission.

Exclusions

(2) Sub-paragraph (1) is subject to the exclusions in Parts 2 and 3 of this Schedule.

Immigration: detention

25 (1) Civil legal services provided in relation to—

(a) detention under the authority of an immigration officer;

(b) detention under Schedule 3 to the Immigration Act 1971;

(c) detention under section 62 of the Nationality, Immigration and Asylum Act 2002;

(d) detention under section 36 of the UK Borders Act 2007.

Exclusions

(2) Sub-paragraph (1) is subject to the exclusions in Parts 2 and 3 of this Schedule.

Immigration: temporary admission

26 (1) Civil legal services provided in relation to temporary admission to the United Kingdom under—

(a) paragraph 21 of Schedule 2 to the Immigration Act 1971;

(b) section 62 of the Nationality, Immigration and Asylum Act 2002.

Exclusions

(2) Sub-paragraph (1) is subject to the exclusions in Parts 2 and 3 of this Schedule.

Immigration: residence etc restrictions

27 (1) Civil legal services provided in relation to restrictions imposed under—

(a) paragraph 2(5) or 4 of Schedule 3 to the Immigration Act 1971 (residence etc restrictions pending deportation);

(b) section 71 of the Nationality, Immigration and Asylum Act 2002 (residence etc restrictions on asylum-seekers).

Exclusions

(2) Sub-paragraph (1) is subject to the exclusions in Parts 2 and 3 of this Schedule.

Immigration: victims of domestic violence and indefinite leave to remain

28 (1) Civil legal services provided to an individual ("V") in relation to an application by V for indefinite leave to remain in the United Kingdom on the grounds that—

(a) V was given leave to enter or remain in the United Kingdom for a limited period as the partner of another individual present and settled in the United Kingdom, and

(b) V's relationship with the other individual broke down permanently because V was the victim of domestic violence.

General exclusions

(2) Sub-paragraph (1) is subject to the exclusions in Parts 2 and 3 of this Schedule.

Specific exclusion

(3) The services described in sub-paragraph (1) do not include attendance at an interview conducted on behalf of the Secretary of State with a view to reaching a decision on an application.

Definitions

(4) For the purposes of this paragraph, one individual is a partner of another if—

(a) they are married to each other,

(b) they are civil partners of each other, or

(c) they are cohabitants.

(5) In this paragraph—

"cohabitant" has the same meaning as in Part 4 of the Family Law Act 1996 (see section 62 of that Act);

"domestic violence" means any incident of threatening behaviour, violence or abuse (whether psychological, physical, sexual, financial or emotional) between individuals who are associated with each other (within the meaning of section 62 of the Family Law Act 1996);

"indefinite leave to remain in the United Kingdom" means leave to remain in the United Kingdom under the Immigration Act 1971 which is not limited as to duration;

"present and settled in the United Kingdom" has the same meaning as in the rules made under section 3(2) of the Immigration Act 1971.

Immigration: victims of domestic violence and residence cards

29 (1) Civil legal services provided to an individual ("V") in relation to a residence card application where V—

(a) has ceased to be a family member of a qualified person on the termination of the marriage or civil partnership of the qualified person,

(b) is a family member who has retained the right of residence by virtue of satisfying the conditions in regulation 10(5) of the Immigration (European Economic Area) Regulations 2006 (S.I. 2006/1003) ("the 2006 Regulations"), and

(c) has satisfied the condition in regulation 10(5)(d)(iv) of the 2006 Regulations on the ground that V or a family member of V was the victim of domestic violence while the marriage or civil partnership of the qualified person was subsisting.

General exclusions

(2) Sub-paragraph (1) is subject to the exclusions in Parts 2 and 3 of this Schedule.

Specific exclusion

(3) The services described in sub-paragraph (1) do not include attendance at an interview conducted on behalf of the Secretary of State with a view to reaching a decision on an application.

Definitions

(4) In this paragraph—

"domestic violence" means any incident of threatening behaviour, violence or abuse (whether psychological, physical, sexual, financial or emotional) between individuals who are associated with each other (within the meaning of section 62 of the Family Law Act 1996);

"family member" has the same meaning as in the 2006 Regulations (see regulations 7 and 9);

"family member who has retained the right of residence" has the same meaning as in the 2006 Regulations (see regulation 10);

"qualified person" has the same meaning as in the 2006 Regulations (see regulation 6);

"residence card application" means—

(a) an application for a residence card under regulation 17 of the 2006 Regulations, or

(b) an application for a permanent residence card under regulation 18(2) of the 2006 Regulations.

Immigration: rights to enter and remain

30 (1) Civil legal services provided in relation to rights to enter, and to remain in, the United Kingdom arising from—

(a) the Refugee Convention;

(b) Article 2 or 3 of the Human Rights Convention;

(c) the Temporary Protection Directive;

(d) the Qualification Directive.

General exclusions

(2) Sub-paragraph (1) is subject to the exclusions in Parts 2 and 3 of this Schedule.

Specific exclusion

(3) The services described in sub-paragraph (1) do not include attendance at an interview conducted on behalf of the Secretary of State with a view to reaching a decision on a claim in respect of the rights mentioned in that sub-paragraph, except where regulations provide otherwise.

Definitions

(4) In this paragraph—

"the Human Rights Convention" means the Convention for the Protection of Human Rights and Fundamental Freedoms, agreed by the Council of Europe at Rome on 4 November 1950 as it has effect for the time being in relation to the United Kingdom;

"the Qualification Directive" means Council Directive 2004/83/EC of 29 April 2004 on minimum standards for the qualification and status of third country nationals or stateless persons as refugees or as persons who otherwise need international protection and the content of the protection granted;

"the Refugee Convention" means the Convention relating to the Status of Refugees done at Geneva on 28 July 1951 and the Protocol to the Convention;

"the Temporary Protection Directive" means Council Directive 2001/55/EC of 20 July 2001 on minimum standards for giving temporary protection in the event of a mass influx of displaced persons and on measures promoting a balance of efforts between Member States in receiving such persons and bearing the consequences thereof.

Immigration: accommodation for asylum-seekers etc

31 (1) Civil legal services provided in relation to the Secretary of State's powers to provide, or arrange for the provision of, accommodation under—

(a) section 4 or 95 of the Immigration and Asylum Act 1999 (accommodation for persons temporarily admitted and asylum-seekers);

(b) section 17 of the Nationality, Immigration and Asylum Act 2002 (support for destitute asylum-seekers).

Exclusions

(2) Sub-paragraph (1) is subject to the exclusions in Parts 2 and 3 of this Schedule.

Victims of trafficking in human beings

32 (1) Civil legal services provided to an individual in relation to an application by the individual for leave to enter, or to remain in, the United Kingdom where—

(a) there has been a conclusive determination that the individual is a victim of trafficking in human beings, or

(b) there are reasonable grounds to believe that the individual is such a victim and there has not been a conclusive determination that the individual is not such a victim.

(2) Civil legal services provided in relation to a claim under employment law arising in connection with the exploitation of an individual who is a victim of trafficking in human beings, but only where—

(a) the services are provided to the individual, or

(b) the individual has died and the services are provided to the individual's personal representative.

(3) Civil legal services provided in relation to a claim for damages arising in connection with the trafficking or exploitation of an individual who is a victim of trafficking in human beings, but only where—

(a) the services are provided to the individual, or

(b) the individual has died and the services are provided to the individual's personal representative.

Exclusions

(4) Sub-paragraph (1) is subject to the exclusions in Parts 2 and 3 of this Schedule.

(5) Sub-paragraphs (2) and (3) are subject to—

(a) the exclusions in Part 2 of this Schedule, with the exception of paragraphs 1, 2, 3, 4, 5, 6 and 8 of that Part, and

(b) the exclusion in Part 3 of this Schedule.

Definitions

(6) For the purposes of sub-paragraph (1)(b) there are reasonable grounds to believe that an individual is a victim of trafficking in human beings if a competent authority has determined for the purposes of Article 10 of the Trafficking Convention (identification of victims) that there are such grounds.

(7) For the purposes of sub-paragraph (1) there is a conclusive determination that an individual is or is not a victim of trafficking in human beings when, on completion of the identification process required by Article 10 of the Trafficking Convention, a competent authority concludes that the individual is or is not such a victim.

(8) In this paragraph—

"competent authority" means a person who is a competent authority of the United Kingdom for the purposes of the Trafficking Convention;

"employment" means employment under a contract of employment or a contract personally to do work and references to "employers" and "employees" are to be interpreted accordingly;

"employment law" means an enactment or rule of law relating to employment, including in particular an enactment or rule of law conferring powers or imposing duties on employers, conferring rights on employees or otherwise regulating the relations between employers and employees;

"exploitation" means a form of exploitation described in section 4(4) of the Asylum and Immigration (Treatment of Claimants, etc) Act 2004 (trafficking people for exploitation);

"personal representative", in relation to an individual who has died, means—

(a) a person responsible for administering the individual's estate under the law of England and Wales, Scotland or Northern Ireland, or

(b) a person who, under the law of another country or territory, has functions equivalent to those of administering the individual's estate;

"the Trafficking Convention" means the Council of Europe Convention on Action against Trafficking in Human Beings (done at Warsaw on 16 May 2005);

"trafficking in human beings" has the same meaning as in the Trafficking Convention.

Loss of home

33 (1) Civil legal services provided to an individual in relation to—

(a) court orders for sale or possession of the individual's home, or

(b) the eviction from the individual's home of the individual or others.

(2) Civil legal services provided to an individual in relation to a bankruptcy order against the individual under Part 9 of the Insolvency Act 1986 where—

(a) the individual's estate includes the individual's home, and

(b) the petition for the bankruptcy order is or was presented by a person other than the individual,

including services provided in relation to a statutory demand under that Part of that Act.

General exclusions

(3) Sub-paragraphs (1) and (2) are subject to the exclusions in Part 2 of this Schedule, with the exception of paragraph 14 of that Part.

(4) But the exclusions described in sub-paragraph (3) are subject to the exceptions in sub-paragraphs (5) and (6).

(5) The services described in sub-paragraph (1) include services provided in relation to proceedings on an application under the Trusts of Land and Appointment of Trustees Act 1996 to which section 335A of the Insolvency Act 1986 applies (application by trustee of bankrupt's estate).

(6) The services described in sub-paragraph (1) include services described in any of paragraphs 3 to 6 or 8 of Part 2 of this Schedule to the extent that they are—

(a) services provided to an individual in relation to a counterclaim in proceedings for a court order for sale or possession of the individual's home, or

(b) services provided to an individual in relation to the unlawful eviction from the individual's home of the individual or others.

(7) Sub-paragraphs (1) and (2) are subject to the exclusion in Part 3 of this Schedule.

Specific exclusion

(8) The services described in sub-paragraph (1) do not include services provided in relation to—

(a) proceedings under the Matrimonial Causes Act 1973;

(b) proceedings under Chapters 2 and 3 of Part 2 of the Civil Partnership Act 2004 (dissolution, nullity and other proceedings and property and financial arrangements).

Definitions

(9) In this paragraph "home", in relation to an individual, means the house, caravan, houseboat or other vehicle or structure that is the individual's only or main residence, subject to sub-paragraph (10).

(10) References in this paragraph to an individual's home do not include a vehicle or structure occupied by the individual if—

(a) there are no grounds on which it can be argued that the individual is occupying the vehicle or structure otherwise than as a trespasser, and

(b) there are no grounds on which it can be argued that the individual's occupation of the vehicle or structure began otherwise than as a trespasser.

(11) In sub-paragraphs (9) and (10), the references to a caravan, houseboat or other vehicle include the land on which it is located or to which it is moored.

(12) For the purposes of sub-paragraph (10) individuals occupying, or beginning occupation, of a vehicle or structure as a trespasser include individuals who do so by virtue of—

(a) title derived from a trespasser, or

(b) a licence or consent given by a trespasser or a person deriving title from a trespasser.

(13) For the purposes of sub-paragraph (10) an individual who is occupying a vehicle or structure as a trespasser does not cease to be a trespasser by virtue of being allowed time to leave the vehicle or structure.

Homelessness

34 (1) Civil legal services provided to an individual who is homeless, or threatened with homelessness, in relation to the provision of accommodation and assistance for the individual under—

(a) Part 6 of the Housing Act 1996 (allocation of housing accommodation);

(b) Part 7 of that Act (homelessness).

Exclusions

(2) Sub-paragraph (1) is subject to the exclusions in Parts 2 and 3 of this Schedule.

Definitions

(3) In this paragraph "homeless" and "threatened with homelessness" have the same meaning as in section 175 of the Housing Act 1996.

Risk to health or safety in rented home

35 (1) Civil legal services provided to an individual in relation to the removal or reduction of a serious risk of harm to the health or safety of the individual or a relevant member of the individual's family where—

(a) the risk arises from a deficiency in the individual's home,

(b) the individual's home is rented or leased from another person, and

(c) the services are provided with a view to securing that the other person makes arrangements to remove or reduce the risk.

Exclusions

(2) Sub-paragraph (1) is subject to—

(a) the exclusions in Part 2 of this Schedule, with the exception of paragraphs 6 and 8 of that Part, and

(b) the exclusion in Part 3 of this Schedule.

Definitions

(3) For the purposes of this paragraph—

(a) a child is a relevant member of an individual's family if the individual is the child's parent or has parental responsibility for the child;

(b) an adult ("A") is a relevant member of an individual's family if—

(i) they are relatives (whether of the full blood or half blood or by marriage or civil partnership) or cohabitants, and

(ii) the individual's home is also A's home.

(4) In this paragraph—

"adult" means a person aged 18 or over;

"building" includes part of a building;

"child" means a person under the age of 18;

"cohabitant" has the same meaning as in Part 4 of the Family Law Act 1996 (see section 62(1) of that Act);

"deficiency" means any deficiency, whether arising as a result of the construction of a building, an absence of maintenance or repair, or otherwise;

"harm" includes temporary harm;

"health" includes mental health;

"home", in relation to an individual, means the house, caravan, houseboat or other vehicle or structure that is the individual's only or main residence, together with any garden or ground usually occupied with it.

Anti-social behaviour

36 (1) Civil legal services provided to an individual in relation to—

(a) an order made in respect of the individual under section 1B of the Crime and Disorder Act 1998 ("the 1998 Act");

(b) an interim order made in respect of the individual under section 1D of the 1998 Act following an application under section 1B of that Act;

(c) an intervention order made in respect of the individual under section 1G of the 1998 Act in connection with an order under section 1B of that Act;

(d) an anti-social behaviour injunction against the individual under section 153A of the Housing Act 1996.

Exclusions

(2) Sub-paragraph (1) is subject to the exclusions in Parts 2 and 3 of this Schedule.

Protection from harassment

37 (1) Civil legal services provided in relation to—

(a) an injunction under section 3 or 3A of the Protection from Harassment Act 1997;

(b) the variation or discharge of a restraining order under section 5 or 5A of that Act.

Exclusions

(2) Sub-paragraph (1) is subject to the exclusions in Parts 2 and 3 of this Schedule.

Gang-related violence

38 (1) Civil legal services provided in relation to injunctions under Part 4 of the Policing and Crime Act 2009 (injunctions to prevent gang-related violence).

Exclusions

(2) Sub-paragraph (1) is subject to the exclusions in Parts 2 and 3 of this Schedule.

Sexual offences

39 (1) Civil legal services provided in relation to a sexual offence, but only where—

(a) the services are provided to the victim of the offence, or

(b) the victim of the offence has died and the services are provided to the victim's personal representative.

Exclusions

(2) Sub-paragraph (1) is subject to—

(a) the exclusions in Part 2 of this Schedule, with the exception of paragraphs 1, 2, 3, 8 and 12 of that Part, and

(b) the exclusion in Part 3 of this Schedule.

Definitions

(3) In this paragraph—

"personal representative", in relation to an individual who has died, means—

(a) a person responsible for administering the individual's estate under the law of England and Wales, Scotland or Northern Ireland, or

(b) a person who, under the law of another country or territory, has functions equivalent to those of administering the individual's estate;

"sexual offence" means—

(a) an offence under a provision of the Sexual Offences Act 2003 ("the 2003 Act"), and

(b) an offence under section 1 of the Protection of Children Act 1978 ("the 1978 Act") (indecent photographs of children).

(4) The references in sub-paragraph (1) to a sexual offence include—

(a) incitement to commit a sexual offence,

(b) an offence committed by a person under Part 2 of the Serious Crime Act 2007 (encouraging or assisting crime) in relation to which a sexual offence is the offence which the person intended or believed would be committed,

(c) conspiracy to commit a sexual offence, and

(d) an attempt to commit a sexual offence.

(5) In this paragraph references to a sexual offence include conduct which would be an offence under a provision of the 2003 Act or section 1 of the 1978 Act but for the fact that it took place before that provision or section came into force.

(6) Conduct falls within the definition of a sexual offence for the purposes of this paragraph whether or not there have been criminal proceedings in relation to the conduct and whatever the outcome of any such proceedings.

Proceeds of crime

40 (1) Civil legal services provided in relation to—

(a) restraint orders under section 41 of the Proceeds of Crime Act 2002 ("the 2002 Act") including orders under section 41(7) of that Act (orders for ensuring that restraint order is effective);

(b) orders under section 47M of the 2002 Act (detention of property);

(c) directions under section 54(3) of the 2002 Act (distribution of funds in the hands of a receiver);

(d) directions under section 62 of the 2002 Act (action to be taken by receiver);

(e) orders under section 67A of the 2002 Act (realising property), including directions under section 67D of that Act (distribution of proceeds of realisation);

(f) orders under section 72 or 73 of the 2002 Act (compensation);

(g) applications under section 351 of the 2002 Act (discharge or variation of a production order or order to grant entry);

(h) applications under section 362 of the 2002 Act (discharge or variation of disclosure order);

(i) applications under section 369 of the 2002 Act (discharge or variation of customer information order);

(j) applications under section 375 of the 2002 Act (discharge or variation of account monitoring orders).

General exclusions

(2) Sub-paragraph (1) is subject to—

(a) the exclusions in Part 2 of this Schedule, with the exception of paragraph 14 of that Part, and

(b) the exclusion in Part 3 of this Schedule.

Specific exclusions

(3) Where a confiscation order has been made under Part 2 of the 2002 Act against a defendant, the services described in sub-paragraph (1) do not include services provided to the defendant in relation to—

(a) directions under section 54(3) of that Act (distribution of funds in the hands of a receiver), or

(b) directions under section 67D of that Act (distribution of proceeds of realisation),

that relate to property recovered pursuant to the order.

(4) Where a confiscation order has been made under Part 2 of the 2002 Act against a defendant and varied under section 29 of that Act, the services described in sub-paragraph (1) do not include services provided in relation to an application by the defendant under section 73 of that Act (compensation).

Inquests

41 (1) Civil legal services provided to an individual in relation to an inquest under the Coroners Act 1988 into the death of a member of the individual's family.

Exclusions

(2) Sub-paragraph (1) is subject to—

(a) the exclusions in Part 2 of this Schedule, with the exception of paragraph 1 of that Part, and

(b) the exclusion in Part 3 of this Schedule.

Definitions

(3) For the purposes of this paragraph an individual is a member of another individual's family if—

(a) they are relatives (whether of the full blood or half blood or by marriage or civil partnership),

(b) they are cohabitants (as defined in Part 4 of the Family Law Act 1996), or

(c) one has parental responsibility for the other.

Environmental pollution

42 (1) Civil legal services provided in relation to injunctions in respect of nuisance arising from prescribed types of pollution of the environment.

Exclusions

(2) Sub-paragraph (1) is subject to the exclusions in Parts 2 and 3 of this Schedule.

Equality

43 (1) Civil legal services provided in relation to contravention of the Equality Act 2010 or a previous discrimination enactment.

Exclusions

(2) Sub-paragraph (1) is subject to—

(a) the exclusions in Part 2 of this Schedule, with the exception of paragraph 15 of that Part, and

(b) the exclusion in Part 3 of this Schedule.

Definitions

(3) In this paragraph "previous discrimination enactment" means—

(a) the Equal Pay Act 1970;

(b) the Sex Discrimination Act 1975;

(c) the Race Relations Act 1976;

(d) the Disability Discrimination Act 1995;

(e) the Employment Equality (Religion or Belief) Regulations 2003 (S.I. 2003/1660);

(f) the Employment Equality (Sexual Orientation) Regulations 2003 (S.I. 2003/1661);

(g) the Equality Act 2006;

(h) the Employment Equality (Age) Regulations 2006 (S.I. 2006/1031);

(i) the Equality Act (Sexual Orientation) Regulations 2007 (S.I. 2007/1263).

(4) The reference in sub-paragraph (1) to contravention of the Equality Act 2010 or a previous discrimination enactment includes—

(a) breach of a term modified by, or included by virtue of, a provision that is an equality clause or equality rule for the purposes of the Equal Pay Act 1970 or the Equality Act 2010, and

(b) breach of a provision that is a non-discrimination rule for the purposes of the Equality Act 2010.

Cross-border disputes

44 (1) Civil legal services provided in relation to proceedings in circumstances in which the services are required to be provided under Council Directive 2002/8/EC of 27 January 2003 to improve access to justice in cross-border disputes by establishing minimum common rules relating to legal aid for such disputes.

No exclusions

(2) Sub-paragraph (1) is not subject to the exclusions in Parts 2 and 3 of this Schedule.

Terrorism prevention and investigation measures etc

45 (1) Civil legal services provided to an individual in relation to a TPIM notice relating to the individual.

(2) Civil legal services provided to an individual in relation to control order proceedings relating to the individual.

Exclusions

(3) Sub-paragraphs (1) and (2) are subject to the exclusions in Parts 2 and 3 of this Schedule.

Definitions

(4) In this paragraph—

"control order proceedings" means proceedings described in paragraph 3(1)(a) to (e) of Schedule 8 to the Terrorism Prevention and Investigation Measures Act 2011 ("the 2011 Act");

"TPIM notice" means a notice under section 2(1) of the 2011 Act.

Connected matters

46 (1) Prescribed civil legal services provided, in prescribed circumstances, in connection with the provision of services described in a preceding paragraph of this Part of this Schedule.

Exclusions

(2) Sub-paragraph (1) is subject to—

(a) the exclusions in Parts 2 and 3 of this Schedule, except to the extent that regulations under this paragraph provide otherwise, and

(b) any other prescribed exclusions.

PART 2

EXCLUDED SERVICES

The services described in Part 1 of this Schedule do not include the services listed in this Part of this Schedule, except to the extent that Part 1 of this Schedule provides otherwise.

1 Civil legal services provided in relation to personal injury or death.

2 Civil legal services provided in relation to a claim in tort in respect of negligence.

3 Civil legal services provided in relation to a claim in tort in respect of assault, battery or false imprisonment.

4 Civil legal services provided in relation to a claim in tort in respect of trespass to goods.

5 Civil legal services provided in relation to a claim in tort in respect of trespass to land.

6 Civil legal services provided in relation to damage to property.

7 Civil legal services provided in relation to defamation or malicious falsehood.

8 Civil legal services provided in relation to a claim in tort in respect of breach of statutory duty.

9 Civil legal services provided in relation to conveyancing.

10 Civil legal services provided in relation to the making of wills.

11 Civil legal services provided in relation to matters of trust law.

12 (1) Civil legal services provided in relation to a claim for damages in respect of a breach of Convention rights by a public authority to the extent that the claim is made in reliance on section 7 of the Human Rights Act 1998.

(2) In this paragraph—

"Convention rights" has the same meaning as in the Human Rights Act 1998;

"public authority" has the same meaning as in section 6 of that Act.

13 Civil legal services provided in relation to matters of company or partnership law.

14 Civil legal services provided to an individual in relation to matters arising out of or in connection with—

(a) a proposal by that individual to establish a business,

(b) the carrying on of a business by that individual (whether or not the business is being carried on at the time the services are provided), or

(c) the termination or transfer of a business that was being carried on by that individual.

15 (1) Civil legal services provided in relation to a benefit, allowance, payment, credit or pension under—

(a) a social security enactment,

(b) the Vaccine Damage Payments Act 1979, or

(c) Part 4 of the Child Maintenance and Other Payments Act 2008.

(2) In this paragraph "social security enactment" means—

(a) the Social Security Contributions and Benefits Act 1992,

(b) the Jobseekers Act 1995,

(c) the State Pension Credit Act 2002,

(d) the Tax Credits Act 2002,

(e) the Welfare Reform Act 2007,

(f) the Welfare Reform Act 2012, or

(g) any other enactment relating to social security.

16 Civil legal services provided in relation to compensation under the Criminal Injuries Compensation Scheme.

17 Civil legal services provided in relation to changing an individual's name.

PART 3

ADVOCACY: EXCLUSION AND EXCEPTIONS

The services described in Part 1 of this Schedule do not include advocacy, except as follows—

(a) those services include the types of advocacy listed in this Part of this Schedule, except to the extent that Part 1 of this Schedule provides otherwise;

(b) those services include other types of advocacy to the extent that Part 1 of this Schedule so provides.

Exceptions: courts

1 Advocacy in proceedings in the Supreme Court.

2 Advocacy in proceedings in the Court of Appeal.

3 Advocacy in proceedings in the High Court.

4 Advocacy in proceedings in the Court of Protection to the extent that they concern—

(a) a person's right to life,

(b) a person's liberty or physical safety,

(c) a person's medical treatment (within the meaning of the Mental Health Act 1983),

(d) a person's capacity to marry, to enter into a civil partnership or to enter into sexual relations, or

(e) a person's right to family life.

5 Advocacy in proceedings in a county court.

6 Advocacy in the following proceedings in the Crown Court—

(a) proceedings for the variation or discharge of an order under section 5 or 5A of the Protection from Harassment Act 1997, and

(b) proceedings under the Proceeds of Crime Act 2002 in relation to matters listed in paragraph 40 of Part 1 of this Schedule.

7 Advocacy in a magistrates' court that falls within the description of civil legal services in any of paragraphs 1, 11 to 13 and 15 to 18 of Part 1 of this Schedule.

8 Advocacy in the following proceedings in a magistrates' court—

(a) proceedings under section 47 of the National Assistance Act 1948,

(b) proceedings in relation to—

(i) bail under Schedule 2 to the Immigration Act 1971, or

(ii) arrest under Schedule 2 or 3 to that Act,

(c) proceedings for the variation or discharge of an order under section 5 or 5A of the Protection from Harassment Act 1997, and

(d) proceedings under the Proceeds of Crime Act 2002 in relation to matters listed in paragraph 40 of Part 1 of this Schedule.

Exceptions: tribunals

9 Advocacy in proceedings in the First-tier Tribunal under—

(a) the Mental Health Act 1983, or

(b) paragraph 5(2) of the Schedule to the Repatriation of Prisoners Act 1984.

10 Advocacy in proceedings in the Mental Health Review Tribunal for Wales.

11 Advocacy in proceedings in the First-tier Tribunal under—

(a) Schedule 2 to the Immigration Act 1971, or

(b) Part 5 of the Nationality, Immigration and Asylum Act 2002.

12 Advocacy in proceedings in the First-tier Tribunal under—

(a) section 40A of the British Nationality Act 1981, or

(b) regulation 26 of the Immigration (European Economic Area) Regulations 2006 (S.I. 2006/1003),

but only to the extent that the proceedings concern contravention of the Equality Act 2010.

13 Advocacy in the First-tier Tribunal that falls within the description of civil legal services in paragraph 28, 29 or 32(1) of Part 1 of this Schedule.

14 Advocacy in proceedings in the First-tier Tribunal under—

(a) section 4 or 4A of the Protection of Children Act 1999 (appeals and applications relating to list of barred from regulated activities with children or vulnerable adults),

(b) section 86 or 87 of the Care Standards Act 2000 (appeals and applications relating to list of persons unsuitable to work with vulnerable adults),

(c) section 32 of the Criminal Justice and Court Services Act 2000 (applications relating to disqualification orders), or

(d) section 144 of the Education Act 2002 (appeals and reviews relating to direction prohibiting person from teaching etc).

15 Advocacy in proceedings in the Upper Tribunal arising out of proceedings within any of paragraphs 9 to 14 of this Part of this Schedule.

16 Advocacy in proceedings in the Upper Tribunal under section 4 of the Safeguarding Vulnerable Groups Act 2006.

17 Advocacy in proceedings in the Upper Tribunal under section 11 of the Tribunals, Courts and Enforcement Act 2007 (appeals on a point of law) from decisions made by the First-tier Tribunal or the Special Educational Needs Tribunal for Wales in proceedings under—

(a) Part 4 of the Education Act 1996 (special educational needs), or

(b) the Equality Act 2010.

18 Advocacy in proceedings which are brought before the Upper Tribunal (wholly or primarily) to exercise its judicial review jurisdiction under section 15 of the Tribunals, Courts and Enforcement Act 2007.

19 Advocacy where judicial review applications are transferred to the Upper Tribunal from the High Court under section 31A of the Senior Courts Act 1981.

20 Advocacy in proceedings in the Employment Appeal Tribunal, but only to the extent that the proceedings concern contravention of the Equality Act 2010.

Other exceptions

21 Advocacy in proceedings in the Special Immigration Appeals Commission.

22 Advocacy in proceedings in the Proscribed Organisations Appeal Commission.

23 Advocacy in legal proceedings before any person to whom a case is referred (in whole or in part) in any proceedings within any other paragraph of this Part of this Schedule.

24 Advocacy in bail proceedings before any court which are related to proceedings within any other paragraph of this Part of this Schedule.

25 Advocacy in proceedings before any person for the enforcement of a decision in proceedings within any other paragraph of this Part of this Schedule.

PART 4

INTERPRETATION

1 For the purposes of this Part of this Act, civil legal services are described in Part 1 of this Schedule if they are described in one of the paragraphs of that

Part (other than in an exclusion), even if they are (expressly or impliedly) excluded from another paragraph of that Part.

2 References in this Schedule to an Act or instrument, or a provision of an Act or instrument—
(a) are references to the Act, instrument or provision as amended from time to time, and
(b) include the Act, instrument or provision as applied by another Act or instrument (with or without modifications).

3 References in this Schedule to services provided in relation to an act, omission or other matter of a particular description (however expressed) include services provided in relation to an act, omission or other matter alleged to be of that description.

4 References in this Schedule to services provided in relation to proceedings, orders and other matters include services provided when such proceedings, orders and matters are contemplated.

5 (1) Where a paragraph of Part 1 or 2 of this Schedule describes services that consist of or include services provided in relation to proceedings, the description is to be treated as including, in particular—
(a) services provided in relation to related bail proceedings,
(b) services provided in relation to preliminary or incidental proceedings,
(c) services provided in relation to a related appeal or reference to a court, tribunal or other person, and
(d) services provided in relation to the enforcement of decisions in the proceedings.

(2) Where a paragraph of Part 3 of this Schedule describes advocacy provided in relation to particular proceedings in or before a court, tribunal or other person, the description is to be treated as including services provided in relation to preliminary or incidental proceedings in or before the same court, tribunal or other person.

(3) Regulations may make provision specifying whether proceedings are or are not to be regarded as preliminary or incidental for the purposes of this paragraph.

6 For the purposes of this Schedule, regulations may make provision about—
(a) when services are provided in relation to a matter;
(b) when matters arise under a particular enactment;
(c) when proceedings are proceedings under a particular enactment;
(d) when proceedings are related to other proceedings.

7 In this Schedule "enactment" includes—
(a) an enactment contained in subordinate legislation (within the meaning of the Interpretation Act 1978), and
(b) an enactment contained in, or in an instrument made under, an Act or Measure of the National Assembly for Wales.

SCHEDULE 2

Section 24

CRIMINAL LEGAL AID: MOTOR VEHICLE ORDERS

Amounts payable in connection with criminal legal aid

1 (1) This Schedule makes provision about the recovery of—

(a) an amount payable in connection with the provision of criminal legal aid which is unpaid after the time when it is required to be paid under section 23,

(b) interest in respect of such an amount which is required to be paid under that section, and

(c) an amount required to be paid under section 24 in respect of costs incurred in connection with the enforcement of an obligation to pay an amount or interest described in paragraph (a) or (b).

(2) Such amounts and interest are referred to in this Schedule as "relevant overdue amounts".

(3) In this Schedule "criminal legal aid" means—

(a) advice and assistance required to be made available under section 13 or 15, and

(b) representation required to be made available made under section 16.

Recovery by means of motor vehicle orders

2 (1) Regulations under section 24 may authorise a court to make motor vehicle orders in respect of an individual for the purpose of enabling a relevant overdue amount required to be paid by the individual to be recovered by the person to whom the amount is due.

(2) Regulations that make such provision are referred to in this Schedule as "MVO regulations".

(3) In this Schedule "court" means the High Court, a county court or a magistrates' court.

Motor vehicle orders

3 (1) In this Schedule "motor vehicle order" means—

(a) a clamping order;

(b) a vehicle sale order.

(2) A clamping order is an order—

(a) that a motor vehicle be fitted with an immobilisation device ("clamped"), and

(b) which complies with any requirements that are imposed by MVO regulations with respect to the making of clamping orders.

(3) A vehicle sale order is an order that—

(a) a motor vehicle which is the subject of a clamping order is to be sold or otherwise disposed of in accordance with provision made by MVO regulations, and

(b) any proceeds are to be applied, in accordance with MVO regulations, in discharging the individual's liability in respect of the relevant overdue amount.

(4) MVO regulations may make provision in connection with—

(a) the procedure for making motor vehicle orders,

(b) the matters which must be included in such orders,

(c) the fitting of immobilisation devices,

(d) the fixing of notices to motor vehicles to which immobilisation devices have been fitted and the content of such notices,

(e) the removal and storage of motor vehicles,

(f) the release of motor vehicles from immobilisation devices or from storage, including the conditions to be met before a motor vehicle is released,

(g) the sale or other disposal of motor vehicles not released,

(h) the imposition of charges in connection with the fitting of immobilisation devices,

(i) the imposition of charges in connection with the removal, storage, release (whether from immobilisation devices or from storage), sale or disposal of motor vehicles, and

(j) the recovery of charges described in paragraphs (h) and (i), including provision for them to be recovered from the proceeds of sale of motor vehicles.

(5) In this Schedule—

"immobilisation device" has the same meaning as in section 104(9) of the Road Traffic Regulation Act 1984 (immobilisation of vehicles illegally parked);

"motor vehicle" means a mechanically propelled vehicle intended or adapted for use on roads, except that section 189 of the Road Traffic Act 1988 (exceptions for certain vehicles) applies for the purposes of this Schedule as it applies for the purposes of the Road Traffic Acts.

Applications

4 MVO regulations must provide that a motor vehicle order may be made in relation to a relevant overdue amount only on the application of the person to whom the amount is due.

Matters of which court to be satisfied

5 (1) MVO regulations must provide that, before a court makes a clamping order in respect of an individual, it must be satisfied—

(a) that the failure to pay the relevant overdue amount is attributable to the individual's wilful refusal or culpable neglect, and

(b) that the value of the motor vehicle or vehicles to be clamped, if sold, would be likely to be an amount which exceeds half of the estimated recoverable amount.

(2) In this paragraph "the estimated recoverable amount" means the aggregate of—

(a) the relevant overdue amount, and

(b) the amount of the likely charges due under MVO regulations in relation to the motor vehicle or vehicles.

Ownership of motor vehicles

6 (1) MVO regulations must provide that a clamping order must not be made except in relation to a motor vehicle which is owned by the individual liable to pay the relevant overdue amount.

(2) For this purpose a motor vehicle is owned by an individual if the individual has an interest in the motor vehicle.

Motor vehicles used by disabled persons

7 (1) MVO regulations must provide that an immobilisation device may not be fitted to a motor vehicle—

(a) which displays a current disabled person's badge or a current recognised badge, or

(b) in relation to which there are reasonable grounds for believing that it is used for the carriage of a disabled person.

(2) In this paragraph—

"disabled person's badge" means a badge issued, or having effect as if issued, under regulations under section 21 of the Chronically Sick and Disabled Persons Act 1970 (badges for display on motor vehicles used by disabled persons);

"recognised badge" has the meaning given by section 21A of the Chronically Sick and Disabled Persons Act 1970 (recognition of badges issued outside Great Britain).

Restrictions on making vehicle sale orders

8 MVO regulations must provide that, where a motor vehicle has been clamped under a clamping order, no vehicle sale order may be made in respect of the motor vehicle before the end of a prescribed period.

SCHEDULE 3

Section 31

LEGAL AID FOR LEGAL PERSONS

Legal persons

1 In this Schedule "legal person" means a person other than an individual.

Exceptional case determinations

2 (1) For the purposes of this Schedule, in relation to a legal person and civil legal services, advice, assistance or representation for the purposes of criminal proceedings, an exceptional case determination is a determination that sub-paragraph (2) or (3) is satisfied.

(2) This sub-paragraph is satisfied if it is necessary to make the services available to the legal person under this Part because failure to do so would be a breach of—

(a) the person's Convention rights (within the meaning of the Human Rights Act 1998), or

(b) any rights of the person to the provision of legal services that are enforceable EU rights.

(3) This sub-paragraph is satisfied if it is appropriate to make the services available to the legal person under this Part, in the particular circumstances of the case, having regard to any risk that failure to do so would be such a breach.

Civil legal aid

3 (1) Civil legal services are to be available to a legal person under this Part only if the Director—

(a) has made an exceptional case determination in relation to the person and the services, and

(b) has determined that the person qualifies for the services in accordance with this Part,

(and has not withdrawn either determination).

(2) Sections 11 and 12(1) apply in relation to a determination under sub-paragraph (1)(b) as they apply in relation to a determination under section 10(2)(b).

(3) Subsections (2) to (6) of section 12 apply in relation to a determination under this paragraph as they apply in relation to a determination under section 10.

(4) In sections 11 and 12 as applied by this paragraph, references to an individual include a legal person.

Advice and assistance for criminal proceedings

4 (1) Regulations may provide that prescribed advice and assistance is to be available under this Part to a legal person described in sub-paragraph (2) if—

(a) prescribed conditions are met,

(b) the Director has made an exceptional case determination in relation to the person and the advice and assistance (and has not withdrawn that determination), and

(c) the Director has determined that the legal person qualifies for such advice and assistance in accordance with the regulations (and has not withdrawn that determination).

(2) Those legal persons are—

(a) legal persons who are involved in investigations which may lead to criminal proceedings, and

(b) legal persons who are before a court, tribunal or other person in criminal proceedings.

(3) Subsections (3) to (9) of section 15 apply in relation to regulations under this paragraph (and decisions made under such regulations) as they apply in

relation to regulations under that section (and decisions made under such regulations).

(4) In those subsections as applied by this paragraph, references to an individual include a legal person.

(5) In this paragraph "assistance" includes, in particular, assistance in the form of advocacy.

Representation for criminal proceedings

5 (1) Representation for the purposes of criminal proceedings is to be available under this Part to a legal person if—

(a) the person is a specified legal person in relation to the proceedings, or

(b) the proceedings involve the person resisting an appeal to the Crown Court otherwise than in an official capacity,

and the conditions in sub-paragraph (2) are met.

(2) Those conditions are that the Director—

(a) has made an exceptional case determination in relation to the legal person and representation for the purposes of the proceedings, and

(b) has determined (provisionally or otherwise) that the legal person qualifies for such representation in accordance with this Part,

(and has not withdrawn either determination).

(3) Where a legal person qualifies under this Part for representation for the purposes of criminal proceedings, representation is also to be available to the legal person for the purposes of any preliminary or incidental proceedings.

(4) Regulations under section 16(4) and (5) apply for the purposes of sub-paragraph (3) as they apply for the purposes of section 16(3), except to the extent that the regulations provide otherwise.

(5) Section 17(1)(b) applies in relation to an exceptional case determination under sub-paragraph (2)(a) as it applies in relation to a determination under section 16.

(6) Paragraphs (a) and (b) of section 17(1) apply in relation to a determination under sub-paragraph (2)(b) as they apply in relation to a determination under section 16.

(7) Subsections (2) to (7) of section 18 apply in relation to a determination under sub-paragraph (2) (and a decision in relation to the interests of justice for the purposes of such a determination) as they apply in relation to a determination under section 16 (and a decision for the purposes of such a determination).

(8) The Director may not make a provisional determination under sub-paragraph (2)(b) unless authorised to do so by regulations under sub-paragraph (9).

(9) Regulations may provide that the Director may make a provisional determination that a legal person qualifies under this Part for representation for the purposes of criminal proceedings where—

(a) the legal person is involved in an investigation which may result in criminal proceedings,

(b) the determination is made for the purposes of criminal proceedings that may result from the investigation, and

(c) any prescribed conditions are met.

(10) Subsections (2) and (3) of section 20 apply in relation to regulations under sub-paragraph (9) (and determinations and decisions made under such regulations) as they apply in relation to regulations under that section (and determinations and decisions made under such regulations).

(11) In sections 17, 18 and 20 as applied by this paragraph—

(a) references to an individual include a legal person,

(b) references to the relevant authority have effect as if they were references to the Director, and

(c) the reference in section 20(2)(d) to a determination made by the Director or a court in reliance on section 18 or 19 has effect as if it were a reference to a determination by the Director under sub-paragraph (2)(b) made otherwise than in reliance on regulations under sub-paragraph (9).

(12) Regulations may prescribe circumstances in which making representation available to a legal person for the purposes of criminal proceedings is to be taken to be in the interests of justice for the purposes of a determination under this paragraph.

(13) In this paragraph "specified legal person", in relation to criminal proceedings, means a description of legal person specified in regulations in relation to those proceedings.

Financial resources

6 Section 21 applies for the purposes of a determination under paragraph 3(1)(b) or 5(2)(b), or under regulations under paragraph 4 or 5(9), as if the references to an individual included a legal person.

Contributions and costs

7 In sections 23, 24, 25 and 26 and Schedule 2, references to an individual include a legal person to whom services are made available under this Part in accordance with this Schedule or regulations under this Schedule.

8 In Schedule 2, references to criminal legal aid include advice, assistance and representation required to be made available under paragraph 4 or 5 of this Schedule.

Providers of services etc

9 (1) Section 27 applies in relation to the provision of services to a legal person in accordance with this Schedule or regulations under this Schedule as it applies in relation to the provision of services to an individual under this Part.

(2) In that section as applied by this paragraph—

(a) references to an individual include a legal person,

(b) the reference to a determination under section 16 includes a determination under paragraph 5(2)(b) of this Schedule, and

(c) the reference to regulations under section 15 includes regulations under paragraph 4 of this Schedule.

(3) In sections 28, 29 and 30, references to an individual include a legal person to whom services are made available under this Part in accordance with this Schedule or regulations under this Schedule.

Supplementary matters

10 In sections 34, 35 and 41(2), references to an individual include a legal person to whom services are made available under this Part in accordance with this Schedule or regulations under this Schedule or who is seeking the provision of such services.

SCHEDULE 4

Section 38

TRANSFER OF EMPLOYEES AND PROPERTY ETC OF LEGAL SERVICES COMMISSION

PART 1

TRANSFER OF EMPLOYEES ETC

Transfer

1 (1) An individual who is an employee of the Legal Services Commission ("the LSC") immediately before the transfer day becomes employed in the civil service of the State on that day.

(2) The terms and conditions of the individual's contract of employment immediately before the transfer day have effect, on and after that day, as if they were terms and conditions of the individual's employment in the civil service of the State, subject to paragraph 4(1) and (2).

(3) All of the rights, powers, duties and liabilities of the LSC in connection with the individual's employment are transferred to the Crown on the transfer day, subject to paragraph 4(1) and (2).

(4) Anything done (or having effect as if done) before the transfer day—

(a) by or in relation to the LSC, and

(b) for the purposes of, or in connection with, anything transferred by virtue of sub-paragraphs (1) to (3),

is to have effect, so far as necessary for continuing its effect on and after that day, as if done by or in relation to the Crown.

(5) Anything which is in the process of being done immediately before the transfer day—

(a) by or in relation to the LSC, and

(b) for the purposes of, or in connection with, anything transferred by virtue of sub-paragraphs (1) to (3),

may be continued by or in relation to the Crown.

(6) A reference to the LSC in a document, including an enactment, constituting or relating to anything transferred by virtue of sub-paragraphs (1) to (3) is to have effect, so far as is necessary for giving effect to those sub-paragraphs, as a reference to the Crown.

Continuity of employment

2 A transfer under paragraph 1 does not break the continuity of the individual's employment and accordingly—

(a) the individual is not to be regarded for the purposes of Part 11 of the Employment Rights Act 1996 (redundancy) as having been dismissed by reason of that transfer, and

(b) the individual's period of employment with the LSC counts as a period of employment in the civil service of the State for the purposes of that Act.

Right to object to transfer

3 (1) This paragraph has effect where, before the transfer day, an individual who is an employee of the LSC informs the LSC or the Lord Chancellor that the individual objects to becoming employed in the civil service of the State by virtue of paragraph 1(1).

(2) Where this paragraph has effect—

(a) the individual does not become employed in the civil service of the State by virtue of paragraph 1(1),

(b) the rights, powers, duties and liabilities under the individual's contract of employment do not transfer by virtue of paragraph 1(3),

(c) the individual's contract of employment terminates immediately before the transfer day, and

(d) the individual is not to be treated, for any purpose, as having been dismissed by the LSC by reason of the termination of the contract under this paragraph.

Pension schemes and compensation schemes

4 (1) On and after the transfer day, the terms and conditions of employment of an individual who is employed in the civil service of the State by virtue of paragraph 1(1) do not include any term or condition that was part of the individual's contract of employment immediately before the transfer day and that relates to—

(a) an occupational pension scheme,

(b) a compensation scheme, or

(c) rights, powers, duties or liabilities under or in connection with such a scheme.

(2) Accordingly, paragraph 1(3) does not apply in relation to rights, powers, duties or liabilities under or in connection with an occupational pension scheme or a compensation scheme.

(3) The Lord Chancellor may make one or more schemes providing for the transfer to the Lord Chancellor or the Secretary of State of the LSC's rights, powers, duties and liabilities under or in connection with—

(a) an occupational pension scheme, or

(b) a compensation scheme,

whether the rights, powers, duties and liabilities arise under the occupational pension scheme or compensation scheme, under an enactment, under a contract of employment or otherwise.

(4) A transfer scheme may provide that anything done (or having effect as if done) before the day on which the transfer scheme takes effect—

(a) by or in relation to the LSC, and

(b) for the purposes of, or in connection with, anything transferred by virtue of the transfer scheme,

is to have effect, so far as is necessary for continuing its effect on and after that day, as if done by or in relation to the transferee.

(5) A transfer scheme may provide that anything which is in the process of being done immediately before the day on which the transfer scheme takes effect—

(a) by or in relation to the LSC, and

(b) for the purposes of, or in connection with, anything transferred by virtue of the transfer scheme,

may be continued by or in relation to the transferee.

(6) A transfer scheme may provide that a reference to the LSC in a document, including an enactment, constituting or relating to anything transferred by virtue of the scheme is to have effect, so far as is necessary for giving effect to that scheme, as a reference to the transferee.

(7) A transfer scheme may, so far as is necessary for giving effect to that scheme, provide that an enactment that applies in relation to compensation schemes or occupational pension schemes applies to a compensation scheme or occupational pension scheme that is the subject of the transfer scheme, the members of such a scheme or the transferee with modifications specified in the transfer scheme.

(8) A transfer scheme may—

(a) amend or otherwise modify a compensation scheme that is the subject of the transfer scheme, and

(b) create, modify or remove rights, powers, duties or liabilities under or in connection with such a scheme.

(9) The powers under sub-paragraph (8) include power to amend or otherwise modify any instrument relating to the constitution, management or operation of a compensation scheme.

(10) Transfer schemes amending or otherwise modifying a compensation scheme have effect in spite of any provision (of any nature) which would otherwise prevent or restrict the amendment or modification.

(11) A transfer scheme may include consequential, incidental, supplementary, transitional, transitory and saving provision.

(12) In this paragraph—

"compensation scheme" means so much of any scheme as makes provision for payment by way of compensation on or in respect of termination of employment;

"occupational pension scheme" has the same meaning as in the Pension Schemes Act 1993;

"transfer scheme" means a scheme made under sub-paragraph (3).

Power to merge LSC occupational pension schemes

5 (1) The Lord Chancellor may make a scheme providing for the merger of LSC occupational pension schemes.

(2) A scheme under this paragraph may in particular—

(a) provide for the assets and liabilities of one LSC occupational pension scheme to become assets and liabilities of another,

(b) create, modify or remove rights, powers, duties or liabilities under or in connection with an LSC occupational pension scheme,

(c) provide for the winding up of an LSC occupational pension scheme,

(d) provide for references to one LSC occupational pension scheme in a document, including an enactment, to have effect as references to another, and

(e) include consequential, incidental, supplementary, transitional, transitory and saving provision.

(3) A scheme under this paragraph may in particular amend or otherwise modify—

(a) the trust deed of an LSC occupational pension scheme,

(b) rules of an LSC occupational pension scheme, and

(c) any other instrument relating to the constitution, management or operation of an LSC occupational pension scheme.

(4) A scheme under this paragraph must ensure that the merger of the LSC occupational pension schemes does not, to any extent, deprive members of the LSC occupational pension schemes, or other beneficiaries under those schemes, of rights that accrue to them under those schemes before the merger takes effect.

(5) Subject to sub-paragraph (4), a scheme under this paragraph has effect in spite of any provision (of any nature) which would otherwise prevent the merger of the LSC occupational pension schemes.

(6) In this paragraph—

"LSC occupational pension scheme" means an occupational pension scheme under which—

(a) the LSC has rights, powers, duties or liabilities, or

(b) the Lord Chancellor or the Secretary of State has rights, powers, duties or liabilities by virtue of a scheme under paragraph 4(3);

"occupational pension scheme" has the same meaning as in the Pension Schemes Act 1993.

PART 2

TRANSFER OF PROPERTY ETC

Transfer of interests in land

6 (1) The LSC's interests in land are by virtue of this sub-paragraph transferred to the Secretary of State for Communities and Local Government on the transfer day.

(2) Anything done (or having effect as if done) before the transfer day—

(a) by or in relation to the LSC, and

(b) for the purposes of, or in connection with, anything transferred by virtue of sub-paragraph (1),

is to have effect, so far as is necessary for continuing its effect on and after that day, as if done by or in relation to the Secretary of State for Communities and Local Government.

(3) Anything which is in the process of being done immediately before the transfer day—

(a) by or in relation to the LSC, and

(b) for the purposes of, or in connection with, anything transferred by virtue of sub-paragraph (1),

may be continued by or in relation to the Secretary of State for Communities and Local Government.

(4) A reference to the LSC in a document, including an enactment, constituting or relating to anything transferred by virtue of sub-paragraph (1) is to have effect, so far as is necessary for giving effect to that sub-paragraph, as a reference to the Secretary of State for Communities and Local Government.

(5) In this paragraph—

"interest in land" means—

(a) an estate or interest in land, and

(b) any rights, powers, duties or liabilities of the LSC in connection with such an estate or interest,

but does not include a charge on an estate or interest in land;

"land" includes buildings and other structures.

Transfer of other property, rights and liabilities

7 (1) The property, rights, powers, duties and liabilities of the LSC are by virtue of this sub-paragraph transferred to the Lord Chancellor on the transfer day.

(2) Sub-paragraph (1) does not apply to—

(a) property, rights, powers, duties and liabilities transferred by virtue of paragraph 1 or 6, or

(b) rights, powers, duties and liabilities described in paragraph 4(3).

(3) Anything done (or having effect as if done) before the transfer day—

(a) by or in relation to the LSC, and

(b) for the purposes of, or in connection with, anything transferred by virtue of sub-paragraph (1),

is to have effect, so far as is necessary for continuing its effect on and after that day, as if done by or in relation to the Lord Chancellor.

(4) Anything which is in the process of being done immediately before the transfer day—

(a) by or in relation to the LSC, and

(b) for the purposes of, or in connection with, anything transferred by virtue of sub-paragraph (1),

may be continued by or in relation to the Lord Chancellor.

(5) A reference to the LSC in a document, including an enactment, constituting or relating to anything transferred by virtue of sub-paragraph (1) is to have effect, so far as is necessary for giving effect to that sub-paragraph, as a reference to the Lord Chancellor.

PART 3

SUPPLEMENTARY

Disapplying restrictions on transfer

8 Paragraphs 1, 6 and 7 and schemes under paragraph 4 have effect in relation to property, rights, powers, duties and liabilities in spite of any provision (of any nature) which would otherwise prevent or restrict their transfer.

Certificate

9 A certificate issued by the Lord Chancellor stating that anything specified in the certificate has vested in a person specified in the certificate by virtue of any of paragraphs 1, 6 and 7 or a scheme under paragraph 4 is conclusive evidence of that fact for all purposes.

Validity

10 The transfer of property, rights, powers, duties or liabilities by any of paragraphs 1, 6 and 7 or a scheme under paragraph 4 does not affect the validity of anything done by or in relation to the LSC before that paragraph or scheme has effect.

Power to make further provision

11 (1) The Lord Chancellor may by regulations make consequential, supplementary, incidental, transitional, transitory or saving provision in connection with—
(a) transfers effected by this Schedule, or
(b) schemes made under this Schedule.

(2) The regulations may, in particular, include provision modifying an enactment (whenever passed or made), including this Schedule.

Interpretation

12 (1) In this Schedule—
"the LSC" means the Legal Services Commission;
"the transfer day" means the day on which section 38(1) comes into force (subject to regulations under sub-paragraph (2));
"enactment" means an enactment contained in an Act or an instrument made under an Act (and "Act" includes an Act or Measure of the National Assembly for Wales).

(2) The Lord Chancellor may by regulations amend or otherwise modify the definition of "the transfer day" in sub-paragraph (1).

SCHEDULE 5

Section 39

LEGAL AID: CONSEQUENTIAL AMENDMENTS

PART 1

AMENDMENTS

Public Records Act 1958 (c. 51)

1 In Schedule 1 to the Public Records Act 1958 (definition of public records), in Part 1 of the Table at the end of paragraph 3, in the second column omit "Legal Services Commission."

Parliamentary Commissioner Act 1967 (c. 13)

2 In Schedule 2 to the Parliamentary Commissioner Act 1967 (departments etc subject to investigation) omit "Legal Services Commission."

Criminal Appeal Act 1968 (c. 19)

3 In section 50 of the Criminal Appeal Act 1968 (meaning of "sentence"), in subsection (3) for "under section 17 of the Access to Justice Act 1999" substitute "relating to a requirement to make a payment under regulations under section 23 or 24 of the Legal Aid, Sentencing and Punishment of Offenders Act 2012".

Children and Young Persons Act 1969 (c. 54)

4 (1) Section 23(5A) of the Children and Young Persons Act 1969 (restrictions on imposing security requirement on child or young person who is not legally represented) is amended as follows.

(2) In paragraph (a)—

(a) for the words from the beginning to "but the right" substitute "representation was provided to the child or young person under Part 1 of the Legal Aid, Sentencing and Punishment of Offenders Act 2012 for the purposes of the proceedings but", and

(b) for "to be granted such a right" substitute "for such representation".

(3) In paragraph (aa) for "to be granted a right to it" substitute "for such representation".

5 (1) In section 23 of that Act as it has effect pursuant to section 98 of the Crime and Disorder Act 1998 (restrictions on remand of boy who is not legally represented), subsection (4A) is amended as follows.

(2) In paragraph (a)—

(a) for the words from the beginning to "but the right" substitute "representation was provided to the person under Part 1 of the Legal Aid, Sentencing and Punishment of Offenders Act 2012 for the purposes of the proceedings but", and

(b) for "to be granted such a right" substitute "for such representation".

(3) In paragraph (aa) for "to be granted a right to it" substitute "for such representation".

Attachment of Earnings Act 1971 (c. 32)

6 In section 1(3)(c) of the Attachment of Earnings Act 1971 (cases in which magistrates' court may make attachment of earnings order) for the words from "paid by" to the end substitute "paid under regulations under section 23 or 24 of the Legal Aid, Sentencing and Punishment of Offenders Act 2012".

Solicitors Act 1974 (c. 47)

7 The Solicitors Act 1974 is amended as follows.

8 (1) Section 47 (jurisdiction and powers of Tribunal) is amended as follows.

(2) In subsections (2)(d), (2B) and (2D) for "providing representation funded by the Legal Services Commission as part of the Criminal Defence Service" substitute "criminal legal aid work".

(3) In subsection (2A)—

(a) for "providing representation" substitute "criminal legal aid work", and

(b) for "funded by the Legal Services Commission as part of the Community Legal Service or Criminal Defence Service" substitute "provided under arrangements made for the purposes of Part 1 of the Legal Aid, Sentencing and Punishment of Offenders Act 2012".

(4) After subsection (3B) insert—

"(3C) In this section "criminal legal aid work" means the provision under arrangements made for the purposes of Part 1 of the Legal Aid, Sentencing and Punishment of Offenders Act 2012 of—

(a) advice or assistance described in section 13 or 15 of that Act, or

(b) representation for the purposes of criminal proceedings."

9 In section 49(3) (appeals from Tribunal) for "providing representation funded by the Legal Services Commission as part of the Criminal Defence Service" substitute "criminal legal aid work (as defined in that section)".

House of Commons Disqualification Act 1975 (c. 24)

10 In Part 2 of Schedule 1 to the House of Commons Disqualification Act 1975 (bodies of which all members are disqualified) omit "The Legal Services Commission."

Northern Ireland Assembly Disqualification Act 1975 (c. 25)

11 In Part 2 of Schedule 1 to the Northern Ireland Assembly Disqualification Act 1975 (bodies of which all members are disqualified) omit "The Legal Services Commission."

Magistrates' Courts Act 1980 (c. 43)

12 The Magistrates' Courts Act 1980 is amended as follows.

13 In section 8(4) (matters which may be contained in report of committal

proceedings without an order) for paragraph (i) substitute—

"(i) whether, for the purposes of the proceedings, representation was provided to the accused or any of the accused under Part 1 of the Legal Aid, Sentencing and Punishment of Offenders Act 2012."

14 In section 8A(5) (power to make ruling at pre-trial hearing)—

(a) in paragraph (a) for the words from "to be granted" to "Criminal Defence Service" substitute "to be provided with representation for the purposes of the proceedings under Part 1 of the Legal Aid, Sentencing and Punishment of Offenders Act 2012", and

(b) in paragraph (b) for "the Legal Services Commission must decide whether or not to grant him that right" substitute "the necessary arrangements must be made for him to apply for it and, where appropriate, obtain it".

15 In section 8C(7) (matters to which reporting restrictions do not apply) for paragraph (g) substitute—

"(g) whether, for the purposes of the proceedings, representation was provided to the accused or any of the accused under Part 1 of the Legal Aid, Sentencing and Punishment of Offenders Act 2012."

16 In section 92(1)(b) (exception to restriction on power to impose imprisonment for default) for the words from "under section 17(2)" to "criminal case" substitute "made by a court under regulations under section 23 of the Legal Aid, Sentencing and Punishment of Offenders Act 2012 (payment by individual in respect of legal aid)".

17 In section 130(3) (powers of alternate court on transfer of remand hearing) for the words from "all the powers" to end substitute "all of the following powers which that court would have had but for the order—

(a) powers in relation to further remand (whether in custody or on bail), and

(b) powers under Part 1 of the Legal Aid, Sentencing and Punishment of Offenders Act 2012."

18 In section 145A(4) (rules about costs orders against legal representatives) for "the Legal Services Commission" substitute "the Lord Chancellor under arrangements made for the purposes of Part 1 of the Legal Aid, Sentencing and Punishment of Offenders Act 2012".

Senior Courts Act 1981 (c. 54)

19 The Senior Courts Act 1981 is amended as follows.

20 In section 28(4) (appeals from Crown Court and inferior courts) for "an order under section 17 of the Access to Justice Act 1999" substitute "a requirement to make a payment under regulations under section 23 or 24 of the Legal Aid, Sentencing and Punishment of Offenders Act 2012".

21 In section 29(6) (mandatory, prohibiting and quashing orders) for "orders under section 17 of the Access to Justice Act 1999" substitute "requirements to make payments under regulations under section 23 or 24 of the Legal Aid, Sentencing and Punishment of Offenders Act 2012".

Prosecution of Offences Act 1985 (c. 23)

22 Part 2 of the Prosecution of Offences Act 1985 (costs in criminal cases) is amended as follows.

23 In section 19(2)(b) (matters of which account to be taken when making order as to costs) for "any grant of a right to representation funded by the Legal Services Commission as part of the Criminal Defence Service" substitute "of whether, for the purposes of the proceedings, representation has been provided under Part 1 of the Legal Aid, Sentencing and Punishment of Offenders Act 2012".

24 In section 20(2) (regulations) for "by the Legal Services Commission or out of central funds" substitute "by the Lord Chancellor under arrangements made for the purposes of Part 1 of the Legal Aid, Sentencing and Punishment of Offenders Act 2012 or out of central funds in accordance with a costs order".

25 (1) Section 21 (interpretation) is amended as follows.

(2) In subsection (1), in the definition of "legally assisted person" for the words from "to whom" to the end of the definition substitute "for whom advice, assistance or representation is provided under arrangements made for the purposes of Part 1 of the Legal Aid, Sentencing and Punishment of Offenders Act 2012".

(3) In subsection (4A)(a) for the words from "not" to "Service" substitute "not to include the cost of advice, assistance or representation provided to the person under arrangements made for the purposes of Part 1 of the Legal Aid, Sentencing and Punishment of Offenders Act 2012".

(4) In subsection (4A)(b) for the words from "the cost" to the end substitute "the cost of such advice, assistance or representation".

Child Abduction and Custody Act 1985 (c. 60)

26 In section 11 of the Child Abduction and Custody Act 1985 (cost of applications for child custody or access), for paragraph (a) (but not the "or" following it) substitute—

"(a) the provision of any civil legal services (within the meaning of Part 1 of the Legal Aid, Sentencing and Punishment of Offenders Act 2012) under arrangements made for the purposes of that Part of that Act,".

Administration of Justice Act 1985 (c. 61)

27 Part 3 of the Administration of Justice Act 1985 (legal aid) is amended as follows.

28 In section 40(1) (legal aid complaints) for the words from "funded by" to "Criminal Defence Service" substitute "under arrangements made for the purposes of Part 1 of the Legal Aid, Sentencing and Punishment of Offenders Act 2012".

29 In section 41(2) (reduction of fees payable where legal aid complaint made)—

(a) for "Legal Services Commission" substitute "Lord Chancellor", and

(b) for "by him as part of the Community Legal Service or Criminal Defence Service" substitute "by the barrister under arrangements made for the purposes of Part 1 of the Legal Aid, Sentencing and Punishment of Offenders Act 2012".

30 (1) Section 42 (exclusion of barristers from legal aid work) is amended as follows.

(2) In subsections (1) and (3) for "providing representation funded by the Legal Services Commission as part of the Criminal Defence Service" substitute "criminal legal aid work".

(3) At the end insert—

"(5) In this section "criminal legal aid work" means the provision under arrangements made for the purposes of Part 1 of the Legal Aid, Sentencing and Punishment of Offenders Act 2012 of—

(a) advice or assistance described in section 13 or 15 of that Act, or

(b) representation for the purposes of criminal proceedings."

31 In section 43(3) (reduction of costs payable where legal aid complaint made)—

(a) for "Legal Services Commission" substitute "Lord Chancellor", and

(b) for "as part of the Community Legal Service or Criminal Defence Service" substitute "under arrangements made for the purposes of Part 1 of the Legal Aid, Sentencing and Punishment of Offenders Act 2012".

32 In paragraph 20(1) of Schedule 2 (powers of Tribunal in respect of legal aid complaints) for "providing representation funded by the Legal Services Commission as part of the Criminal Defence Service" substitute "criminal legal aid work (as defined in that section)".

Housing Act 1985 (c. 68)

33 In section 170(5) of the Housing Act 1985 (charges to recover costs of assistance in legal proceedings)—

(a) for "section 10(7) of the Access to Justice Act 1999" substitute "section 25 of the Legal Aid, Sentencing and Punishment of Offenders Act 2012", and

(b) for "Legal Services Commission" substitute "Lord Chancellor".

Criminal Justice Act 1987 (c. 38)

34 The Criminal Justice Act 1987 is amended as follows.

35 In section 4(1) (notices of transfer to Crown Court) for "paragraph 2 of Schedule 3 to the Access to Justice Act 1999" substitute "regulations under section 19 of the Legal Aid, Sentencing and Punishment of Offenders Act 2012".

36 In section 11(12) (matters to which reporting restrictions do not apply) for paragraph (h) substitute—

"(h) whether, for the purposes of the proceedings, representation was provided to the accused or any of the accused under Part

1 of the Legal Aid, Sentencing and Punishment of Offenders Act 2012."

Housing Act 1988 (c. 50)

37 In section 82(4) of the Housing Act 1988 (charges to recover costs of assistance in legal proceedings)—
(a) for "section 10(7) of the Access to Justice Act 1999" substitute "section 25 of the Legal Aid, Sentencing and Punishment of Offenders Act 2012", and
(b) for "Legal Services Commission" substitute "Lord Chancellor".

Children Act 1989 (c. 41)

38 In section 25(6) of the Children Act 1989 (child without legal representation not to be placed in secure accommodation without having been informed of right to apply for legal aid), for the words from "representation" to "Criminal Defence Service" substitute "the provision of representation under Part 1 of the Legal Aid, Sentencing and Punishment of Offenders Act 2012".

Courts and Legal Services Act 1990 (c. 41)

39 (1) Section 31B of the Courts and Legal Services Act 1990 (advocates and litigators employed by Legal Services Commission) is amended as follows.

(2) In the heading of the section for "Legal Services Commission" substitute "Lord Chancellor".

(3) In subsection (1) for paragraph (b) substitute—
"(b) is employed by the Lord Chancellor, or by any body established and maintained by the Lord Chancellor, under arrangements made for the purposes of Part 1 of the Legal Aid, Sentencing and Punishment of Offenders Act 2012."

Criminal Justice Act 1991 (c. 53)

40 In section 53(3) of the Criminal Justice Act 1991 (effect of notices transferring certain cases involving children) for "paragraph 2 of Schedule 3 to the Access to Justice Act 1999" substitute "regulations under section 19 of the Legal Aid, Sentencing and Punishment of Offenders Act 2012".

Social Security Administration Act 1992 (c. 5)

41 (1) Section 108(7) of the Social Security Administration Act 1992 is amended as follows.

(2) For "Legal Services Commission", in the first place, substitute "Lord Chancellor".

(3) In paragraph (a)—
(a) at the end of sub-paragraph (iii) for "and" substitute "or", and
(b) after that sub-paragraph insert—
"(iv) was provided with civil legal services (within the meaning of Part 1 of the Legal Aid,

Sentencing and Punishment of Offenders Act 2012) under arrangements made for the purposes of that Part of that Act; and".

(4) In paragraph (b) after sub-paragraph (iii) insert "or

(iv) under regulations under section 23 or 24 of the Legal Aid, Sentencing and Punishment of Offenders Act 2012 in respect of civil legal services (within the meaning of Part 1 of that Act) provided under arrangements made for the purposes of that Part of that Act,".

Criminal Procedure and Investigations Act 1996 (c. 25)

42 In section 37(9) of the Criminal Procedure and Investigations Act 1996 (matters to which reporting restrictions do not apply) for paragraph (g) substitute—

"(g) whether, for the purposes of the proceedings, representation was provided to the accused or any of the accused under Part 1 of the Legal Aid, Sentencing and Punishment of Offenders Act 2012."

Family Law Act 1996 (c. 27)

43 The Family Law Act 1996 is amended as follows.

44 (1) Section 8 (attendance at information meetings) is amended as follows.

(2) In subsection (9)(h) for "services funded by the Legal Services Commission as part of the Community Legal Service" substitute "civil legal services under Part 1 of the Legal Aid, Sentencing and Punishment of Offenders Act 2012".

(3) In subsection (12) for "funded for him by the Legal Services Commission as part of the Community Legal Service" substitute "provided for the person under arrangements made for the purposes of Part 1 of the Legal Aid, Sentencing and Punishment of Offenders Act 2012".

(4) In subsection (13), after "section" insert—

""civil legal services" has the meaning given in Part 1 of the Legal Aid, Sentencing and Punishment of Offenders Act 2012;".

45 (1) Section 23 (provision of marriage counselling) is amended as follows.

(2) In subsection (3) for "funded for them by the Legal Services Commission as part of the Community Legal Service" substitute "provided for them under arrangements made for the purposes of Part 1 of the Legal Aid, Sentencing and Punishment of Offenders Act 2012".

(3) Omit subsection (8) (powers of Legal Services Commission).

Crime and Disorder Act 1998 (c. 37)

46 The Crime and Disorder Act 1998 is amended as follows.

47 (1) Section 50 (early administrative hearings) is amended as follows.

(2) In subsection (2)—

(a) after "this section" insert "—

(a) ", and

(b) for the words from "to be granted" to the end substitute "to be provided with representation for the purposes of the proceedings under Part 1 of the Legal Aid, Sentencing and Punishment of Offenders Act 2012, and

(b) if he indicates that he does, the necessary arrangements must be made for him to apply for it and, where appropriate, obtain it."

(3) Omit subsection (2A).

48 In section 51B(6)(b) (effect of notice given under section 51B in serious or complex fraud cases) for "paragraph 2 of Schedule 3 to the Access to Justice Act 1999" substitute "regulations under section 19 of the Legal Aid, Sentencing and Punishment of Offenders Act 2012".

49 In section 52A(7) (matters to which reporting restrictions do not apply) for paragraph (h) substitute—

"(h) whether, for the purposes of the proceedings, representation was provided to the accused or any of the accused under Part 1 of the Legal Aid, Sentencing and Punishment of Offenders Act 2012."

50 In paragraph 3(8) of Schedule 3 (matters to which reporting restrictions do not apply) for paragraph (g) substitute—

"(g) whether, for the purposes of the proceedings, representation was provided to the accused or any of the accused under Part 1 of the Legal Aid, Sentencing and Punishment of Offenders Act 2012."

Access to Justice Act 1999 (c. 22)

51 In the Access to Justice Act 1999 omit—

(a) sections 1 to 26 and Schedules 1 to 3A (legal aid), and

(b) Part 2 of Schedule 14 (transitional provision: Legal Services Commission).

Powers of Criminal Courts (Sentencing) Act 2000 (c. 6)

52 The Powers of Criminal Courts (Sentencing) Act 2000 is amended as follows.

53 (1) Section 83(3) (exception to restriction on imposition of custodial sentence on persons not legally represented) is amended as follows.

(2) In paragraph (a)—

(a) for the words from the beginning to "but the right" substitute "representation was made available to him for the purposes of the proceedings under Part 1 of the Legal Aid, Sentencing and Punishment of Offenders Act 2012 but", and

(b) for "to be granted such a right" substitute "for such representation".

(3) In paragraph (aa) for "to be granted a right to it" substitute "for such representation".

54 In section 155(8) (alteration of Crown Court sentence) for "under section 17(2) of the Access to Justice Act 1999" substitute "relating to a requirement to make a payment under regulations under section 23 or 24 of the Legal Aid, Sentencing and Punishment of Offenders Act 2012".

Freedom of Information Act 2000 (c. 36)

55 In Part 6 of Schedule 1 to the Freedom of Information Act 2000 (public authorities) omit "The Legal Services Commission."

International Criminal Court Act 2001 (c. 17)

56 In section 6(2)(c) of the International Criminal Court Act 2001 (supplementary provisions as to proceedings before competent court) for "Access to Justice Act 1999 (c.22) (advice, assistance and representation)" substitute "Legal Aid, Sentencing and Punishment of Offenders Act 2012".

Anti-terrorism, Crime and Security Act 2001 (c. 24)

57 In Schedule 4 to the Anti-terrorism, Crime and Security Act 2001 (extension of disclosure powers)—

(a) omit paragraph 47, and

(b) after paragraph 53D insert—

"53E Sections 34(2) and 35 of the Legal Aid, Sentencing and Punishment of Offenders Act 2012."

Proceeds of Crime Act 2002 (c. 29)

58 The Proceeds of Crime Act 2002 is amended as follows.

59 In section 245C(6)(b) (exclusion from property freezing order or prohibition on dealing with property to which order applies) for "funded by the Legal Services Commission or" substitute "made available under arrangements made for the purposes of Part 1 of the Legal Aid, Sentencing and Punishment of Offenders Act 2012 or funded by".

60 In section 252(4A)(b) (exclusion from restriction on dealing with property) for "funded by the Legal Services Commission or" substitute "made available under arrangements made for the purposes of Part 1 of the Legal Aid, Sentencing and Punishment of Offenders Act 2012 or funded by".

Communications Act 2003 (c. 21)

61 In section 119(7)(a) of the Communications Act 2003 (charges to recover costs of assistance in proceedings)—

(a) for "section 10(7) of the Access to Justice Act 1999 (c.22)" substitute "section 25 of the Legal Aid, Sentencing and Punishment of Offenders Act 2012", and

(b) for "Legal Services Commission" substitute "Lord Chancellor".

Extradition Act 2003 (c. 41)

62 The Extradition Act 2003 is amended as follows.

63 In section 45(7) (consent to extradition) for paragraph (a) substitute—

"(a) in England and Wales, representation for the purposes of criminal proceedings provided under arrangements made for the purposes of Part 1 of the Legal Aid, Sentencing and Punishment of Offenders Act 2012;".

64 In section 127(8) (consent to extradition: general) for paragraph (a) substitute—

"(a) in England and Wales, representation for the purposes of criminal proceedings provided under arrangements made for the purposes of Part 1 of the Legal Aid, Sentencing and Punishment of Offenders Act 2012;".

Criminal Justice Act 2003 (c. 44)

65 In section 71(8) of the Criminal Justice Act 2003 (matters to which reporting restrictions do not apply) for paragraph (g) substitute—

"(g) whether, for the purposes of the proceedings, representation was provided to the defendant or any of the defendants under Part 1 of the Legal Aid, Sentencing and Punishment of Offenders Act 2012."

Domestic Violence, Crime and Victims Act 2004 (c. 28)

66 In Schedule 9 to the Domestic Violence, Crime and Victims Act 2004 (authorities within remit of Commissioner for Victims and Witnesses) omit paragraph 21 (Legal Services Commission).

Equality Act 2006 (c. 3)

67 In section 29(3) of the Equality Act 2006 (costs of Equality and Human Rights Commission in providing legal assistance) for "section 11(4)(f) of the Access to Justice Act 1999 (c. 22) (recovery of costs in funded cases)" substitute "section 25 of the Legal Aid, Sentencing and Punishment of Offenders Act 2012 (statutory charge in connection with civil legal aid)".

Legal Services Act 2007 (c. 29)

68 In section 194(6) of the Legal Services Act 2007 (payments in respect of pro bono representation) for paragraph (b) substitute—

"(b) provided under arrangements made for the purposes of Part 1 of the Legal Aid, Sentencing and Punishment of Offenders Act 2012."

Criminal Justice and Immigration Act 2008 (c. 4)

69 In paragraph 19(2) of Schedule 1 to the Criminal Justice and Immigration Act 2008 (preconditions to imposing local authority residence requirement or fostering requirement) for paragraph (a) (but not the "or" following it) substitute—

"(a) that representation was made available to the offender for the purposes of the proceedings under Part 1 of the Legal Aid, Sentencing and Punishment of Offenders Act 2012 but was withdrawn because of the offender's conduct,".

Equality Act 2010 (c. 15)

70 In Part 1 of Schedule 19 to the Equality Act 2010 (public authorities) omit "The Legal Services Commission."

Terrorist Asset-Freezing etc Act 2010 (c. 38)

71 In section 23(1)(d) (general power to disclose information) omit "the Legal Services Commission,".

PART 2

REPEALS CONSEQUENTIAL ON PART 1 OF THIS SCHEDULE

Short title and chapter	*Extent of repeal*
Legal Aid Act 1988 (c. 34)	In Schedule 5, paragraph 13.
Access to Justice Act 1999 (c. 22)	In Schedule 4— (a) paragraph 1; (b) paragraph 8; (c) paragraphs 10 to 12; (d) paragraphs 15 to 19; (e) paragraphs 29 and 30(2) and (3)(a); (f) paragraph 33; (g) paragraph 35; (h) paragraphs 38 to 40; (i) paragraph 45; (j) paragraph 47; (k) paragraph 49; (l) paragraphs 51(3) and 52; (m) paragraph 55.
Terrorism Act 2000 (c. 11)	In Schedule 15, paragraph 19.
Child Support, Pensions and Social Security Act 2000 (c. 19)	In Schedule 8, paragraph 15.
Criminal Defence Service (Advice and Assistance) Act 2001 (c. 4)	The whole Act.
Anti-terrorism, Crime and Security Act 2001 (c. 24)	Section 2(1) to (3).
Proceeds of Crime Act 2002 (c. 29)	In Schedule 11, paragraph 36.
Adoption and Children Act 2002 (c. 38)	In Schedule 3, paragraph 102.
Nationality, Immigration and Asylum Act 2002 (c. 41)	Section 116.
Extradition Act 2003 (c. 41)	Section 182.
Criminal Justice Act 2003 (c. 44)	In Schedule 26, paragraph 51.

Short title and chapter	*Extent of repeal*
Civil Partnership Act 2004 (c. 33)	In Schedule 27, paragraph 156.
Constitutional Reform Act 2005 (c. 4)	In Schedule 9, paragraph 68(3).
Mental Capacity Act 2005 (c. 9)	In Schedule 6, paragraph 44.
Criminal Defence Service Act 2006 (c. 9)	Sections 1 to 3. Section 4(1).
Serious Crime Act 2007 (c. 27)	In Schedule 8, paragraph 159.
Legal Services Act 2007 (c. 29)	In Schedule 16, paragraphs 51(4) and 108(c). In Schedule 21, paragraph 128.
Criminal Justice and Immigration Act 2008 (c. 4)	Sections 56 to 58.
Human Fertilisation and Embryology Act 2008 (c. 22)	Schedule 6, paragraph 38.
Coroners and Justice Act 2009 (c. 25)	Section 51. Sections 149 to 153. Schedule 18.
Policing and Crime Act 2009 (c. 26)	In Schedule 7, paragraphs 65 and 98.

SCHEDULE 6

Section 40

NORTHERN IRELAND: INFORMATION ABOUT FINANCIAL RESOURCES

Obtaining information

1 (1) The relevant authority may make an information request to—
(a) the Secretary of State,
(b) a relevant Northern Ireland Department, or
(c) the Commissioners for Her Majesty's Revenue and Customs ("the Commissioners").

(2) An information request may be made under this paragraph only for the purposes of facilitating a determination about an individual's financial resources for the purposes of —
(a) the Legal Aid, Advice and Assistance (Northern Ireland) Order 1981 (S.I. 1981/228 (N.I. 8)), or
(b) the Access to Justice (Northern Ireland) Order 2003 (S.I. 2003/435) (N.I. 10)).

(3) An information request made to the Secretary of State or a relevant Northern Ireland Department under this paragraph may request the disclosure of some or all of the following information—
(a) a relevant individual's full name and any previous names;
(b) a relevant individual's address and any previous addresses;
(c) a relevant individual's date of birth;
(d) a relevant individual's national insurance number;

(e) a relevant individual's benefit status at a time specified in the request;

(f) information of a prescribed description.

(4) An information request made to the Commissioners under this paragraph may request the disclosure of some or all of the following information—

(a) whether or not a relevant individual is employed or was employed at a time specified in the request;

(b) the name and address of the employer;

(c) whether or not a relevant individual is carrying on a business, trade or profession or was doing so at a time specified in the request;

(d) the name under which it is or was carried on;

(e) the address of any premises used for the purposes of carrying it on;

(f) a relevant individual's national insurance number;

(g) a relevant individual's benefit status at a time specified in the request;

(h) information of a prescribed description.

(5) The information that may be prescribed under sub-paragraphs (3)(f) and (4)(h) includes, in particular, information relating to—

(a) prescribed income of a relevant individual for a prescribed period, and

(b) prescribed capital of a relevant individual.

(6) Information may not be prescribed under sub-paragraph (4)(h) without the Commissioners' consent.

(7) The Secretary of State, the relevant Northern Ireland Departments and the Commissioners may disclose to the relevant authority information specified in an information request made under this paragraph.

(8) In this paragraph—

"benefit status", in relation to an individual, means whether or not the individual is in receipt of a prescribed benefit or benefits and, if so—

(a) which benefit or benefits the individual is receiving,

(b) whether the individual is entitled to the benefit or benefits alone or jointly,

(c) in prescribed cases, the amount the individual is receiving by way of the benefit (or each of the benefits) ("the benefit amount"), and

(d) in prescribed cases, where the benefit consists of a number of elements, what those elements are and the amount included in respect of each element in calculating the benefit amount;

"financial resources", in relation to an individual, includes an individual's means, disposable income and disposable capital;

"the relevant authority" means—

(a) a prescribed person, or

(b) in relation to circumstances for which no person is prescribed, the chief executive of the Northern Ireland Legal Services Commission;

"a relevant individual", in relation to an information request under this paragraph for the purposes of a determination about an individual's financial resources, means—

(a) that individual, and

(b) any other individual whose financial resources are or may be relevant for the purposes of the determination;

"relevant Northern Ireland Department" means the Department for Social Development in Northern Ireland or the Department of Finance and Personnel in Northern Ireland.

Restrictions on disclosing information

2 (1) A person to whom information is disclosed under paragraph 1 of this Schedule or this sub-paragraph may disclose the information to any person to whom its disclosure is necessary or expedient in connection with facilitating a determination described in paragraph 1(2).

(2) A person to whom such information is disclosed must not—

(a) disclose the information other than in accordance with sub-paragraph (1), or

(b) use the information other than for the purpose of facilitating a determination described in paragraph 1(2).

(3) Sub-paragraph (2) does not prevent—

(a) the disclosure of information in accordance with an enactment or an order of a court,

(b) the disclosure of information for the purposes of the investigation or prosecution of an offence (or suspected offence) under the law of England and Wales or Northern Ireland or any other jurisdiction, except as otherwise prescribed,

(c) the disclosure of information for the purposes of instituting, or otherwise for the purposes of, proceedings before a court, or

(d) the disclosure of information which has previously been lawfully disclosed to the public.

(4) A person who discloses or uses information in contravention of this paragraph is guilty of an offence and liable—

(a) on conviction on indictment, to imprisonment for a term not exceeding 2 years or a fine (or both);

(b) on summary conviction—

(i) in England and Wales, to imprisonment for a term not exceeding 12 months or a fine not exceeding the statutory maximum (or both), and

(ii) in Northern Ireland, to imprisonment for a term not exceeding 6 months or a fine not exceeding the statutory maximum (or both).

(5) It is a defence for a person charged with an offence under this paragraph to prove that the person reasonably believed that the disclosure or use was lawful.

(6) In this paragraph "enactment" includes—

(a) an enactment contained subordinate legislation (within the meaning of the Interpretation Act 1978), and

(b) an enactment contained in, or in an instrument made under, an Act or Measure of the National Assembly for Wales or Northern Ireland legislation.

(7) In relation to an offence under this paragraph committed before the commencement of section 154(1) of the Criminal Justice Act 2003, the reference in sub-paragraph (4)(b)(i) to 12 months has effect as if it were a reference to 6 months.

Power to make consequential and supplementary provision etc

3 (1) The Department of Justice in Northern Ireland may by regulations make consequential, supplementary, incidental or transitional provision in relation to this Schedule extending to Northern Ireland.

(2) The regulations may, in particular—

(a) amend, repeal, revoke or otherwise modify Northern Ireland legislation passed before this Schedule comes into force or an instrument made under such legislation, and

(b) include transitory or saving provision.

Regulations

4 (1) In this Schedule "prescribed" means prescribed by regulations made by the Department of Justice in Northern Ireland.

(2) The powers under this Schedule to make regulations are exercisable by statutory rule for the purposes of the Statutory Rules (Northern Ireland) Order 1979 (S.I. 1979/1573 (N.I. 12)).

(3) Regulations under this Schedule are subject to negative resolution within the meaning of section 41(6) of the Interpretation Act (Northern Ireland) 1954, subject to sub-paragraph (4).

(4) The following regulations may not be made unless a draft of the regulations has been laid before, and approved by a resolution of, the Northern Ireland Assembly—

(a) the first regulations under paragraph 1, and

(b) regulations under paragraph 3 that amend or repeal Northern Ireland legislation (whether alone or with other provision).

(5) Section 41(3) of the Interpretation Act (Northern Ireland) 1954 applies for the purposes of sub-paragraph (4) in relation to the laying of a draft as it applies in relation to the laying of a statutory document under an enactment (as defined in that Act).

(6) Subsections (1) to (3) of section 41 of this Act apply in relation to regulations made under paragraph 1 or 2 of this Schedule as they apply in relation to regulations made by the Lord Chancellor under this Part.

SCHEDULE 7

Section 62

COSTS IN CRIMINAL CASES

PART 1

PROSECUTION OF OFFENCES ACT 1985

Introduction

1 The Prosecution of Offences Act 1985 is amended as follows.

Defence costs

2 (1) Section 16 (defence costs) is amended as follows.

(2) After subsection (6) insert—

"(6A) Where the court considers that there are circumstances that make it inappropriate for the accused to recover the full amount mentioned in subsection (6), a defendant's costs order must be for the payment out of central funds of such lesser amount as the court considers just and reasonable.

(6B) Subsections (6) and (6A) have effect subject to—

(a) section 16A, and

(b) regulations under section 20(1A)(d).

(6C) When making a defendant's costs order, the court must fix the amount to be paid out of central funds in the order if it considers it appropriate to do so and—

(a) the accused agrees the amount, or

(b) subsection (6A) applies.

(6D) Where the court does not fix the amount to be paid out of central funds in the order—

(a) it must describe in the order any reduction required under subsection (6A), and

(b) the amount must be fixed by means of a determination made by or on behalf of the court in accordance with procedures specified in regulations made by the Lord Chancellor."

(3) Omit subsections (7) and (9).

Legal costs

3 After section 16 insert—

"16A Legal costs

(1) A defendant's costs order may not require the payment out of central funds of an amount that includes an amount in respect of the accused's legal costs, subject to the following provisions of this section.

(2) Subsection (1) does not apply where condition A, B or C is met.

(3) Condition A is that the accused is an individual and the order is made under—
   (a) section 16(1),
   (b) section 16(3), or
   (c) section 16(4)(a)(ii) or (iii) or (d).

(4) Condition B is that the accused is an individual and the legal costs were incurred in proceedings in a court below which were—
   (a) proceedings in a magistrates' court, or
   (b) proceedings on an appeal to the Crown Court under section 108 of the Magistrates' Courts Act 1980 (right of appeal against conviction or sentence).

(5) Condition C is that the legal costs were incurred in proceedings in the Supreme Court.

(6) The Lord Chancellor may by regulations make provision about exceptions from the prohibition in subsection (1), including—
   (a) provision amending this section by adding, modifying or removing an exception, and
   (b) provision for an exception to arise where a determination has been made by a person specified in the regulations.

(7) Regulations under subsection (6) may not remove or limit the exception provided by condition C.

(8) Where a court makes a defendant's costs order requiring the payment out of central funds of an amount that includes an amount in respect of legal costs, the order must include a statement to that effect.

(9) Where, in a defendant's costs order, a court fixes an amount to be paid out of central funds that includes an amount in respect of legal costs incurred in proceedings in a court other than the Supreme Court, the latter amount must not exceed an amount specified by regulations made by the Lord Chancellor.

(10) In this section—

"legal costs" means fees, charges, disbursements and other amounts payable in respect of advocacy services or litigation services including, in particular, expert witness costs;

"advocacy services" means any services which it would be reasonable to expect a person who is exercising, or contemplating exercising, a right of audience in relation to any proceedings, or contemplated proceedings, to provide;

"expert witness costs" means amounts payable in respect of the services of an expert witness, including amounts payable in connection with attendance by the witness at court or elsewhere;

"litigation services" means any services which it would be reasonable to expect a person who is exercising, or contemplating exercising, a right to conduct litigation in relation to proceedings, or contemplated proceedings, to provide."

Prosecution costs

4 (1) Section 17 (prosecution costs) is amended as follows.

(2) In subsection (1) for "subsection (2)" substitute "subsections (2) and (2A)".

(3) After subsection (2) insert—

"(2A) Where the court considers that there are circumstances that make it inappropriate for the prosecution to recover the full amount mentioned in subsection (1), an order under this section must be for the payment out of central funds of such lesser amount as the court considers just and reasonable.

(2B) When making an order under this section, the court must fix the amount to be paid out of central funds in the order if it considers it appropriate to do so and—

(a) the prosecutor agrees the amount, or

(b) subsection (2A) applies.

(2C) Where the court does not fix the amount to be paid out of central funds in the order—

(a) it must describe in the order any reduction required under subsection (2A), and

(b) the amount must be fixed by means of a determination made by or on behalf of the court in accordance with procedures specified in regulations made by the Lord Chancellor."

(4) Omit subsections (3) and (4).

Costs of witnesses and appellants not in custody

5 (1) Section 19 (provision for orders as to costs in other circumstances) is amended as follows.

(2) After subsection (3) insert—

"(3ZA) In relation to a sum that may be required by a court other than the Supreme Court to be paid out of central funds under regulations under subsection (3)—

(a) the requirement under that subsection for the sum to be such sum as the court considers reasonably necessary to cover or compensate for expenses, fees, costs, trouble or losses is subject to regulations made under section 20(1A)(d), and

(b) regulations under subsection (3) may make provision accordingly."

(3) After subsection (3C) insert—

"(3D) Regulations under subsection (3) may make provision generally or only in relation to particular descriptions of persons, expenses, fees, costs, trouble or losses."

(4) After subsection (4) insert—

"(4A) Subsection (4) has effect subject to regulations under section 20(1A)(d).

(4B) An order under subsection (4) may not require the payment out of central funds of a sum that includes a sum in respect of legal costs (as defined in section 16A), except where regulations made by the Lord Chancellor provide otherwise.

(4C) Regulations under subsection (4B) may, in particular, include—

(a) provision for an exception to arise where a determination has been made by a person specified in the regulations,

(b) provision requiring the court, when it orders the payment of a sum that includes a sum in respect of legal costs, to include a statement to that effect in the order, and

(c) provision that the court may not order the payment of a sum in respect of legal costs exceeding an amount specified in the regulations."

Regulations

6 (1) Section 20 (regulations) is amended as follows.

(2) In subsection (1) omit the words from "and the regulations" to the end.

(3) After that subsection insert—

"(1A) The Lord Chancellor may by regulations—

(a) make provision as to the amounts that may be ordered to be paid out of central funds in pursuance of a costs order, whether by specifying rates or scales or by making other provision as to the calculation of the amounts,

(b) make provision as to the circumstances in which and conditions under which such amounts may be paid or ordered to be paid,

(c) make provision requiring amounts required to be paid out of central funds by a costs order to be calculated having regard to regulations under paragraphs (a) and (b),

(d) make provision requiring amounts required to be paid to a person out of central funds by a relevant costs order to be calculated in accordance with such regulations (whether or not that results in the fixing of an amount that the court considers reasonably sufficient or necessary to compensate the person), and

(e) make provision as to the review of determinations of amounts required to be paid out of central funds by costs orders.

(1B) In subsection (1A)(d) "relevant costs order" means a costs order other than—

(a) an order made by any court under section 17, and

(b) so much of a costs order made by the Supreme Court as relates to expenses, fees, costs, trouble or losses incurred in proceedings in that court.

(1C) Regulations under subsection (1A) may, in particular—

(a) make different provision in relation to amounts to be paid in respect of different expenses, fees, costs, trouble and losses,

(b) make different provision in relation to different costs orders and different areas, and

(c) make different provision in relation to the fixing of an amount in a costs order and the fixing of an amount by means of a determination."

(4) In subsection (3)—

(a) for "subsection (1)" substitute "subsection (1A)",

(b) for "rates or scales of allowances" substitute "provision as to the calculation of amounts", and

(c) after "order" insert "(whether in the form of rates or scales or other provision)".

Interpretation

7 (1) Section 21 (interpretation) is amended as follows.

(2) In subsection (4) after "16" insert ", 16A".

(3) In subsection (4A)(a) after "16" insert ", 16A".

Supplementary

8 (1) Section 29 (regulations) is amended as follows.

(2) For subsection (1) substitute—

"(1) A power to make regulations under this Act is exercisable by statutory instrument.

(1A) A statutory instrument containing regulations under this Act is subject to annulment in pursuance of a resolution of either House of Parliament, subject to subsection (1B).

(1B) A statutory instrument containing (whether alone or with other provision) regulations under section 16A(6) or 19(4B) may not be made unless a draft of the instrument has been laid before, and approved by a resolution of, each House of Parliament."

(3) In subsection (2) for "Any such regulations" substitute "Regulations under this Act".

PART 2

ATTORNEY GENERAL'S REFERENCES

Reference of point of law following acquittal on indictment

9 (1) Section 36 of the Criminal Justice Act 1972 (reference of point of law following acquittal on indictment) is amended as follows.

(2) In subsection (5) omit "to his costs, that is to say".

(3) Omit subsection (5A).

(4) After that subsection insert—

"(5A) Subsection (5) has effect subject to—

(a) subsection (5B), and
(b) regulations under section 20(1A)(d) of the Prosecution of Offences Act 1985 (as applied by this section).

(5B) A person is not entitled under subsection (5) to the payment of sums in respect of legal costs (as defined in section 16A of the Prosecution of Offences Act 1985) incurred in proceedings in the Court of Appeal.

(5C) Subsections (1A) to (1C) and (3) of section 20 of the Prosecution of Offences Act 1985 (regulations as to amounts ordered to be paid out of central funds) apply in relation to amounts payable out of central funds under subsection (5) as they apply in relation to amounts payable out of central funds in pursuance of costs orders made under section 16 of that Act."

10 In consequence of the amendments made by paragraph 9, omit paragraph 8 of Schedule 1 to the Prosecution of Offences Act 1985.

Reference of sentence of Crown Court appearing to be unduly lenient

11 (1) Schedule 3 to the Criminal Justice Act 1988 (reference of sentence of Crown Court appearing to be unduly lenient) is amended as follows.

(2) In paragraph 11 (recovery of costs of representation)—
(a) number the existing provision sub-paragraph (1),
(b) in that sub-paragraph, omit "to his costs, that is to say", and
(c) after that sub-paragraph insert—

"(2) Sub-paragraph (1) has effect subject to—
(a) sub-paragraph (3), and
(b) regulations under section 20(1A)(d) of the Prosecution of Offences Act 1985 (as applied by this paragraph).

(3) A person is not entitled under sub-paragraph (1) to the payment of sums in respect of legal costs (as defined in section 16A of the Prosecution of Offences Act 1985) incurred in proceedings in the Court of Appeal.

(4) Subsections (1A) to (1C) and (3) of section 20 of the Prosecution of Offences Act 1985 (regulations as to amounts ordered to be paid out of central funds) apply in relation to funds payable out of central funds under sub-paragraph (1) as they apply in relation to amounts payable out of central funds in pursuance of costs orders made under section 16 of that Act."

(3) In paragraph 12 (application to Northern Ireland)—
(a) for "11", in each place, substitute "11(1)", and
(b) after sub-paragraph (d) insert—

"(e) paragraph 11 has effect as if sub-paragraphs (2) to (4) were omitted."

PART 3

EXTRADITION ACT 2003

Introduction

12 The Extradition Act 2003 is amended as follows.

Extradition to Category 1 Territories

13 (1) Section 61 (costs where discharge ordered) is amended as follows.

(2) After subsection (5) insert—

"(5A) In England and Wales, an order under subsection (5) is to be made, and the appropriate amount is to be determined, in accordance with sections 62A and 62B.

(5B) In Scotland and Northern Ireland, an order under subsection (5) is to be made, and the appropriate amount is to be determined, in accordance with subsections (6) to (9)."

14 In section 62 (supplementary provision about costs where discharge ordered) omit subsections (1) and (2).

15 After section 62 insert—

"62A Appropriate amount: England and Wales

(1) For the purposes of an order under section 61(5), the appropriate amount is such amount as the judge or court making the order considers reasonably sufficient to compensate the person in whose favour the order is made for any expenses properly incurred by the person in the proceedings under this Part.

(2) But if the judge or court considers that there are circumstances that make it inappropriate for the person to recover the full amount mentioned in subsection (1), the order under section 61(5) must be for the payment out of money provided by Parliament of such lesser amount as the judge or court considers just and reasonable.

(3) Subsections (1) and (2) have effect subject to—
(a) section 62B, and
(b) regulations under section 20(1A)(d) of the Prosecution of Offences Act 1985 (as applied by this section).

(4) When making an order under section 61(5), the judge or court must fix the amount to be paid out of money provided by Parliament in the order if the judge or court considers it appropriate to do so and—
(a) the person in whose favour the order is made agrees the amount, or
(b) subsection (2) applies.

(5) Where the judge or court does not fix the amount to be paid out of money provided by Parliament in the order—
(a) the judge or court must describe in the order any reduction required under subsection (2), and

(b) the amount must be fixed by means of a determination made by or on behalf of the judge or court in accordance with procedures specified in regulations made by the Lord Chancellor.

(6) Subsections (1A) to (1C) and (3) of section 20 of the Prosecution of Offences Act 1985 (regulations as to amounts ordered to be paid out of central funds) apply in relation to amounts payable out of money provided by Parliament in pursuance of an order under section 61 as they apply in relation to amounts payable out of central funds in pursuance of costs orders made under section 16 of that Act.

(7) This section extends to England and Wales only.

62B Legal costs: England and Wales

(1) An order under section 61(5) may not require the payment out of money provided by Parliament of an amount that includes an amount in respect of legal costs incurred by the person in whose favour the order is made, subject to the following provisions of this section.

(2) Subsection (1) does not apply in relation to legal costs incurred in—
(a) proceedings in a magistrates' court, or
(b) proceedings in the Supreme Court.

(3) The Lord Chancellor may by regulations make provision about exceptions from the prohibition in subsection (1), including—
(a) provision amending this section by adding, modifying or removing an exception, and
(b) provision for an exception to arise where a determination has been made by a person specified in the regulations.

(4) Regulations under subsection (3) may not remove or limit the exception provided by subsection (2)(b).

(5) Where a judge or court makes an order under section 61(5) requiring the payment out of money provided by Parliament of an amount that includes an amount in respect of legal costs, the order must include a statement to that effect.

(6) Where, in an order under section 61(5), a judge or court fixes an amount to be paid out of money provided by Parliament that includes an amount in respect of legal costs incurred in proceedings in a court other than the Supreme Court, the latter amount must not exceed an amount specified by regulations made by the Lord Chancellor.

(7) In this section—
"legal costs" means fees, charges, disbursements and other amounts payable in respect of advocacy services or litigation services including, in particular, expert witness costs;
"advocacy services" means any services which it would be reasonable to expect a person who is exercising, or contemplating exercising, a right of audience in relation to any proceedings, or contemplated proceedings, to provide;

"expert witness costs" means amounts payable in respect of the services of an expert witness, including amounts payable in connection with attendance by the witness at court or elsewhere;

"litigation services" means any services which it would be reasonable to expect a person who is exercising, or contemplating exercising, a right to conduct litigation in relation to proceedings, or contemplated proceedings, to provide.

(8) This section extends to England and Wales only."

Extradition to Category 2 Territories

16 (1) Section 134 (costs where discharge ordered) is amended as follows.

(2) After subsection (5) insert—

"(5A) In England and Wales, an order under subsection (5) is to be made, and the appropriate amount is to be determined, in accordance with sections 135A and 135B.

(5B) In Scotland and Northern Ireland, an order under subsection (5) is to be made, and the appropriate amount is to be determined, in accordance with subsections (6) to (9)."

17 In section 135 (supplementary provision about costs where discharge ordered) omit subsections (1) and (2).

18 After section 135 insert—

"135A Appropriate amount: England and Wales

(1) For the purposes of an order under section 134(5), the appropriate amount is such amount as the judge or court making the order considers reasonably sufficient to compensate the person in whose favour the order is made for any expenses properly incurred by the person in the proceedings under this Part.

(2) But if the judge or court considers that there are circumstances that make it inappropriate for the person to recover the full amount mentioned in subsection (1), the order under section 134(5) must be for the payment out of money provided by Parliament of such lesser amount as the judge or court considers just and reasonable.

(3) Subsections (1) and (2) have effect subject to—
  (a) section 135B, and
  (b) regulations under section 20(1A)(d) of the Prosecution of Offences Act 1985 (as applied by this section).

(4) When making an order under section 134(5), the judge or court must fix the amount to be paid out of money provided by Parliament in the order if the judge or court considers it appropriate to do so and—
  (a) the person in whose favour the order is made agrees the amount, or
  (b) subsection (2) applies.

(5) Where the judge or court does not fix the amount to be paid out of money provided by Parliament in the order—

(a) the judge or court must describe in the order any reduction required under subsection (2), and

(b) the amount must be fixed by means of a determination made by or on behalf of the court in accordance with procedures specified in regulations made by the Lord Chancellor.

(6) Subsections (1A) to (1C) and (3) of section 20 of the Prosecution of Offences Act 1985 (regulations as to amounts ordered to be paid out of central funds) apply in relation to amounts payable out of money provided by Parliament in pursuance of an order under section 134 as they apply in relation to amounts payable out of central funds in pursuance of costs orders made under section 16 of that Act.

(7) This section extends to England and Wales only.

135B Legal costs: England and Wales

(1) An order under section 134(5) may not require the payment out of money provided by Parliament of an amount that includes an amount in respect of legal costs incurred by the person in whose favour the order is made, subject to the following provisions of this section.

(2) Subsection (1) does not apply in relation to legal costs incurred in—

(a) proceedings in a magistrates' court, or

(b) proceedings in the Supreme Court.

(3) The Lord Chancellor may by regulations make provision about exceptions from the prohibition in subsection (1), including—

(a) provision amending this section by adding, modifying or removing an exception, and

(b) provision for an exception to arise where a determination has been made by a person specified in the regulations.

(4) Regulations under subsection (3) may not remove or limit the exception provided by subsection (2)(b).

(5) Where a judge or court makes an order under section 134(5) requiring the payment out of money provided by Parliament of an amount that includes an amount in respect of legal costs, the order must include a statement to that effect.

(6) Where, in an order under section 134(5), a judge or court fixes an amount to be paid out of money provided by Parliament that includes an amount in respect of legal costs incurred in proceedings in a court other than the Supreme Court, the latter amount must not exceed an amount specified by regulations made by the Lord Chancellor.

(7) In this section—

"legal costs" means fees, charges, disbursements and other amounts payable in respect of advocacy services or litigation services including, in particular, expert witness costs;

"advocacy services" means any services which it would be reasonable to expect a person who is exercising, or contemplating exercising, a right of audience in relation to any proceedings, or contemplated proceedings, to provide;

"expert witness costs" means amounts payable in respect of the services of an expert witness, including amounts payable in connection with attendance by the witness at court or elsewhere;

"litigation services" means any services which it would be reasonable to expect a person who is exercising, or contemplating exercising, a right to conduct litigation in relation to proceedings, or contemplated proceedings, to provide.

(8) This section extends to England and Wales only."

Regulations

19 In section 223(6) (orders and regulations subject to affirmative procedure), at the appropriate places insert—

"section 62B(3)";

"section 135B(3)".

PART 4

SAVINGS

20 The amendments made by paragraphs 2 to 5 do not have effect in relation to costs orders made by a court in proceedings which commenced before the relevant day.

21 The amendments made by paragraphs 9 to 11 do not have effect in relation to a person's entitlement to costs in connection with a reference made before the relevant day.

22 The amendments made by paragraphs 12 to 19 do not have effect in relation to orders made by a judge or court in proceedings which commenced before the relevant day.

23 In paragraphs 20 to 22 "the relevant day", in relation to an amendment, means the day on which the amendment comes into force.

24 For the purposes of paragraphs 20 and 22—

(a) proceedings commence in a magistrates' court when a warrant, requisition or summons relating to the proceedings is issued;

(b) proceedings commence on an appeal to the Crown Court when a notice of appeal is served;

(c) other proceedings commence in the Crown Court when they are committed, transferred or sent to that court;

(d) proceedings commence in the High Court when an application for leave to appeal by way of case stated is made or (in the absence of such an application) when notice of appeal is given;

(e) proceedings commence in the Court of Appeal when an application for leave to appeal is made or (in the absence of such an application) when notice of appeal is given;

(f) proceedings commence in the Supreme Court when an application for leave to appeal is made.

SCHEDULE 8

Section 62

COSTS IN CRIMINAL CASES: SERVICE COURTS

PART 1

APPEALS FROM COURT MARTIAL

Introduction

1 Part 2 of the Court Martial Appeals Act 1968 (appeals from Court Martial) is amended as follows.

Costs of successful appellant

2 (1) Section 31 (costs of successful appellant) is amended as follows.

(2) In subsection (1) omit "other than an appeal against sentence".

(3) In subsection (2) at the end insert ", subject to subsection (3), section 31A and regulations under section 33B(1)(d)."

(4) After subsection (2) insert—

"(3) Where the Appeal Court consider that there are circumstances that make it inappropriate for the appellant to recover the whole of the sums mentioned in subsection (2), a direction under this section must be for the payment of such lesser sums as they consider just and reasonable.

(4) The Appeal Court must fix the sums to be paid by the Secretary of State in the direction if they consider it appropriate to do so and—
(a) the appellant agrees the sums, or
(b) subsection (3) applies.

(5) Where the Appeal Court do not fix the sums to be paid by the Secretary of State in the direction—
(a) they must describe in the direction any reduction required under subsection (3), and
(b) the sums must be fixed by means of a determination made by or on behalf of the Appeal Court in accordance with procedures specified in regulations made by the Lord Chancellor."

Legal costs

3 After section 31 insert—

"31A Legal costs

(1) The costs which the Appeal Court may direct the Secretary of State to pay under section 31 do not include legal costs, except where regulations made by the Lord Chancellor provide otherwise.

(2) Regulations under this section may, in particular, include—
(a) provision for an exception to arise where a determination has been made by a person specified in the regulations,

(b) provision requiring the Appeal Court, when they direct the payment of a sum that includes a sum in respect of legal costs, to include a statement to that effect in the direction, and

(c) provision that the Appeal Court may not direct the payment of a sum in respect of legal costs exceeding an amount specified in the regulations.

(3) In this section—

"legal costs" means fees, charges, disbursements and other amounts payable in respect of advocacy services or litigation services including, in particular, expert witness costs;

"advocacy services" means any services which it would be reasonable to expect a person who is exercising, or contemplating exercising, a right of audience in relation to any proceedings, or contemplated proceedings, to provide;

"expert witness costs" means amounts payable in respect of the services of an expert witness, including amounts payable in connection with attendance by the witness at court or elsewhere;

"litigation services" means any services which it would be reasonable to expect a person who is exercising, or contemplating exercising, a right to conduct litigation in relation to proceedings, or contemplated proceedings, to provide."

Witnesses' expenses

4 (1) Section 33 (witnesses' expenses) is amended as follows.

(2) In subsection (1) at the end insert ", subject to subsection (3) and regulations under section 33B(1)(d)".

(3) At the end insert—

"(3) Sums ordered to be paid out of money provided by Parliament under subsection (1) may not include sums in respect of expert witness costs (as defined in section 31A), unless regulations made by the Lord Chancellor provide otherwise."

Expenses of appellant not in custody

5 (1) Section 33A (appellant's expenses) is amended as follows.

(2) Number the existing provision subsection (1).

(3) After that subsection insert—

"(2) The expenses which the Appeal Court may direct the Secretary of State to pay under this section do not include legal costs (as defined in section 31A), except where regulations made by the Lord Chancellor provide otherwise.

(3) Regulations under this section may, in particular, include—

(a) provision for an exception to arise where a determination has been made by a person specified in the regulations,

(b) provision requiring the Appeal Court, when they direct the payment of a sum that includes a sum in respect of legal costs, to include a statement to that effect in the direction, and

(c) provision that the Appeal Court may not direct the payment of a sum in respect of legal costs exceeding an amount specified in the regulations."

Further provision about costs

6 After section 33A insert—

"33B Further provision about costs

(1) The Lord Chancellor may by regulations—

(a) make provision as to the sums that may be directed or ordered to be paid under section 31, 33 or 33A, whether by specifying rates or scales or by making other provision as to the calculation of the sums,

(b) make provision as to the circumstances in which and conditions under which such sums may be paid or directed or ordered to be paid,

(c) make provision requiring such sums to be fixed having regard to regulations under paragraphs (a) and (b),

(d) make provision requiring such sums to be calculated in accordance with such regulations (whether or not that results in the fixing of an amount that the court considers reasonably sufficient to compensate the person concerned), and

(e) make provision as to the review of determinations of sums directed to be paid under section 31.

(2) Regulations under this section may provide that provision as to the calculation of sums (whether in the form of rates or scales or other provision) may be determined by the Lord Chancellor with the consent of the Treasury."

Regulations

7 After section 33B insert—

"33C Regulations

(1) Regulations under sections 31, 31A, 33, 33A and 33B may, in particular—

(a) make different provision in relation to different cases and different classes of case, including different provision in relation to different expenses, trouble and loss, different directions and orders and different areas, and

(b) make different provision in relation to the fixing of a sum in a direction or order and the fixing of a sum by means of a determination.

(2) A power to make regulations under those sections is exercisable by statutory instrument.

(3) A statutory instrument containing regulations under those sections is subject to annulment in pursuance of a resolution of either House of Parliament, subject to subsection (4).

(4) A statutory instrument containing (whether alone or with other provision) regulations under section 31A, 33 or 33A may not be made unless a draft of the instrument has been laid before, and approved by a resolution of, each House of Parliament."

Consequential repeal

8 In consequence of the amendment made by paragraph 2(2), omit paragraph 1(6) of Schedule 2 to the Armed Forces Act 1971.

PART 2

APPEALS FROM COURT MARTIAL APPEAL COURT

Introduction

9 Part 3 of the Court Martial Appeals Act 1968 (appeals from Court Martial Appeal Court) is amended as follows.

Application to Appeal Court

10 Before section 47 insert—

"46A Costs: application to Appeal Court by Director of Service Prosecutions

(1) Where the Appeal Court dismiss an application for leave to appeal to the Supreme Court made by the Director of Service Prosecutions, the Appeal Court may direct the payment by the Secretary of State of such sums as appear to them to be reasonably sufficient to compensate the accused for any expenses properly incurred by the accused in resisting the application, subject to—

(a) subsection (2), and

(b) regulations under section 47A(1)(d).

(2) The sums which the Appeal Court may direct the Secretary of State to pay do not include legal costs (as defined in section 31A), except where regulations made by the Lord Chancellor provide otherwise.

(3) Regulations under subsection (2) may, in particular, include—

(a) provision for an exception to arise where a determination has been made by a person specified in the regulations,

(b) provision requiring the Appeal Court, when they direct the payment of a sum that includes a sum in respect of legal costs, to include a statement to that effect in the direction, and

(c) provision that the Appeal Court may not direct the payment of a sum in respect of legal costs exceeding an amount specified in the regulations.

46B Costs: application to Appeal Court by accused

Where the Appeal Court dismiss an application for leave to appeal to the Supreme Court made by the accused—

(a) the Appeal Court may make the like order as may be made by the Court under section 32(1) of this Act where they dismiss an application for leave to appeal to the Court,

(b) an order made under this section may be enforced in the manner described in section 32(2) of this Act, and

(c) section 32(3) of this Act applies in relation to any sum recovered by virtue of section 32(2)(a) (as applied by this section)."

Application to Supreme Court

11 (1) Section 47 (costs) is amended as follows.

(2) In subsections (1) and (2) omit "the Appeal Court or" (in each place).

(3) After subsection (2) insert—

"(2A) Section 32(3) of this Act applies in relation to any sum recovered by virtue of section 32(2)(a) (as applied by subsection (2))."

(4) In subsection (3), at the end insert "subject to—

(a) subsection (3A), and

(b) regulations under section 47A(1)(d)."

(5) After subsection (3) insert—

"(3A) The costs which the Supreme Court may direct the Secretary of State to pay do not include legal costs (as defined in section 31A) incurred in proceedings in a court below, except where regulations made by the Lord Chancellor provide otherwise.

(3B) Regulations under subsection (3A) may, in particular, include—

(a) provision for an exception to arise where a determination has been made by a person specified in the regulations,

(b) provision requiring the Supreme Court, when they direct the payment of a sum that includes a sum in respect of legal costs, to include a statement to that effect in the direction, and

(c) provision that the Supreme Court may not direct the payment of a sum in respect of legal costs exceeding an amount specified in the regulations."

(6) In subsection (4) for "the foregoing provisions of" substitute "sections 46A, 46B and".

12 Accordingly, in the heading of section 47, at the end insert ": application to Supreme Court".

Further provision about costs

13 After section 47 insert—

"47A Further provision about costs

(1) The Lord Chancellor may by regulations—

(a) make provision as to the sums that may be directed to be paid under section 46A or 47(3), whether by specifying rates or scales or by making other provision as to the calculation of the sums,

(b) make provision as to the circumstances in which and conditions under which such sums may be paid or directed to be paid,

(c) make provision requiring such sums to be fixed having regard to regulations under paragraphs (a) and (b), and

(d) make provision requiring such sums to be calculated in accordance with such regulations (whether or not that results in the fixing of an amount that the court considers reasonably sufficient to compensate the person concerned).

(2) The power under subsection (1)(d) may not be exercised in respect of sums ordered to be paid by the Supreme Court in respect of expenses incurred in proceedings before that court.

(3) Regulations under this section may provide that provision as to the calculation of sums (whether in the form of rates or scales or other provision) may be determined by the Lord Chancellor with the consent of the Treasury."

Regulations

14 After section 47A insert—

"47B Regulations

(1) Regulations under sections 46A, 47 and 47A may, in particular, make different provision in relation to different cases and different classes of case, including different provision in relation to different expenses, trouble and loss, different directions and orders and different areas.

(2) A power to make regulations under those sections is exercisable by statutory instrument.

(3) A statutory instrument containing regulations under those sections is subject to annulment in pursuance of a resolution of either House of Parliament, subject to subsection (4).

(4) A statutory instrument containing (whether alone or with other provision) regulations under section 46A or 47 may not be made unless a draft of the instrument has been laid before, and approved by a resolution of, each House of Parliament."

PART 3

SAVINGS

15 The amendments made by this Schedule do not have effect in relation to directions and orders made by a court in proceedings commenced before the relevant day.

16 For the purposes of paragraph 15—

(a) "the relevant day", in relation to an amendment, means the day on which the amendment comes into force;

(b) proceedings commence in the Court Martial Appeal Court when an application for leave to appeal is made or (in the absence of such an application) when notice of appeal is given;

(c) proceedings commence in the Supreme Court when an application for leave to appeal is made.

SCHEDULE 9

Section 68

CHANGES TO POWERS TO MAKE SUSPENDED SENTENCE ORDERS: CONSEQUENTIAL AND TRANSITORY PROVISION

PART 1

CONSEQUENTIAL AMENDMENTS

Powers of Criminal Courts (Sentencing) Act 2000 (c. 6)

1 In section 163(1) of the Powers of Criminal Courts (Sentencing) Act 2000 omit the definition of "operational period".

Criminal Justice Act 2003 (c. 44)

2 The Criminal Justice Act 2003 is amended as follows.

3 For the heading of Chapter 3 of Part 12 substitute "SUSPENDED SENTENCE ORDERS".

4 In section 190(2) (limits on power to impose requirements by suspended sentence order), for "189(1)(a)" substitute "189(1A)".

5 In section 191(1) (power to provide for review of suspended sentence order), after "suspended sentence order" insert "that imposes one or more community requirements".

6 (1) Section 195 (interpretation of Chapter 3) is amended as follows.

(2) For the definition of "operational period" and "supervision period" substitute—

""the operational period", in relation to a suspended sentence, has the meaning given by section 189(1)(a);".

(3) After the definition of "sentence of imprisonment" insert—

""the supervision period", in relation to a suspended sentence, has the meaning given by section 189(1A)."

7 (1) Section 196 (meaning of "relevant order") is amended as follows.

(2) In the heading, after ""relevant order"" insert "etc".

(3) After subsection (1) insert—

"(1A) In this Chapter "suspended sentence order" means a suspended sentence order that imposes one or more community requirements."

8 In section 200(4) (supervision period and operational period where unpaid work requirement imposed by suspended sentence order)—

(a) for "189(1)(a)" substitute "189(1A)", and
(b) for "189(1)(b)(ii)" substitute "189(1)(a)".

9 In section 213(3)(d) (supervision requirement: meaning of "relevant period") for "189(1)(a)" substitute "189(1A)".

10 (1) Paragraph 8 of Schedule 12 (powers of court in case of breach of community requirement or conviction of further offence) is amended as follows.

(2) In sub-paragraph (2), at the beginning of paragraph (c) insert "in the case of a suspended sentence order that imposes one or more community requirements,".

(3) After that paragraph insert—

"(d) in the case of a suspended sentence order that does not impose any community requirements, the court may, subject to section 189(3), amend the order by extending the operational period."

(4) In sub-paragraph (4)(a), for "the community requirements" substitute "any community requirements".

(5) In sub-paragraph (8), for "the community" substitute "any community".

11 In Part 3 of Schedule 12 (amendment of suspended sentence order), before paragraph 13 (and before the italic heading before that paragraph) insert—

"*Application of Part*

12B This Part of this Schedule applies only in relation to a suspended sentence order that imposes one or more community requirements."

12 (1) Schedule 13 (transfer of suspended sentence orders to Scotland or Northern Ireland) is amended as follows.

(2) In paragraph 1(1) (suspended sentence order in respect of an offender residing in Scotland)—

(a) after "a suspended sentence order" in the first place those words appear insert "that imposes one or more community requirements", and
(b) before "a suspended sentence order" in the second place those words appear insert "such".

(3) In paragraph 6(1) (suspended sentence order in respect of an offender residing in Northern Ireland)—

(a) after "a suspended sentence order" in the first place those words appear insert "that imposes one or more community requirements", and
(b) before "a suspended sentence order" in the second place those words appear insert "such".

Criminal Justice Act 2003 (Sentencing) (Transitory Provisions) Order 2005 (S.I. 2005/643)

13 In the Criminal Justice Act 2003 (Sentencing) (Transitory Provisions) Order 2005 omit—

(a) article 2(2) (modifications to section 189 of the Criminal Justice Act 2003 pending the commencement of the repeal of section 78 of the Powers of Criminal Courts (Sentencing) Act 2000), and

(b) article 3(2)(a) (modifications to section 189 of the Criminal Justice Act 2003 pending the commencement of section 61 of the Criminal Justice and Court Services Act 2000).

Armed Forces Act 2006 (c. 52)

14 The Armed Forces Act 2006 is amended as follows.

15 (1) Section 200 (suspended sentence orders with or without community requirements) is amended as follows.

(2) In the heading omit "with or without community requirements".

(3) Omit subsections (1) to (4) (power of relevant service court to make suspended sentence order with or without community requirements, and meanings of those terms).

(4) In subsection (5) (modification of section 189(1) of the Criminal Justice Act 2003 in its application to a relevant service court)—

(a) for "(b)(ii)" substitute "(a)",

(b) for "the end of sub-paragraph (ii)" substitute ""imprisonment),"", and

(c) in the words treated as substituted, for "(a)" substitute "(i)" and for "(b)" substitute "(ii)".

(5) After subsection (6) insert—

"(7) In this Chapter "a suspended sentence order with community requirements" means a suspended sentence order that imposes one or more community requirements within the meaning of section 189(7)(c) of the 2003 Act."

16 Omit section 201 (provisions of the Criminal Justice Act 2003 that do not apply to suspended sentence orders without community requirements).

17 In section 207 (definitions for purposes of Chapter 4 of Part 8)—

(a) in the definition of "suspended sentence order with community requirements" for "200(3)" substitute "200(7)", and

(b) omit the definition of "suspended sentence order without community requirements".

18 (1) Schedule 7 (suspended prison sentence: further conviction or breach of requirement) is amended as follows.

(2) For the heading before paragraph 1 substitute "Modifications of Part 2 of Schedule 12 to the 2003 Act".

(3) In paragraph 1 (modifications of Part 2 of Schedule 12 to the Criminal Justice Act 2003 in case of suspended sentence orders with community requirements) omit "with community requirements".

(4) Omit paragraph 2 (modifications of Part 2 of Schedule 12 to the Criminal Justice Act 2003 in case of suspended sentence orders without community requirements) and the heading before that paragraph.

(5) After paragraph 6 insert—

"6A Paragraph 8(2)(ba) of that Schedule has effect as if at the beginning there were inserted "where the court dealing with the offender is the Crown Court,"."

Armed Forces Act 2006 (Transitional Provisions etc) Order 2009 (SI 2009/1059)

19 In Schedule 2 to the Armed Forces Act 2006 (Transitional Provisions etc) Order 2009 omit paragraph 2(2) (modifications to section 189 of the Criminal Justice Act 2003 pending the commencement of the repeal of section 78 of the Powers of Criminal Courts (Sentencing) Act 2000).

PART 2

TRANSITORY PROVISION

20 In relation to any time before the coming into force of section 61 of the Criminal Justice and Court Services Act 2000 (abolition of sentences of detention in a young offender institution, custody for life etc), section 189 of the Criminal Justice Act 2003 has effect with the following modifications—

(a) in subsection (1), after the first "imprisonment" insert "or, in the case of a person aged at least 18 but under 21, a sentence of detention in a young offender institution",

(b) in that subsection, after the second "imprisonment" insert "or detention in a young offender institution", and

(c) in subsection (1B), after "imprisonment" insert "or detention in a young offender institution".

SCHEDULE 10

Section 89

REPEAL OF SECTIONS 181 TO 188 OF CRIMINAL JUSTICE ACT 2003: CONSEQUENTIAL AMENDMENTS

Prison Act 1952 (c. 52)

1 Omit section 49(4A) of the Prison Act 1952 (persons unlawfully at large).

Criminal Justice Act 1961 (c. 39)

2 In section 23 of the Criminal Justice Act 1961 (prison rules)—

(a) in subsection (3), for "Subject to subsection (3A), the days" substitute "The days";

(b) omit subsection (3A).

Firearms Act 1968 (c. 27)

3 In section 21 of the Firearms Act 1968 (possession of firearms by persons previously convicted of crime), omit—

(a) subsection (2A)(d);

(b) subsection (2B);

(c) in subsection (6), ", (2B)".

Magistrates' Courts Act 1980 (c. 43)

4 Omit section 131(2A) of the Magistrates' Courts Act 1980 (remand of accused already in custody).

Road Traffic Offenders Act 1988 (c. 53)

5 In section 35A of the Road Traffic Offenders Act 1988 (extension of disqualification where custodial sentence also imposed), omit subsection (4)(c) and (d).

Football Spectators Act 1989 (c. 37)

6 In the Football Spectators Act 1989, omit—
(a) section 14E(7) (banning orders);
(b) section 18(5) (information).

Prisoners (Return to Custody) Act 1995 (c. 3)

7 Omit section 1(1A) of the Prisoners (Return to Custody) Act 1995 (remaining at large after temporary release).

Goods Vehicles (Licensing of Operators) Act 1995 (c. 23)

8 In Schedule 3 to the Goods Vehicles (Licensing of Operators) Act 1995 (qualifications for standard licence), in paragraph 3(2)(a), for the words from "of 12 months or more" to the end substitute "exceeding 3 months".

Crime (Sentences) Act 1997 (c. 43)

9 (1) Schedule 1 to the Crime (Sentences) Act 1997 (transfers of prisoners within the British Islands) is amended as follows.

(2) In paragraph 6(4), omit the definitions of "custody plus order" and "intermittent custody order".

(3) In paragraph 8, in sub-paragraphs (2) and (4)—
(a) after paragraph (aa) insert "and";
(b) omit paragraph (ab).

(4) In paragraph 9, in sub-paragraphs (2) and (4)—
(a) after paragraph (aa) insert "and";
(b) omit paragraph (ab).

Powers of Criminal Courts (Sentencing) Act 2000 (c. 6)

10 In section 147A of the Powers of Criminal Courts (Sentencing) Act 2000 (extension of disqualification where custodial sentence also imposed), omit subsection (4)(c) and (d).

Extradition Act 2003 (c. 41)

11 (1) The Extradition Act 2003 is amended as follows.

(2) In the following provisions, omit "(other than temporarily on licence pursuant to an intermittent custody order under section 183(1)(b) of the Criminal Justice Act 2003)"—
- (a) section 59(11)(b) (return of person to serve remainder of sentence);
- (b) section 132(11)(b) (return of person to serve remainder of sentence);
- (c) section 153B(10)(a)(ii) (return of person in pursuance of undertaking).

(3) In section 216 (interpretation), omit subsection (6A).

Criminal Justice Act 2003 (c. 44)

12 The Criminal Justice Act 2003 is amended as follows.

13 In section 195 (interpretation of Chapter 3), omit the definitions of "custodial period", "licence period" and "the number of custodial days".

14 (1) Section 196 (meaning of "relevant order" in Chapter 4) is amended as follows.

(2) In subsection (1)—
- (a) at the end of paragraph (a) insert "or";
- (b) omit paragraph (b);
- (c) omit paragraph (d) and the word "or" preceding it.

(3) Omit subsection (2).

15 In section 197(1)(a)(i) (meaning of "responsible officer), omit "182(1) or".

16 In section 202(4)(b) (circumstances in which court must not include programme requirement), omit "(or, where the relevant order is a custody plus order or an intermittent custody order, will be)".

17 Omit section 204(4) and (5) (restrictions on imposing curfew requirement).

18 In section 213(3) (definition of "relevant period" for supervision requirement), omit paragraphs (b) and (c).

19 Omit section 216(2) (requirement to specify area in which offender will reside).

20 In section 241 (effect of direction under section 240 or 240A)—
- (a) in subsection (1), omit "or Chapter 3 (prison sentences of less than twelve months)";
- (b) omit subsection (2).

21 (1) Section 244 (duty to release prisoners) is amended as follows.

(2) Omit subsection (2).

(3) In subsection (3)—
- (a) omit paragraphs (b) and (c);
- (b) in paragraph (d), omit "none of which falls within paragraph (c)".

22 Omit section 245 (restrictions on duty to release intermittent custody prisoners).

23 (1) Section 246 (power to release prisoners on licence early) is amended as follows.

(2) In subsection (1)—
  (a) in paragraph (a), omit ", other than an intermittent custody prisoner,";
  (b) omit paragraph (b) and the word "and" preceding it.

(3) Omit subsection (3).

(4) In subsection (4)(i), omit from "or, where the sentence is one of intermittent custody" to the end.

(5) In subsection (5)—
  (a) in paragraph (a), omit "or (b), (3)";
  (b) in paragraph (c), omit "or (3)(b)(ii)".

(6) In subsection (6)—
  (a) omit the definition of "the required custodial days";
  (b) in the definition of "the requisite custodial period", omit "other than a sentence of intermittent custody" and ", (b)";
  (c) omit the definition of "sentence of intermittent custody".

24 In section 249 (duration of licence)—
  (a) in subsection (1), for "subsections (2) and (3)" substitute "subsection (3)";
  (b) omit subsection (2);
  (c) in subsection (3), omit the words from "and subsection (2)" to the end;
  (d) omit subsection (4).

25 In section 250 (licence conditions)—
  (a) omit subsections (2), (2A), (3) and (6);
  (b) in subsection (7), for the words from "section 264(3)" to the end substitute "and section 264(3) (consecutive terms)".

26 Omit section 251 (licence conditions on re-release of those serving less than 12 months).

27 In section 252(2) (duty to comply with licence conditions: overseas)—
  (a) at the end of paragraph (a) insert "and";
  (b) omit paragraph (b).

28 Omit section 253(4) (curfew conditions for those subject to intermittent custody order).

29 In section 260(7) (early removal of persons liable to removal from UK: definition of "requisite custodial period"), omit ", (b)".

30 In section 261(6) (re-entry to UK of offender removed early: definitions), in the definition of "requisite custodial period", omit ", (b)".

31 Omit section 263(3) (concurrent terms: requirements of licence).

32 (1) Section 264 (consecutive terms) is amended as follows.

(2) Omit subsection (1)(c) and the "and" preceding it.

(3) In subsection (6) omit—
  (a) paragraph (a)(iii) and the "and" preceding it;

(b) paragraph (b).

33 Omit section 264A (consecutive terms: intermittent custody).

34 Omit section 265(1B) (restriction on consecutive sentences: intermittent custody).

35 In section 268 (interpretation of Chapter 6), omit the definitions of "intermittent custody prisoner", "release" and "relevant court order".

36 In section 302 (execution of process between England and Wales and Scotland), omit "paragraph 8(1) of Schedule 10".

37 In section 305(1) (interpretation of Part 12)—

(a) omit the definition of "custody plus order";

(b) omit the definition of "intermittent custody order";

(c) omit the words "custody plus order, intermittent custody order" (wherever they appear);

(d) in the definition of "responsible officer", omit the words "a custody plus order, an intermittent custody order".

38 (1) Schedule 12 (breach or amendment of suspended sentence order etc) is amended as follows.

(2) In paragraph 8(2) (powers of court on breach of community requirement or conviction of further offence)—

(a) in paragraph (a), omit "and custodial period";

(b) in paragraph (b), for the words from "with either or both" to the end substitute "with the substitution for the original term of a lesser term".

(3) In paragraph 9(1) (further provision as to order that suspended sentence is to take effect)—

(a) omit "and custodial period";

(b) omit paragraph (a).

39 In Schedule 32 (amendments relating to sentencing), omit paragraphs 12(2), (3) and (6), 29, 57, 58 and 68(2).

Domestic Violence, Crime and Victims Act 2004 (c. 28)

40 (1) The Domestic Violence, Crime and Victims Act 2004 is amended as follows.

(2) Omit section 31 and Schedule 6 (intermittent custody).

(3) In Schedule 11 (repeals), omit the entries relating to the Criminal Justice Act 2003.

Armed Forces Act 2006 (c. 52)

41 (1) The Armed Forces Act 2006 is amended as follows.

(2) In section 196 (term of sentence etc), omit—

(a) the reference to sections 181 and 182 of the Criminal Justice Act 2003;

(b) in the reference to Chapter 4 of Part 12 of that Act, the words "custody plus order or".

(3) Omit sections 197 to 199 (imprisonment with or without custody plus order).

(4) In section 207 (definitions), omit the definition of "custody plus order".

(5) In Schedule 7 (suspended sentence: further conviction or breach of requirement), omit paragraph 9(1)(a) (modification of paragraph 9(1)(a) of Schedule 12 to the Criminal Justice Act 2003).

(6) In Schedule 16 (minor and consequential amendments), omit paragraphs 222 and 223.

Criminal Justice and Immigration Act 2008 (c. 4)

42 Omit section 20(2) and (3) of the Criminal Justice and Immigration Act 2008.

Policing and Crime Act 2009 (c. 26)

43 Omit section 71(10) of the Policing and Crime Act 2009.

Criminal Justice Act 2003 (Sentencing) (Transitory Provisions) Order 2005 (S.I. 2005/643)

44 Article 2(4) of the Criminal Justice Act 2003 (Sentencing) (Transitory Provisions) Order 2005 is revoked.

SCHEDULE 11

Section 90

AMENDMENT OF ENACTMENTS RELATING TO BAIL

Bail Act 1976 (c. 63)

1 The Bail Act 1976 is amended as follows.

2 In section 2(2) (definitions)—

(a) insert the following definitions at the appropriate places—

""bail in non-extradition proceedings" means bail in criminal proceedings of the kind mentioned in section 1(1)(a),";

""custodial sentence" means a sentence or order mentioned in section 76(1) of the Powers of Criminal Courts (Sentencing) Act 2000 or any corresponding sentence or order imposed or made under any earlier enactment,";

""imprisonable offence" means an offence punishable in the case of an adult with imprisonment,";

""sexual offence" means an offence specified in Part 2 of Schedule 15 to the Criminal Justice Act 2003,";

""violent offence" means murder or an offence specified in Part 1 of Schedule 15 to the Criminal Justice Act 2003,", and

(b) in the definition of "young person" for "seventeen" substitute "eighteen".

3 (1) Section 3 (general provisions) is amended as follows.

(2) In subsection (6ZAA), for "person)," substitute "person granted bail in criminal proceedings of the kind mentioned in section 1(1)(a) or (b)), section

3AAA (in the case of a child or young person granted bail in connection with extradition proceedings),".

(3) In subsection (7)—

(a) for "a child or young person" substitute "a person under the age of seventeen",

(b) for the words "the child or young person", in both places they appear, substitute "the person", and

(c) in paragraph (a)—

(i) omit "of a young person", and

(ii) omit "young" in the second place it appears.

4 (1) Section 3AA (conditions for the imposition of electronic monitoring requirements: children and young persons) is amended as follows.

(2) In the heading after "young persons" insert "released on bail other than in extradition proceedings".

(3) In subsection (1) (conditions for the imposition of electronic monitoring conditions: children and young persons) after "young person" insert "released on bail in criminal proceedings of the kind mentioned in section 1(1)(a) or (b)".

5 After section 3AA insert—

"3AAA Conditions for the imposition of electronic monitoring requirements: children and young persons released on bail in extradition proceedings

(1) A court may not impose electronic monitoring requirements on a child or young person released on bail in connection with extradition proceedings unless each of the following conditions is met.

(2) The first condition is that the child or young person has attained the age of twelve years.

(3) The second condition is that—

(a) the conduct constituting the offence to which the extradition proceedings relate, or one or more of those offences, would, if committed in England and Wales, constitute a violent or sexual offence or an offence punishable in the case of an adult with imprisonment for a term of fourteen years or more, or

(b) the offence or offences to which the extradition proceedings relate, together with any other imprisonable offences of which the child or young person has been convicted in any proceedings—

(i) amount, or

(ii) would, if the child or young person were convicted of that offence or those offences, amount,

to a recent history of committing imprisonable offences while on bail or subject to a custodial remand.

(4) The third condition is that the court is satisfied that the necessary provision for dealing with the child or young person concerned can be made under arrangements for the electronic monitoring of persons released on bail that are currently available in each local justice area which is a relevant area.

(5) The fourth condition is that a youth offending team has informed the court that in its opinion the imposition of electronic monitoring requirements will be suitable in the case of the child or young person.

(6) The references in subsection (3)(b) to an imprisonable offence include a reference to an offence—

(a) of which the child or young person has been accused or convicted outside England and Wales, and

(b) which is equivalent to an offence that is punishable with imprisonment in England and Wales.

(7) The reference in subsection (3)(b) to a child or young person being subject to a custodial remand is to the child or young person being—

(a) remanded to local authority accommodation or youth detention accommodation under section 91 of the Legal Aid, Sentencing and Punishment of Offenders Act 2012,

(b) remanded to local authority accommodation under section 23 of the Children and Young Persons Act 1969 or to prison under that section as modified by section 98 of the Crime and Disorder Act 1998 or under section 27 of the Criminal Justice Act 1948, or

(c) subject to a form of custodial detention in a country or territory outside England and Wales while awaiting trial or sentence in that country or territory or during a trial in that country or territory."

6 (1) Section 3AB (conditions for the imposition of electronic monitoring requirements: other persons) is amended as follows.

(2) In subsection (1) for "seventeen" substitute "eighteen".

(3) Omit subsection (4).

7 In section 3AC (electronic monitoring: general provisions) in each of subsections (7) and (8) after "3AA" insert ", 3AAA".

8 (1) Section 7 (liability to arrest for absconding or breaking conditions of bail) is amended as follows.

(2) In subsection (5) for "subsection (6)" substitute "subsections (5A) and (6)".

(3) After subsection (5) insert—

"(5A) A justice of the peace may not remand a person in, or commit a person to, custody under subsection (5) if—

(a) the person has attained the age of eighteen,

(b) the person was released on bail in non-extradition proceedings,

(c) the person has not been convicted of an offence in those proceedings, and

(d) it appears to the justice of the peace that there is no real prospect that the person will be sentenced to a custodial sentence in the proceedings."

(4) In subsection (6) for "the person so brought before the justice" substitute "a person brought before a justice under subsection (4) or (4B)".

9 (1) Section 9A (bail decisions relating to persons aged under 18 who are accused of offences mentioned in Schedule 2 to the Magistrates' Courts Act 1980) is amended as follows.

(2) In the heading for "persons aged under 18" substitute "children or young persons".

(3) In subsection (1)(a) for "person aged under 18" substitute "child or young person".

(4) In subsections (2) and (3)(b) after "accused" insert "child or young".

10 Part 1 of Schedule 1 (bail for defendants accused or convicted of certain imprisonable offences) is amended in accordance with paragraphs 11 to 21.

11 For the heading immediately before paragraph 1 (defendants to whom Part 1 applies) substitute "Application of Part 1".

12 In paragraph 1 (defendants to whom Part 1 applies) in sub-paragraph (1) after "sub-paragraph (2)" insert "and paragraph 1A".

13 After paragraph 1 insert—

"1A (1) The paragraphs of this Part of this Schedule mentioned in sub-paragraph (2) do not apply in relation to bail in non-extradition proceedings where—

(a) the defendant has attained the age of 18,

(b) the defendant has not been convicted of an offence in those proceedings, and

(c) it appears to the court that there is no real prospect that the defendant will be sentenced to a custodial sentence in the proceedings.

(2) The paragraphs are—

(a) paragraph 2 (refusal of bail where defendant may fail to surrender to custody, commit offences on bail or interfere with witnesses),

(b) paragraph 2A (refusal of bail where defendant appears to have committed indictable or either way offence while on bail), and

(c) paragraph 6 (refusal of bail where defendant has been arrested under section 7)."

14 In paragraph 2 (exceptions to bail where defendant may fail to surrender to custody, commit offences on bail or interfere with witnesses) for sub-paragraph (2) substitute—

"(2) Where the defendant falls within paragraph 6B, this paragraph does not apply unless—

(a) the court is of the opinion mentioned in paragraph 6A, or

(b) paragraph 6A does not apply by virtue of paragraph 6C."

15 After paragraph 2 insert—

"2ZA(1) The defendant need not be granted bail if the court is satisfied that there are substantial grounds for believing that the defendant, if released on bail (whether subject to conditions or not), would commit an offence while on bail by engaging in conduct that would, or would be likely to, cause—

(a) physical or mental injury to an associated person; or

(b) an associated person to fear physical or mental injury.

(2) In sub-paragraph (1) "associated person" means a person who is associated with the defendant within the meaning of section 62 of the Family Law Act 1996."

16 For paragraph 2A (refusal of bail where defendant appears to have committed offence while on bail) substitute—

"2A The defendant need not be granted bail if—

(a) the offence is an indictable offence or an offence triable either way, and

(b) it appears to the court that the defendant was on bail in criminal proceedings on the date of the offence."

17 For paragraph 6 (refusal of bail where defendant fails to surrender to custody or has been arrested under section 7) substitute—

"6 The defendant need not be granted bail if, having previously been released on bail in, or in connection with, the proceedings, the defendant has been arrested in pursuance of section 7."

18 In paragraph 6A (certain drug users to be refused bail unless no significant risk of offending while on bail) for "is satisfied" substitute "is of the opinion".

19 In paragraph 9 (considerations to which the court must have regard)—

(a) for "2A(1), 6(1) or 6A" substitute "2ZA(1)", and

(b) after "paragraph 6ZA" insert "or 6A".

20 In paragraph 9AA (court to give particular weight to the fact that an under 18 defendant was on bail when the offence was committed) in sub-paragraph (1)(a) for "under the age of 18" substitute "a child or young person".

21 In paragraph 9AB (factors to be given particular weight by the court when making a decision for the purposes of section 2(1)(a), in the case of an under 18 defendant who has failed to surrender) in sub-paragraph (1)(a) for "under the age of 18" substitute "a child or young person".

22 Part 1A of Schedule 1 (bail for defendants accused or convicted of imprisonable offences to which Part 1 of that Schedule does not apply) is amended in accordance with paragraphs 23 to 26.

23 For the heading immediately before paragraph 1 (defendants to whom Part 1A applies) substitute "Application of Part 1A".

24 In paragraph 1 (defendants to whom Part 1A applies) for "The" substitute "Subject to paragraph 1A, the".

25 After paragraph 1 insert—

"1A (1) The paragraphs of this Part of this Schedule mentioned in sub-paragraph (2) do not apply in relation to bail in, or in connection with, proceedings where—

(a) the defendant has attained the age of 18,

(b) the defendant has not been convicted of an offence in those proceedings, and

(c) it appears to the court that there is no real prospect that the defendant will be sentenced to a custodial sentence in the proceedings.

(2) The paragraphs are—

(a) paragraph 2 (refusal of bail for failure to surrender to custody),

(b) paragraph 3 (refusal of bail where defendant would commit further offences on bail), and

(c) paragraph 7 (refusal of bail in certain circumstances when arrested under section 7)."

26 (1) Paragraph 4 (refusal of bail to defendants who are likely to cause injury or fear of injury) is amended as follows.

(2) The existing words become sub-paragraph (1).

(3) In paragraphs (a) and (b) of that sub-paragraph for "any person other than the defendant", in both places those words appear, substitute "an associated person".

(4) After that sub-paragraph insert—

"(2) In sub-paragraph (1) "associated person" means a person who is associated with the defendant within the meaning of section 62 of the Family Law Act 1996."

27 Part 2 of Schedule 1 (bail for defendants accused or convicted of non-imprisonable offences) is amended in accordance with paragraphs 28 to 30.

28 In paragraph 2 (refusal of bail for failure to surrender to custody) after "bail if—" insert—

"(za) the defendant—

(i) is a child or young person, or

(ii) has been convicted in the proceedings of an offence;".

29 In paragraph 5 (refusal of bail in certain circumstances when arrested under section 7) after "bail if—" insert—

"(za) the defendant—

(i) is a child or young person, or

(ii) has been convicted in the proceedings of an offence;".

30 After paragraph 5 insert—

"6 (1) The defendant need not be granted bail if—

(a) having been released on bail in, or in connection with, the proceedings for the offence, the defendant has been arrested in pursuance of section 7, and

(b) the court is satisfied that there are substantial grounds for believing that the defendant, if released on bail (whether subject to conditions or not), would commit an offence while on bail by engaging in conduct that would, or would be likely to, cause—

(i) physical or mental injury to an associated person, or

(ii) an associated person to fear physical or mental injury.

(2) In sub-paragraph (1) "associated person" means a person who is associated with the defendant within the meaning of section 62 of the Family Law Act 1996."

31 (1) Paragraph 2 of Part 3 of Schedule 1 (references to previous grants of bail) is amended as follows.

(2) In paragraph (b) for "section 14(1) of the Criminal Justice Act 2003" substitute "paragraph 16 of Schedule 11 to the Legal Aid, Sentencing and Punishment of Offenders Act 2012".

(3) In paragraph (c) for "section 15(1) of the Criminal Justice Act 2003" substitute "paragraph 17 of Schedule 11 to the Legal Aid, Sentencing and Punishment of Offenders Act 2012".

(4) After paragraph (f) insert ";

(g) as respects the reference in paragraph 6 of Part 2 of this Schedule, bail granted before the coming into force of that paragraph."

Bail (Amendment) Act 1993 (c. 26)

32 (1) Section 1 of the Bail (Amendment) Act 1993 (prosecution right of appeal where bail is granted) is amended as follows.

(2) After subsection (1A) insert—

"(1B) Where a judge of the Crown Court grants bail to a person who is charged with, or convicted of, an offence punishable by imprisonment, the prosecution may appeal to the High Court against the granting of bail.

(1C) An appeal under subsection (1B) may not be made where a judge of the Crown Court has granted bail on an appeal under subsection (1)."

(3) In subsection (2) for "Subsection (1) above applies" substitute "Subsections (1) and (1B) above apply".

(4) In subsections (3), (4) and (8) for "or (1A)" substitute ", (1A) or (1B)".

(5) In subsection (10)(a)—

(a) for "reference in subsection (1)" substitute "references in subsections (1) and (1B)", and

(b) for "is to be read as a reference" substitute "are to be read as references".

Criminal Justice and Public Order Act 1994 (c. 33)

33 In section 25 of the Criminal Justice and Public Order Act 1994 (no bail for defendants charged with or convicted of homicide or rape after previous conviction for such offences) in subsection (1) for "is satisfied" substitute "is of the opinion".

Consequential amendments

34 In section 38(2A) of the Police and Criminal Evidence Act 1984 (considerations applicable to paragraph 2 of Part 1 of Schedule 1 to the 1976 Act to be taken into account by custody officer when making decision about bail after charge) for "paragraph 2(2)" substitute "paragraphs 1A and 2(2)".

35 In section 200 of the Extradition Act 2003 (amendments to section 1 of the Bail (Amendment) Act 1993) omit subsections (4)(a) and (7)(a).

SCHEDULE 12

Section 105

REMANDS OF CHILDREN OTHERWISE THAN ON BAIL: MINOR AND CONSEQUENTIAL AMENDMENTS

Criminal Justice Act 1948 (c. 58)

1 Section 27 of the Criminal Justice Act 1948 (remand of persons aged 17 to 20) is amended as follows.

2 In the heading, for "17" substitute "18".

3 In subsection (1) for "seventeen" substitute "eighteen".

Prison Act 1952 (c. 52)

4 In section 43(1) of the Prison Act 1952 (power of Secretary of State to provide young offender institutions, secure training centres etc), at the end of paragraph (d) insert "and in which children who have been remanded to youth detention accommodation under section 91(4) of the Legal Aid, Sentencing and Punishment of Offenders Act 2012 may be detained".

Children and Young Persons Act 1969 (c. 54)

5 The Children and Young Persons Act 1969 is amended as follows.

6 Omit section 23 (remands and committals to local authority accommodation).

7 Omit section 23AA (electronic monitoring of conditions of remand).

8 Omit section 23A (liability to arrest for breaking conditions of remand).

9 (1) Section 23B (report by local authority in certain cases where person remanded on bail) is amended as follows.

(2) In subsection (2), at the end insert "under section 91(3) of the Legal Aid, Sentencing and Punishment of Offenders Act 2012."

(3) In subsection (3), for "section 23(2) of this Act" substitute "section 92(2) of the Legal Aid, Sentencing and Punishment of Offenders Act 2012".

(4) In subsection (6)—

(a) in paragraph (a), for "17" substitute "18", and

(b) for paragraph (b) and the "and" at the end of that paragraph substitute—

"(b) the requirements in section 94(3) and (4) or 95(3) and (4) of the Legal Aid, Sentencing and Punishment of Offenders Act 2012 would have been fulfilled if the person had not been remanded on bail, and".

(5) In subsection (7), in the definition of "serious offence", after "means" insert "(subject to subsection (8))".

(6) After subsection (7) insert—

"(8) For the purposes of the application of this section to a person remanded on bail in connection with proceedings under the Extradition Act 2003—

(a) an offence is a "serious offence" if the conduct constituting the offence would, if committed in England and Wales, constitute an offence punishable in the case of an adult with imprisonment for a term of two years or more, and

(b) the reference in subsection (1)(a) to a person being charged with a serious offence includes a reference to the person having been accused of such an offence."

10 (1) Section 32 (detention of absentees) is amended as follows.

(2) In subsection (1A)—

(a) in paragraph (b), omit sub-paragraph (iii), and

(b) after that paragraph insert—

"(c) from a place in which the child or young person has been accommodated pursuant to a remand under section 91 of the Legal Aid, Sentencing and Punishment of Offenders Act 2012,".

(3) In subsection (1B), for the "or" at the end of paragraph (b) substitute—

"(ba) the place mentioned in subsection (1A)(c); or".

(4) In subsection (1C), for paragraph (d) and the "or" preceding that paragraph substitute—

"(d) where the child or young person was accommodated pursuant to a remand under section 91(3) of the Legal Aid, Sentencing and Punishment of Offenders Act 2012 (remands to local authority accommodation), the designated authority within the meaning of section 107(1) of that Act; or

(e) where the child or young person was accommodated pursuant to a remand under section 91(4) of that Act (remands to youth detention accommodation), the Secretary of State."

11 In section 34(1) (transitional modifications of Part 1 for persons of specified ages)—

(a) in paragraph (c) omit ", 23(1)", and

(b) omit paragraph (e).

12 In section 69 (orders and regulations etc) omit subsection (4A).

Local Authority Social Services Act 1970 (c. 42)

13 In Schedule 1 to the Local Authority Social Services Act 1970 (social services functions for the purposes of the Act), at the end insert—

"Legal Aid, Sentencing and Punishment of Offenders Act 2012	
Section 92	Functions in relation to a child remanded to local authority accommodation."

Bail Act 1976 (c. 63)

14 The Bail Act 1976 is amended as follows.

15 (1) Section 3AA (conditions for the imposition of electronic monitoring requirements: children and young persons) is amended as follows.

(2) In subsection (3)(b), for "to local authority accommodation" substitute "subject to a custodial remand".

(3) For subsection (11) substitute—

"(11) The references in subsection (3)(b) to an imprisonable offence include a reference to an offence—

(a) of which the child or young person has been convicted outside England and Wales, and

(b) which is equivalent to an offence that is punishable with imprisonment in England and Wales.

(12) The reference in subsection (3)(b) to a child or young person being subject to a custodial remand is to the child or young person being—

(a) remanded to local authority accommodation or youth detention accommodation under section 91 of the Legal Aid, Sentencing and Punishment of Offenders Act 2012,

(b) remanded to local authority accommodation under section 23 of the Children and Young Persons Act 1969 or to prison under that section as modified by section 98 of the Crime and Disorder Act 1998 or under section 27 of the Criminal Justice Act 1948, or

(c) subject to a form of custodial detention in a country or territory outside England and Wales while awaiting trial or sentence in that country or territory or during a trial in that country or territory."

16 In section 7(6) (arrest for absconding or breaking conditions of bail: powers of justice), for the words from "section 23" to the end of the subsection substitute "section 91 of the Legal Aid, Sentencing and Punishment of Offenders Act 2012 (remands of children otherwise than on bail)".

17 In Part 3 of Schedule 1 (supplementary provisions about persons entitled to bail: interpretation), in paragraph 3, for the words from "the care of" to the end of the paragraph substitute "accommodation pursuant to a remand

under section 91(3) or (4) of the Legal Aid, Sentencing and Punishment of Offenders Act 2012 (remands to local authority accommodation or youth detention accommodation)."

Child Abduction Act 1984 (c. 37)

18 The Child Abduction Act 1984 is amended as follows.

19 In section 1(8) (offence of child abduction: modifications in relation to children remanded to local authority accommodation etc), for "to a local authority accommodation" substitute "otherwise than on bail".

20 In paragraph 2 of the Schedule (modifications of section 1 in case of children in places of safety etc)—

(a) in sub-paragraph (1), in paragraph (b) omit "section 23 of the Children and Young Persons Act 1969,",

(b) in that sub-paragraph, at the end of paragraph (ba) insert "; or

(bb) remanded to local authority accommodation or youth detention accommodation under section 91 of the Legal Aid, Sentencing and Punishment of Offenders Act 2012.", and

(c) in sub-paragraph (2)(a), after "place of safety" insert ", local authority accommodation or youth detention accommodation".

Police and Criminal Evidence Act 1984 (c. 60)

21 In section 17(1)(ca) of the Police and Criminal Evidence Act 1984 (powers of entry and search of premises for purpose of arresting child or young person remanded to local authority accommodation), for the words from "or committed" to "that Act" substitute "to local authority accommodation or youth detention accommodation under section 91 of the Legal Aid, Sentencing and Punishment of Offenders Act 2012".

Prosecution of Offences Act 1985 (c. 23)

22 In section 22(11) of the Prosecution of Offences Act 1985 (time limits in relation to preliminary stages of criminal proceedings: interpretation), in the definition of "custody" for the words from "to which" to "Act 1969" substitute "or youth detention accommodation to which a person is remanded under section 91 of the Legal Aid, Sentencing and Punishment of Offenders Act 2012".

Children Act 1989 (c. 41)

23 The Children Act 1989 is amended as follows.

24 In section 21(2)(c) (duty to receive and provide accommodation for certain kinds of children) omit sub-paragraph (i) (children on remand under section 23(1) of the Children and Young Persons Act 1969).

25 In Schedule 12 (minor amendments), omit paragraph 28(b).

Criminal Justice Act 1991 (c. 53)

26 The Criminal Justice Act 1991 is amended as follows.

27 Omit section 60(1).

28 In section 60(3) (applications under section 25 of the Children Act 1989 in case of child remanded or committed to local authority accommodation)—

(a) omit "or committed", and

(b) after "local authority accommodation" insert "under section 91(3) of the Legal Aid, Sentencing and Punishment of Offenders Act 2012".

29 Omit section 61 (provision by local authorities of secure accommodation).

30 Omit section 61A (cost of secure accommodation).

31 In section 92(3) (application of prisoner escort provisions to persons remanded etc under section 23 of the Children and Young Persons Act 1969)—

(a) in paragraph (a), for the words from "or committed" to "1969 Act" substitute "to local authority accommodation or youth detention accommodation under section 91 of the Legal Aid, Sentencing and Punishment of Offenders Act 2012", and

(b) in paragraph (b) for "such accommodation" substitute "accommodation in which a person is or is to be accommodated pursuant to such a remand".

Bail (Amendment) Act 1993 (c. 26)

32 In section 1(10) of the Bail (Amendment) Act 1993 (prosecution right of appeal against grant of bail: application to children and young persons)—

(a) for the words from "child" to "Act 1969)" substitute "person under the age of 18", and

(b) in paragraph (b) for the words from "section 23" to "accommodation)" substitute "Chapter 3 of Part 3 of the Legal Aid, Sentencing and Punishment of Offenders Act 2012 (remands of children otherwise than on bail)".

Criminal Justice and Public Order Act 1994 (c. 33)

33 The Criminal Justice and Public Order Act 1994 is amended as follows.

34 Omit sections 19(1) and (3), 21 and 23.

35 In Schedule 9 (minor amendments) omit paragraph 38.

Crime and Disorder Act 1998 (c. 37)

36 The Crime and Disorder Act 1998 is amended as follows.

37 In section 38(4)(d) (definition of "youth justice services": placements pursuant to remands to local authority accommodation), for the words from "or committed" to "1969 Act")" substitute "to such accommodation under section 91(3) of the Legal Aid, Sentencing and Punishment of Offenders Act 2012".

38 In section 41(5) (functions of the Youth Justice Board for England and Wales) omit—

(a) paragraph (i)(iii) (agreements for the provision of accommodation for detention under section 23(4)(c) of the Children and Young

Persons Act 1969 as modified by section 98 of the Crime and Disorder Act 1998), and

(b) paragraph (k) (assistance to local authorities in discharging duty under section 61 of the Criminal Justice Act 1991).

39 In section 57A(3) (use of live link for accused's attendance at preliminary or sentencing hearing: interpretation), in paragraph (a) of the definition of "custody", for the words from "to which" to "Act 1969" substitute "or youth detention accommodation to which a person is remanded under section 91 of the Legal Aid, Sentencing and Punishment of Offenders Act 2012".

40 Omit sections 97 and 98.

Access to Justice Act 1999 (c. 22)

41 In Schedule 4 to the Access to Justice Act 1999 (amendments consequential on Part 1), omit paragraphs 4, 6 and 7.

Powers of Criminal Courts (Sentencing) Act 2000 (c. 6)

42 The Powers of Criminal Courts (Sentencing) Act 2000 is amended as follows.

43 In section 101 (taking account of remands in relation to a detention and training order)—

(a) in subsection (11), for paragraph (c) and the "or" at the end of that paragraph substitute—

"(c) remanded to youth detention accommodation under section 91(4) of the Legal Aid, Sentencing and Punishment of Offenders Act 2012; or", and

(b) in subsection (12) omit the words from "and in that subsection" to the end of the subsection.

44 In Schedule 9 (consequential amendments), omit paragraphs 93 and 126.

Care Standards Act 2000 (c. 14)

45 In Schedule 4 to the Care Standards Act 2000 (minor and consequential amendments), omit paragraphs 3 and 17.

Criminal Justice and Court Services Act 2000 (c. 43)

46 (1) Schedule 7 to the Criminal Justice and Court Services Act 2000 (minor and consequential amendments) is amended as follows.

(2) In paragraph 4(2), in the entry for the Children and Young Persons Act 1969, omit the words from "section 23(4)" to "15 and 16 year old boys)),".

(3) Omit paragraph 39.

Criminal Justice and Police Act 2001 (c. 16)

47 In the Criminal Justice and Police Act 2001, omit sections 130, 132 and 133(1).

Courts Act 2003 (c. 39)

48 In Schedule 8 to the Courts Act 2003 (minor and consequential amendments), omit paragraph 135.

Extradition Act 2003 (c. 41)

49 In the Extradition Act 2003, omit section 201.

Criminal Justice Act 2003 (c. 44)

50 The Criminal Justice Act 2003 is amended as follows.

51 In section 242 (interpretation of provisions about crediting periods of remand in custody)—

(a) in subsection (2)(b), for the words from "or committed" to "that section" substitute "to youth detention accommodation under section 91(4) of the Legal Aid, Sentencing and Punishment of Offenders Act 2012", and

(b) omit subsection (3).

52 In Schedule 32 (amendments relating to sentencing), omit paragraph 15.

Criminal Defence Service Act 2006 (c. 9)

53 In section 4(2) of the Criminal Defence Service Act 2006 (provisions to which certain consequential amendments apply), omit paragraphs (a) and (b).

Violent Crime Reduction Act 2006 (c. 38)

54 In the Violent Crime Reduction Act 2006, omit section 61.

Criminal Justice and Immigration Act 2008 (c. 4)

55 In Schedule 26 to the Criminal Justice and Immigration Act 2008 (minor and consequential amendments), omit paragraph 5.

Children and Young Persons Act 2008 (c. 23)

56 In Schedule 1 to the Children and Young Persons Act 2008 (children looked after by local authorities: supplementary and consequential provision), omit paragraph 8.

Offender Management Act 2007 (Consequential Amendments) Order 2008 (SI 2008/912)

57 In Schedule 1 to the Offender Management Act 2007 (Consequential Amendments) Order 2008 (amendments of Acts), omit paragraph 13(6).

Policing and Crime Act 2009 (c. 26)

58 In paragraph 14(3) of Schedule 5A to the Policing and Crime Act 2009 (detention order for breach of injunction: meaning of youth detention

accommodation) for paragraph (c) substitute—

"(c) a secure children's home, as defined by section 102(11) of the Legal Aid, Sentencing and Punishment of Offenders Act 2012."

SCHEDULE 13

Section 110

CREDITING OF TIME IN CUSTODY

PART 1

ARMED FORCES AMENDMENTS

1 The Armed Forces Act 2006 is amended as follows.

2 (1) Section 246 (crediting of time in service custody: terms of imprisonment and detention) is amended as follows.

(2) For subsections (2) to (5) substitute—

"(2) The number of days for which the offender was kept in service custody in connection with the offence in question or any related offence since being so charged is to count as time served by the offender as part of the sentence.

But this is subject to subsections (2A) to (2C).

(2A) If, on any day on which the offender was kept in service custody, the offender was also detained in connection with any other matter, that day is not to count as time served.

(2B) A day counts as time served—

(a) in relation to only one sentence, and

(b) only once in relation to that sentence.

(2C) A day is not to count as time served as part of any period of 28 days served by the offender before automatic release (see section 255B(1) of the 2003 Act)."

(3) In subsection (6)—

(a) omit "and" at the end of paragraph (a), and

(b) after paragraph (b) insert ", and

(c) a determinate sentence of detention in a young offender institution,".

3 (1) Section 247 (crediting of time in service custody: supplementary) is amended as follows.

(2) In subsection (2)—

(a) after "in connection with other offences" insert "(but see section 246(2B))", and

(b) omit ", or has also been detained in connection with other matters".

(3) After subsection (2) insert—

"(2A) The reference in section 246(2A) to detention in connection with any other matter does not include remand in custody in connection with another offence but includes—

(a) detention pursuant to any custodial sentence;

(b) committal in default of payment of any sum of money;

(c) committal for want of sufficient distress to satisfy any sum of money;

(d) committal for failure to do or abstain from doing anything required to be done or left undone."

(4) In subsection (4) for "the reference in section 246(2)" substitute "the references in section 246(2) and (2B)".

4 In section 373(3) (orders, regulations and rules) in paragraph (g) omit "or 246".

5 In Schedule 16 (minor and consequential amendments), omit paragraph 228.

PART 2

OTHER AMENDMENTS

Criminal Appeal Act 1968 (c. 19)

6 In Schedule 2 to the Criminal Appeal Act 1968 (procedural and other provisions applicable on order for retrial), in paragraph 2(4), for "Sections 240" substitute "Sections 240ZA".

Immigration Act 1971 (c. 77)

7 In section 7 of the Immigration Act 1971 (exemption from deportation for certain existing residents), in subsection (4), after "section 240" insert ", 240ZA or 240A".

Road Traffic Offenders Act 1988 (c. 53)

8 In section 35A of the Road Traffic Offenders Act 1988 (extension of disqualification where custodial sentence also imposed), in subsection (6)—

(a) omit "a direction under";

(b) in paragraph (a), for "section 240" substitute "section 240ZA";

(c) in paragraph (b), before "section 240A" insert "a direction under".

Powers of Criminal Courts (Sentencing) Act 2000 (c. 6)

9 The Powers of Criminal Courts (Sentencing) Act 2000 is amended as follows.

10 In section 82A (determination of tariffs), in subsection (3)(b), for "section 240" substitute "section 240ZA".

11 In section 101 (term of detention and training order), in subsection (12A), for "the reference in subsection (2) of that section to section 240" substitute "the reference in subsection (2A) of that section to section 240ZA".

12 In section 147A (extension of disqualification where custodial sentence also imposed), in subsection (6)—
(a) omit "a direction under";
(b) in paragraph (a), for "section 240" substitute "section 240ZA";
(c) in paragraph (b), before "section 240A" insert "a direction under".

International Criminal Court Act 2001 (c. 17)

13 In Schedule 7 to the International Criminal Court Act 2001 (domestic provisions not applicable to ICC prisoners), in paragraph 2(1)(d), for "sections 240" substitute "sections 240ZA".

SCHEDULE 14

Section 111

PRISONERS SERVING LESS THAN 12 MONTHS: CONSEQUENTIAL AMENDMENTS

Road Traffic Offenders Act 1988 (c. 53)

1 In section 35A of the Road Traffic Offenders Act 1988 (extension of disqualification where custodial sentence also imposed)—
(a) in subsection (8), after "section" insert "243A(3)(a),";
(b) in subsection (9)(a), after "in respect of section" insert "243A(3)(a) or".

Crime (Sentences) Act 1997 (c. 43)

2 In Schedule 1 to the Crime (Sentences) Act 1997 (transfer of prisoners within the British Islands), in paragraphs 8(2)(a) and 9(2)(a), after "sections 241," insert "243A,".

Powers of Criminal Courts (Sentencing) Act 2000 (c. 6)

3 In section 147A of the Powers of Criminal Courts (Sentencing) Act 2000 (extension of disqualification where custodial sentence also imposed)—
(a) in subsection (8), after "section" insert "243A(3)(a),";
(b) in subsection (9)(a), after "in respect of section" insert "243A(3)(a) or".

International Criminal Court Act 2001 (c. 17)

4 In Schedule 7 to the International Criminal Court Act 2001 (domestic provisions not applicable to ICC prisoners), in paragraph 3(1), for "sections 244" substitute "sections 243A".

Criminal Justice Act 2003 (c. 44)

5 The Criminal Justice Act 2003 is amended as follows.

6 (1) Section 244 (duty to release prisoners on licence) is amended as follows.

(2) In subsection (1)—
(a) after "section" in the first place it appears insert "243A or";

(b) after "the requisite custodial period" insert "for the purposes of this section".

(3) In subsection (3)—

(a) for "In this section" substitute "For the purposes of this section";

(b) in paragraph (a)—

(i) for "any" substitute "a";

(ii) after "the Sentencing Act" insert "for such a term".

7 In section 246(6) (power to release prisoners early: definitions), in the definition of "the requisite custodial period", after "has the meaning given by" insert "paragraph (a) or (b) of section 243A(3) or (as the case may be)".

8 (1) Section 249 (duration of licence) is amended as follows.

(2) In subsection (1), after "a fixed-term prisoner" insert ", other than one to whom section 243A applies,".

(3) After subsection (1) insert—

"(1A) Where a prisoner to whom section 243A applies is released on licence, the licence shall, subject to any revocation under section 254 or 255, remain in force until the date on which, but for the release, the prisoner would have served one-half of the sentence.
This is subject to subsection (3)."

(4) In subsection (3)—

(a) for "Subsection (1) has" substitute "Subsections (1) and (1A) have";

(b) omit "and (4)".

9 In section 250(4) (licence conditions) omit "for a term of twelve months or more" and "such" in the first place it appears.

10 In section 253(3) (period for which curfew condition to remain in force), after "fall to be released" insert "unconditionally under section 243A or".

11 In section 260 (early removal of prisoners liable to removal from UK)—

(a) in subsection (5), after "section" in the second place it appears insert "243A,";

(b) in subsection (7), after "has the meaning given by" insert "paragraph (a) or (b) of section 243A(3) or (as the case may be)".

12 (1) Section 261 (re-entry to UK of offender removed early) is amended as follows.

(2) In subsection (5), for "section 244" substitute "section 243A or 244 (as the case may be)".

(3) In subsection (6)—

(a) in the definition of "requisite custodial period", after "has the meaning given by" insert "paragraph (a) or (b) of section 243A(3) or (as the case may be)";

(b) in the definition of "sentence expiry date"—

(i) after "but for his" insert "release from prison and";

(ii) for "ceased to be subject to a licence" substitute "served the whole of the sentence".

13 In section 263(2) (concurrent terms)—

(a) after paragraph (a) insert—

"(aa) the offender's release is to be unconditional if section 243A so requires in respect of each of the sentences (and in any other case is to be on licence),";

(b) in paragraph (b), after "each of the others" insert "to which that section applies";

(c) in paragraph (c), after "release under this Chapter" insert "(unless that release is unconditional)".

14 In section 264 (consecutive terms)—

(a) in subsection (2), omit "on licence";

(b) in subsection (3), for "any of the terms of imprisonment is a term of twelve months or more" substitute "the aggregate length of the terms of imprisonment is 12 months or more";

(c) after subsection (3) insert—

"(3A) Where the aggregate length of the terms of imprisonment is less than 12 months, the offender's release under this Chapter is to be unconditional.";

(d) omit subsections (4) and (5);

(e) in subsection (6)(a)(ii)—

(i) for "a term of twelve months or more" substitute "any other sentence";

(ii) for "the term" substitute "the sentence";

(f) in subsection (7), omit "of 12 months or more".

15 In section 267 (alteration by order of proportion of sentence), after "any reference in" insert "section 243A(3)(a),".

16 The heading of Chapter 6 of Part 12 becomes "Release, licences and recall".

Commencement of repeal

17 The repeal by section 303(a) of the Criminal Justice Act 2003 of sections 33 to 51 of the Criminal Justice Act 1991 has effect in relation to any sentence of imprisonment which—

(a) is of less than 12 months (whether or not such a sentence is imposed to run concurrently or consecutively with another such sentence), and

(b) is imposed in respect of an offence committed on or after 4 April 2005,

and paragraph 14 of Schedule 2 to the Criminal Justice Act 2003 (Commencement No. 8 and Transitional and Savings Provisions) Order 2005 (S.I. 2005/950) is accordingly revoked.

SCHEDULE 15

Section 120

APPLICATION OF SECTIONS 108 TO 119 AND TRANSITIONAL AND TRANSITORY PROVISION

1 In this Schedule—

(a) "the commencement date", in relation to any of sections 108 to 118, means the day appointed under section 151 for the coming into force of that section;

(b) "Chapter 6" means Chapter 6 of Part 12 of the 2003 Act, as amended by those sections;

(c) "the 2003 Act" means the Criminal Justice Act 2003.

2 (1) The following provisions apply in relation to any person who falls to be released under Chapter 6 on or after the commencement date—

(a) section 108 (but this is subject to sub-paragraph (3));

(b) in section 110—

(i) subsections (1) to (7), (9) and (12) so far as they relate to section 240ZA of the 2003 Act, and

(ii) subsection (10);

(c) section 111;

(d) section 115;

(e) section 116;

(f) Part 1 of Schedule 13 and section 110(13) so far as it relates to that Part (but this is subject to sub-paragraph (3)).

(2) Section 117 applies in relation to any person who falls to be released under Chapter 6, or (as the case may be) under Chapter 2 of Part 2 of the Crime (Sentences) Act 1997, on or after the commencement date.

(3) Where a court, before the commencement date, has given a direction under section 240(3) of the 2003 Act or section 246(2) of the Armed Forces Act 2006—

(a) if the number of days in relation to which the direction is given is greater than the number of days calculated under the new provisions, the direction continues to have effect (in place of the new provisions);

(b) in any other case, the direction ceases to have effect.

(4) In sub-paragraph (3) "the new provisions" means—

(a) where the direction was given under section 240(3) of the 2003 Act, section 240ZA of that Act;

(b) where the direction was given under section 246(2) of the Armed Forces Act 2006, section 246 of that Act as amended by Part 1 of Schedule 13.

3 The following provisions apply in relation to any person sentenced on or after the commencement date—

(a) section 109;

(b) in section 110—

(i) subsections (1) to (7), (9) and (12) so far as they relate to section 240A of the 2003 Act, and

(ii) subsection (8).

4 The amendments made by section 112 do not affect the release under Chapter 6 of any prisoner before the commencement date.

5 Section 113 applies in relation to any person recalled under section 254 of the 2003 Act before the commencement date (as well as in relation to any person recalled under that section on or after that date).

6 Section 114 applies in relation to any person recalled under that section on or after the commencement date.

7 Section 119 applies in relation to any person who, on the day on which this Act is passed, has served the relevant part of the sentence (as well as in relation to any person who, on that date, has not served that part).

SCHEDULE 16

Section 121

AMENDMENTS OF CRIMINAL JUSTICE ACT 2003: TRANSITIONAL AND CONSEQUENTIAL PROVISION

PART 1

TRANSITIONAL PROVISION

1 The Criminal Justice Act 2003 is amended as follows.

2 After section 267 insert—

"267A Application of Chapter 6 to pre-4 April 2005 cases

Schedule 20A (which modifies certain provisions of this Chapter as they apply to persons serving a sentence for an offence committed before 4 April 2005) has effect."

3 After Schedule 20 insert—

"SCHEDULE 20A

Section 267A

APPLICATION OF CHAPTER 6 OF PART 12 TO PRE-4 APRIL 2005 CASES

1 In this Schedule—

"the 1991 Act" means the Criminal Justice Act 1991;

"the commencement date" means the date on which section 121 of the Legal Aid, Sentencing and Punishment of Offenders Act 2012 comes into force.

2 Paragraphs 3 to 9 apply in relation to any person serving a sentence for an offence committed before 4 April 2005, whenever that sentence was imposed (see section 121(1) of the Legal Aid, Sentencing and Punishment of Offenders Act 2012).

3 (1) Any relevant period is to be treated, for the purposes of section 240ZA, as if it were a period for which the offender was remanded in custody in connection with the offence.

(2) "Relevant period" means any period which would (but for the repeal of section 67 of the Criminal Justice Act 1967) be a relevant period within the meaning of that section (reduction of sentences by period spent in custody etc).

4 Section 246 applies as if, in subsection (4)—

(a) the reference in paragraph (a) to section 227 or 228 were a reference to section 85 of the Sentencing Act;

(b) the reference in paragraph (d) to paragraph 9(1)(b) or (c) or 10(1)(b) or (c) of Schedule 8 were a reference to paragraph 4(1)(d) or 5(1)(d) of Schedule 3 to the Sentencing Act;

(c) in paragraph (g)—

(i) the reference to section 246 included a reference to section 34A of the 1991 Act,

(ii) the reference to section 255(1)(a) included a reference to section 38A(1)(a) or 39(1) or (2) of the 1991 Act, and

(iii) the reference to section 255(3) included a reference to section 38A(3) of the 1991 Act;

(d) the references in paragraph (h) to sections 248 and 254 included references to, respectively, sections 36 and 39(1) or (2) of the 1991 Act; and

(e) in paragraph (i), the words from "in the case of" to "relates" were omitted.

5 (1) Where the person has been released on licence under Part 2 of the 1991 Act or under section 60 of the Criminal Justice Act 1967 before the commencement date, the person is to be treated as if the release had been under this Chapter.

(2) In particular, the following provisions apply.

(3) A licence under section 34A of the 1991 Act is to be treated as if it were a licence under section 246.

(4) A licence under section 36 of the 1991 Act is to be treated as if it were a licence under section 248.

(5) Any condition of a licence specified under section 37 of the 1991 Act is to have effect as if it were included under section 250 (whether or not the condition is of a kind which could otherwise be included under that section).

(6) Where the licence is, on the commencement date, subject to a suspension under section 38(2) of the 1991 Act, the suspension continues to have effect for the period specified by the court despite the repeal of that section.

(7) A licence under section 40A of the 1991 Act is to be treated as if it were a licence under this Chapter, except that in respect of any failure (before or after the commencement date) to comply with the conditions of the licence, the person is liable to be dealt with in accordance with section 40A(4) to (6) (despite the repeal of that section) and is not liable to be dealt with in any other way.

(8) Sub-paragraph (1) does not affect the duration of the licence.

6 (1) Where a person has been recalled under Part 2 of the 1991 Act before the commencement date, the person is to be treated as if the recall had been under section 254.

(2) In particular, the following provisions apply.

(3) If the Secretary of State has not referred the person's case to the Board under section 39(4) or 44A of the 1991 Act, the Secretary of State must refer the case under section 255C(4).

(4) If the Secretary of State has referred the person's case to the Board under section 39(4) or 44A of the 1991 Act, that reference is to be treated as if it had been made under section 255C(4).

(5) A determination of a reference under section 39(4) or 44A of the 1991 Act is to be treated as a determination under section 256(1).

(6) If the person is released on licence, the duration of that licence is determined in accordance with section 249 (subject to paragraphs 17, 19 and 26 of Schedule 20B).

7 Rules made by virtue of section 42 of the 1991 Act have effect as if made by virtue of section 257.

8 (1) A person removed from prison under section 46A of the 1991 Act before the commencement date is to be treated as having been removed from prison under section 260.

(2) Section 260 applies as if, in subsection (7)—

(a) the reference to an extended sentence imposed under section 227 or 228 were a reference to an extended sentence imposed under section 85 of the Sentencing Act, and

(b) the reference to the appropriate custodial term determined under section 227 or 228 were a reference to the custodial term determined under section 85.

9 An order made under section 47 of the 1991 Act is to have effect as if it were an order made under section 243.

10 Section 264 applies as if the definition of "custodial period" in subsection (6) included, in relation to an extended sentence imposed under section 85 of the Sentencing Act, one-half of the custodial term determined under that section."

PART 2

CONSEQUENTIAL AMENDMENTS

Repatriation of Prisoners Act 1984 (c. 47)

4 In section 2(4)(b)(i) of the Repatriation of Prisoners Act 1984 (power to provide for prisoner to be treated as having been released) for "section 244 or 246" substitute "Chapter 6 of Part 12".

Criminal Justice Act 1991 (c. 53)

5 In Schedule 12 to the Criminal Justice Act 1991, omit paragraphs 8 to 13 (transitional provisions relating to the coming into force of Part 2 of that Act).

Crime (Sentences) Act 1997 (c. 43)

6 Schedule 1 to the Crime (Sentences) Act 1997 (transfer of prisoners within the British Islands) is amended as follows.

7 In paragraph 8 (transfers to Scotland)—

(a) in sub-paragraph (2)(a), after "246 to 264A" insert ", 267A and 267B";

(b) in sub-paragraph (4)(a), for "and 249 to 264A" substitute ", 249 to 264A, 267A and 267B".

8 In paragraph 9(2)(a) and (4)(a) (transfers to Northern Ireland), for "and 254 to 264A" substitute ", 254 to 264A, 267A and 267B".

Extradition Act 2003 (c. 41)

9 The Extradition Act 2003 is amended as follows.

10 In section 59 (return of person to serve remainder of sentence), in subsection (11)—

(a) omit paragraph (a);

(b) in paragraph (b), for "section 244" substitute "Chapter 6 of Part 12".

11 In section 132 (return of person to serve remainder of sentence), in subsection (11)—

(a) omit paragraph (a);

(b) in paragraph (b), for "section 244" substitute "Chapter 6 of Part 12".

12 In section 153B (return of person in pursuance of undertaking), in subsection (10)(a)—

(a) omit sub-paragraph (i);

(b) in sub-paragraph (ii), for "section 244" substitute "Chapter 6 of Part 12".

Criminal Justice Act 2003 (c. 44)

13 The Criminal Justice Act 2003 is amended as follows.

14 In section 240A(1)(a) (crediting of periods of remand on bail), omit the words "committed on or after 4th April 2005".

15 (1) The repeal by section 25 of the Criminal Justice and Immigration Act 2008 of provisions in section 247 of the Criminal Justice Act 2003 comes fully into force.

(2) Accordingly, in paragraph 2 of Schedule 2 to the Criminal Justice and Immigration Act 2008 (Commencement No.2 and Transitional and Savings Provisions) Order 2008 (S.I. 2008/1586), omit "and 25".

16 Omit section 262 and Schedule 20 (prisoners liable to removal from United Kingdom).

17 Omit section 265(1A) (restriction on consecutive sentences for released prisoners).

Domestic Violence, Crime and Victims Act 2004 (c. 28)

18 Omit paragraph 46 of Schedule 10 to the Domestic Violence, Crime and Victims Act 2004.

Police and Justice Act 2006 (c. 48)

19 Omit paragraph 33 of Schedule 13 to the Police and Justice Act 2006.

Criminal Justice and Immigration Act 2008 (c. 4)

20 In the Criminal Justice and Immigration Act 2008, omit—
(a) sections 20(4)(b), 26 to 28, 32 and 33(1), (3), (5) and (6);
(b) paragraph 29(2) to (5) of Schedule 26;
(c) paragraphs 8 and 9 of Schedule 27.

Coroners and Justice Act 2009 (c. 25)

21 In the Coroners and Justice Act 2009, omit—
(a) section 145;
(b) paragraph 43 of Schedule 22.

Criminal Justice and Immigration Act 2008 (Commencement No.1 and Transitional Provisions) Order 2008 (S.I. 2008/1466)

22 Article 3 of the Criminal Justice and Immigration Act 2008 (Commencement No.1 and Transitional Provisions) Order 2008 (S.I. 2008/1466) is revoked.

SCHEDULE 17

Section 121

CRIMINAL JUSTICE ACT 2003: RESTATEMENT OF TRANSITIONAL PROVISION

1 The Criminal Justice Act 2003 is amended as follows.

2 In section 244 (duty to release prisoners on licence), after subsection (3) insert—

"(4) This section is subject to paragraphs 5, 6, 8, 25 and 28 of Schedule 20B (transitional cases)."

3 In section 247 (release on licence of prisoner serving extended sentence), after subsection (7) insert—

"(8) In its application to a person serving a sentence imposed before 14 July 2008, this section is subject to the modifications set out in paragraph 15 of Schedule 20B (transitional cases)."

4 In section 249 (duration of licence), at the end insert—

"(5) This section is subject to paragraphs 17, 19 and 26 of Schedule 20B (transitional cases)."

5 (1) Section 258 (early release of fine defaulters and contemnors) is amended as follows.

(2) After subsection (2) insert—

"(2A) Subsection (2) is subject to paragraph 35 of Schedule 20B (transitional cases)."

(3) In subsection (3) after "in this section" insert "or in paragraph 35 of Schedule 20B".

6 In section 260 (early removal of prisoners liable to removal from UK), after

subsection (7) insert—

"(8) Paragraphs 36 and 37 of Schedule 20B (transitional cases) make further provision about early removal of certain prisoners."

7 In section 263 (concurrent terms), after subsection (4) insert—

"(5) This section is subject to paragraphs 21, 31 and 32 of Schedule 20B (transitional cases)."

8 In section 264 (consecutive terms), after subsection (7) insert—

"(8) This section is subject to paragraphs 21, 22, 31, 32 and 33 of Schedule 20B (transitional cases)."

9 After section 267A (inserted by Schedule 16) insert—

"267B Modification of Chapter 6 in certain transitional cases

Schedule 20B (which modifies this Chapter so as to restate, with minor amendments, the effect of transitional provisions relating to the coming into force of this Chapter) has effect."

10 After Schedule 20A (inserted by Schedule 16) insert—

"SCHEDULE 20B Section 267B

MODIFICATIONS OF CHAPTER 6 OF PART 12 IN CERTAIN TRANSITIONAL CASES

PART 1

INTRODUCTORY

Interpretation

1 (1) The following provisions apply for the purposes of this Schedule.

(2) "The commencement date" means the date on which section 121 of the Legal Aid, Sentencing and Punishment of Offenders Act 2012 comes into force.

(3) "The 1967 Act" means the Criminal Justice Act 1967.

(4) "The 1991 Act" means the Criminal Justice Act 1991.

(5) A "section 85 extended sentence" means an extended sentence under section 85 of the Sentencing Act and includes (in accordance with paragraph 1(3) of Schedule 11 to that Act) a sentence under section 58 of the Crime and Disorder Act 1998.

(6) In relation to a section 85 extended sentence, "the custodial term" and "the extension period" have the meaning given by that section.

(7) References to section 86 of the Sentencing Act include (in accordance with paragraph 1(3) of Schedule 11 to that Act) section 44 of the 1991 Act as originally enacted.

(8) A "1967 Act sentence" is a sentence imposed before 1 October 1992.

(9) A "1991 Act sentence" is a sentence which is—
(a) imposed on or after 1 October 1992 but before 4 April 2005, or
(b) imposed on or after 4 April 2005 but before the commencement date and is either—
(i) imposed in respect of an offence committed before 4 April 2005, or
(ii) for a term of less than 12 months.

(10) A "2003 Act sentence" is a sentence which is—
(a) imposed on or after the commencement date, or
(b) imposed on or after 4 April 2005 but before the commencement date and is both—
(i) imposed in respect of an offence committed on or after 4 April 2005, and
(ii) for a term of 12 months or more.

(11) Where an offence is found to have been committed over a period of two or more days, or at some time during a period of two or more days, it is to be taken for the purposes of this Schedule to have been committed on the last of those days.

Explanation of dates

2 The following dates (which are mentioned in this Schedule) are dates on which changes to the law relating to the release and recall of prisoners came into force—

1 October 1992 is the date on which Part 2 of the 1991 Act came into force;

30 September 1998 is the date on which certain provisions of the Crime and Disorder Act 1998 came into force;

4 April 2005 is the date on which this Chapter came into force;

9 June 2008 is the date on which section 26 of the Criminal Justice and Immigration Act 2008 came into force;

14 July 2008 is the date on which certain other provisions of that Act came into force;

2 August 2010 is the date on which section 145 of the Coroners and Justice Act 2009 came into force.

PART 2

PRISONERS SERVING 1991 ACT SENTENCES ETC

3 (1) This Part applies to certain persons serving a 1991 Act sentence.

(2) This Part also applies to a person serving a 2003 Act sentence which is—
(a) a section 85 extended sentence, or
(b) an extended sentence imposed under section 227 or 228 before 14 July 2008.

(3) But this Part does not apply to a person who—
(a) has been released on licence under Part 2 of the 1991 Act,

(b) has been recalled to prison, and
(c) (whether or not having returned to custody in consequence of that recall) is unlawfully at large on the commencement date.

Duty to release on licence at two-thirds of sentence

4 (1) This paragraph applies to a person in relation to whom—
(a) all the conditions in sub-paragraph (2) are met, and
(b) the condition in any one or more of sub-paragraphs (3) to (5) is met.

(2) The conditions in this sub-paragraph are that—
(a) the person has been convicted of an offence committed before 4 April 2005,
(b) the person is serving a sentence of imprisonment imposed in respect of that offence on or after 1 October 1992 but before the commencement date,
(c) the sentence or (in the case of a section 85 extended sentence) the custodial term is for a term of 4 years or more, and
(d) the person has not previously been released from prison on licence in respect of that sentence.

(3) The condition in this sub-paragraph is that the offence (or one of the offences) in respect of which the sentence was imposed is—
(a) an offence specified in Schedule 15 (specified violent offences and specified sexual offences) as it had effect on 4 April 2005,
(b) an offence under any of sections 11, 12, 15 to 18, 54 and 56 to 63 of the Terrorism Act 2000,
(c) an offence under any of sections 47, 50 and 113 of the Anti-terrorism, Crime and Security Act 2001,
(d) an offence under section 12 of the Sexual Offences Act 1956,
(e) an offence of aiding, abetting counselling, procuring or inciting the commission of an offence listed in any of paragraphs (b) to (d), or
(f) an offence of conspiring or attempting to commit an offence listed in any of paragraphs (b) to (d).

(4) The condition in this sub-paragraph is that the person has served one-half of the sentence or (in the case of a section 85 extended sentence) of the custodial term before 9 June 2008.

(5) The condition in this sub-paragraph is that—
(a) the person is serving the sentence by virtue of having been transferred to the United Kingdom in pursuance of a warrant under section 1 of the Repatriation of Prisoners Act 1984,
(b) the warrant was issued before 9 June 2008, and
(c) the offence (or one of the offences) for which the person is serving the sentence corresponds to murder or to any

offence specified in Schedule 15 as it had effect on 4 April 2005.

5 (1) As soon as a person to whom paragraph 4 applies has served two-thirds of the sentence, it is the duty of the Secretary of State to release the person on licence under this paragraph.

(2) If the person is serving a section 85 extended sentence, the reference in sub-paragraph (1) to two-thirds of the sentence is a reference to two-thirds of the custodial term.

(3) Sub-paragraphs (1) and (2) apply in place of section 244 (release on licence of prisoners serving 12 months or more).

Duty to release on direction of Parole Board

6 (1) After a person to whom paragraph 4 applies has served one-half of the sentence, the Secretary of State must, if directed to do so by the Board, release the person on licence under this paragraph.

(2) The Board must not give a direction under sub-paragraph (1) unless the Board is satisfied that it is no longer necessary for the protection of the public that the person should be confined.

(3) If the person is serving a section 85 extended sentence, the reference in sub-paragraph (1) to one-half of the sentence is a reference to one-half of the custodial term.

(4) Sub-paragraphs (1) to (3) apply in place of section 244 (release on licence of prisoners serving 12 months or more).

Release on licence at one-half of sentence: section 85 extended sentence prisoners

7 (1) This paragraph applies to a person if—
(a) the person has been convicted of an offence committed on or after 30 September 1998 but before 4 April 2005,
(b) the person is serving a section 85 extended sentence in respect of that offence,
(c) the person has not previously been released from prison on licence in respect of that sentence, and
(d) paragraph 4 does not apply to the person.

8 (1) As soon as a person to whom paragraph 7 applies has served one-half of the custodial term, it is the duty of the Secretary of State to release the person on licence under this paragraph.

(2) Sub-paragraph (1) applies in place of section 243A or 244, as the case may be (release of prisoners serving less than 12 months, or serving 12 months or more).

Duty to release unconditionally at three-quarters of sentence

9 (1) This paragraph applies to a person if—
(a) the person has been convicted of an offence committed before 30 September 1998,
(b) the person is serving a sentence of imprisonment imposed in respect of that offence on or after 1 October 1992,

(c) the sentence is for a term of 12 months or more,

(d) the person has been released on licence under Part 2 of the 1991 Act, and

(e) the person has been recalled before 14 July 2008 (and has not been recalled after that date).

(2) But this paragraph does not apply if the court by which the person was sentenced ordered that section 86 of the Sentencing Act (extension of periods in custody and on licence in the case of certain sexual offences) should apply.

10 As soon as a person to whom paragraph 9 applies would (but for the earlier release) have served three-quarters of the sentence, it is the duty of the Secretary of State to release the person unconditionally.

Duty to release on licence at three-quarters of sentence

11 (1) This paragraph applies to a person who—

(a) has been convicted of an offence committed on or after 30 September 1998 but before 4 April 2005,

(b) is serving a sentence of imprisonment for a term of 12 months or more imposed in respect of that offence,

(c) has been released on licence under Part 2 of the 1991 Act, and

(d) has been recalled before 14 July 2008 (and has not been recalled after that date).

(2) But this paragraph does not apply if the person has been released and recalled more than once.

(3) Nor does this paragraph apply if the sentence is a section 85 extended sentence (paragraph 13 applying to such a case instead).

12 As soon as a person to whom paragraph 11 applies would (but for the earlier release) have served three-quarters of the sentence, it is the duty of the Secretary of State to release the person on licence.

Release on licence: re-release of section 85 extended sentence prisoners

13 (1) This paragraph applies to a person who—

(a) has been convicted of an offence committed on or after 30 September 1998 but before 4 April 2005,

(b) is serving a section 85 extended sentence imposed in respect of that offence,

(c) has been released on licence under Part 2 of the 1991 Act, and

(d) has been recalled before 14 July 2008 (and has not been recalled after that date).

(2) But this paragraph does not apply if the person has been released and recalled more than once.

14 (1) If a person to whom paragraph 13 applies is serving a sentence with a custodial term of less than 12 months, it is the duty of the Secretary of State to release the person on licence as soon as the

person would (but for the earlier release) have served the period found by adding—
(a) one-half of the custodial term, and
(b) the extension period.

(2) If a person to whom paragraph 13 applies is serving a sentence with a custodial term of 12 months or more, it is the duty of the Secretary of State to release the person on licence as soon as the person would (but for the earlier release) have served the period found by adding—
(a) three-quarters of the custodial term, and
(b) the extension period.

Release of section 227 or 228 extended sentence prisoners: Parole Board direction

15 (1) This paragraph applies to a person ("P") who is serving an extended sentence imposed under section 227 or 228 before 14 July 2008.

(2) Section 247 (release of prisoner on licence) applies to P with the following modifications.

(3) The Secretary of State must not release P under subsection (2) of that section unless the Board has directed P's release under that subsection.

(4) The Board must not give a direction under sub-paragraph (3) unless the Board is satisfied that it is no longer necessary for the protection of the public that the person should be confined.

(5) As soon as P has served the appropriate custodial term, the Secretary of State must release P on licence, unless P has previously been recalled under section 254.

Licence to remain in force to three-quarters of sentence

16 (1) This paragraph applies to a person to whom paragraph 4 applies.

(2) This paragraph also applies to a person if—
(a) the person has been convicted of an offence committed before 4 April 2005,
(b) the person is serving a sentence of imprisonment imposed in respect of that offence on or after 1 October 1992 but before the commencement date,
(c) that sentence is for a term of 12 months or more but less than 4 years, and
(d) the person has not previously been released from prison on licence in respect of that sentence.

(3) This paragraph also applies to a person if—
(a) the person has been convicted of an offence committed before 4 April 2005,
(b) the person is serving a sentence of imprisonment imposed in respect of that offence on or after 1 October 1992,
(c) that sentence is for a term of 12 months or more,

(d) the person has been released on licence under Part 2 of the 1991 Act, and

(e) the person has been recalled before 14 July 2008 (and has not been recalled after that date).

(4) But this paragraph does not apply if the person has been released and recalled more than once.

(5) Nor does this paragraph apply if—

(a) the person is serving a section 85 extended sentence, or

(b) the court by which the person was sentenced ordered that section 86 of the Sentencing Act (extension of periods in custody and on licence in the case of certain sexual offences) should apply.

(6) If a person has been—

(a) released under section 34A of the 1991 Act or section 246 (home detention curfew), and

(b) recalled under section 38A(1)(b) of the 1991 Act or section 255(1)(b) (no longer possible to monitor curfew),

the release and recall are to be disregarded for the purposes of this paragraph.

17 (1) Where a person to whom paragraph 16 applies is released on licence under section 244 or paragraph 5 or 6, the licence shall remain in force until the date on which the person would (but for the release) have served three-quarters of the sentence.

(2) Sub-paragraph (1) is subject to any revocation under section 254.

(3) Sub-paragraphs (1) and (2) apply in place of section 249 (duration of licence).

Period for which licence to remain in force: section 85 extended sentence prisoners

18 This paragraph applies to a person who—

(a) has been convicted of an offence committed on or after 30 September 1998 but before 4 April 2005,

(b) is serving a section 85 extended sentence imposed in respect of that offence, and

(c) has not previously been released from prison on licence in respect of that sentence.

19 (1) Where a person to whom paragraph 18 applies is released on licence and the custodial term is less than 12 months, the licence shall remain in force until the end of the period found by adding—

(a) one-half of the custodial term, and

(b) the extension period.

(2) Where a person to whom paragraph 18 applies is released on licence and the custodial term is 12 months or more, the licence shall remain in force until the end of the period found by adding—

(a) three-quarters of the custodial term, and

(b) the extension period.

(3) Sub-paragraphs (1) and (2) are subject to any revocation under section 254.

(4) Sub-paragraphs (1) to (3) apply in place of section 249 (duration of licence).

Concurrent or consecutive terms

20 Paragraphs 21 and 22 apply where a person ("P") is serving two or more sentences of imprisonment imposed on or after 1 October 1992 and—

(a) the sentences were passed on the same occasion, or

(b) where they were passed on different occasions, the person has not been released under Part 2 of the 1991 Act or under this Chapter at any time during the period beginning with the first and ending with the last of those occasions.

21 (1) This paragraph applies if each of the sentences is a 1991 Act sentence.

(2) Sections 263 and 264 (consecutive and concurrent terms) do not apply in relation to the sentences.

(3) For the purposes of any reference in this Chapter, however expressed, to the term of imprisonment to which P has been sentenced or which, or part of which, P has served, the terms are to be treated as a single term.

(4) If one or more of the sentences is a section 85 extended sentence—

(a) for the purpose of determining the single term mentioned in sub-paragraph (3), the extension period or periods is or are to be disregarded, and

(b) the period for which P is to be on licence in respect of the single term is to be increased in accordance with sub-paragraph (5).

(5) That period is to be increased—

(a) if only one of the sentences is a section 85 extended sentence, by the extension period;

(b) if there is more than one such sentence and they are wholly or partly concurrent, by the longest of the extension periods;

(c) if there is more than one such sentence and they are consecutive, by the aggregate of the extension periods.

22 (1) This paragraph applies where two or more sentences are to be served consecutively on each other and—

(a) one or more of those sentences is a 1991 Act sentence, and

(b) one or more of them is a 2003 Act sentence.

(2) Section 264 does not affect the length of the period which P must serve in prison in respect of the 1991 Act sentence or sentences.

(3) Nothing in this Chapter requires the Secretary of State to release P until P has served a period equal in length to the aggregate of the length of the periods which P must serve in relation to each of the sentences mentioned in sub-paragraph (1).

(4) If P is also serving one or more 1967 Act sentences, paragraphs 32 and 33 apply instead of this paragraph.

PART 3

PRISONERS SERVING 1967 ACT SENTENCES

23 (1) This Part applies to certain persons serving a 1967 Act sentence.

(2) But this Part does not apply to a person who—
(a) has been released on licence,
(b) has been recalled to prison, and
(c) (whether or not having returned to custody in consequence of that recall) is unlawfully at large on the commencement date.

(3) In this Part, references to release under Part 2 of the 1991 Act include release under section 60 of the 1967 Act.

Sentence of more than 12 months imposed before 1 October 1992

24 (1) This paragraph applies to a person if—
(a) the person is serving a sentence of imprisonment imposed before 1 October 1992,
(b) the sentence is for a term of more than 12 months, and
(c) the person has not previously been released from prison on licence in respect of that sentence.

(2) This paragraph also applies to a person if—
(a) the person is serving a sentence of imprisonment imposed before 1 October 1992,
(b) the sentence is for a term of more than 12 months,
(c) the person has been released on licence under Part 2 of the 1991 Act, and
(d) the person has been recalled before 14 July 2008 (and has not been recalled after that date).

(3) But this paragraph does not apply if, on the passing of the sentence, an extended sentence certificate was issued (see paragraph 27).

(4) If a person has been—
(a) released under section 34A of the 1991 Act or section 246 (home detention curfew), and
(b) recalled under section 38A(1)(b) of the 1991 Act or section 255(1)(b) (no longer possible to monitor curfew),

the release and recall are to be disregarded for the purposes of this paragraph.

25 (1) It is the duty of the Secretary of State to release a person to whom paragraph 24 applies unconditionally under this paragraph—
(a) in the case of a person falling within paragraph 24(1), as soon as the person has served two-thirds of the sentence;

(b) in the case of a person falling within paragraph 24(2), as soon as the person would (but for the earlier release) have served two-thirds of the sentence.

(2) After a person falling within paragraph 24(1) has served one-third of the sentence or six months, whichever is longer, the Secretary of State must, if directed to do so by the Board, release the person on licence under this paragraph.

(3) The Board must not give a direction under sub-paragraph (2) unless the Board is satisfied that it is no longer necessary for the protection of the public that the person should be confined.

(4) Sub-paragraphs (1) to (3) apply in place of section 244 (release on licence of prisoners serving 12 months or more).

26 (1) Where a person to whom paragraph 24 applies is released on licence under paragraph 25(2), the licence shall remain in force until the date on which the person would (but for the release) have served two-thirds of the sentence.

(2) Sub-paragraph (1) is subject to any revocation under section 254.

(3) Sub-paragraphs (1) and (2) apply in place of section 249 (duration of licence).

Extended sentence of more than 12 months imposed before 1 October 1992

27 (1) This paragraph applies to a person if—

(a) the person is serving a sentence of imprisonment imposed before 1 October 1992,

(b) the sentence is for a term of more than 12 months,

(c) on the passing of the sentence an extended sentence certificate was issued, and

(d) the person has not previously been released from prison on licence in respect of that sentence.

(2) This paragraph also applies to a person if—

(a) the person is serving a sentence of imprisonment imposed before 1 October 1992,

(b) the sentence is for a term of more than 12 months,

(c) on the passing of the sentence an extended sentence certificate was issued,

(d) the person has been released on licence under Part 2 of the 1991 Act, and

(e) the person has been recalled before 14 July 2008 (and has not been recalled after that date).

(3) In this paragraph "extended sentence certificate" means a certificate was issued under section 28 of the Powers of Criminal Courts Act 1973 (punishment of persistent offenders) stating that an extended term of imprisonment was imposed on the person under that section.

28 (1) It is the duty of the Secretary of State to release a person to whom paragraph 27 applies on licence under this paragraph—

(a) in the case of a person falling within paragraph 27(1), as soon as the person has served two-thirds of the sentence;

(b) in the case of a person falling within paragraph 27(2), as soon as the person would (but for the earlier release) have served two-thirds of the sentence.

(2) After a person falling within paragraph 27(1) has served one-third of the sentence or six months, whichever is longer, the Secretary of State must, if directed to do so by the Board, release the person on licence under this paragraph.

(3) The Board must not give a direction under sub-paragraph (2) unless the Board is satisfied that it is no longer necessary for the protection of the public that the person should be confined.

(4) Sub-paragraphs (1) to (3) apply in place of section 244 (release on licence of prisoners serving twelve months or more).

Additional days

29 (1) Prison rules made by virtue of section 257 may include provision for applying any provisions of this Chapter, in relation to any person falling within sub-paragraph (2), as if the person had been awarded such number of additional days as may be determined by or under the rules.

(2) A person falls within this sub-paragraph if—

(a) the person was released on licence under section 60 of the 1967 Act before 1 October 1992 and the licence was in force on that date, or

(b) the person was, on that date, serving a custodial sentence,

and (in either case) the person has forfeited any remission of the sentence.

Concurrent or consecutive terms

30 Paragraphs 31 to 33 apply where a person ("P") is serving two or more sentences of imprisonment and—

(a) the sentences were passed on the same occasion, or

(b) where they were passed on different occasions, the person has not been released under Part 2 of the 1991 Act or under this Chapter at any time during the period beginning with the first and ending with the last of those occasions.

31 (1) This paragraph applies where each of the sentences is a 1967 Act sentence.

(2) Sections 263 and 264 (consecutive and concurrent terms) do not apply in relation to the sentences.

(3) For the purposes of any reference in this Chapter, however expressed, to the term of imprisonment to which P has been sentenced or which, or part of which, P has served, the terms are to be treated as a single term.

32 (1) This paragraph applies where—

(a) one or more of the sentences is a 1967 Act sentence, and

(b) one or more of them is a 1991 Act sentence.

(2) Sections 263 and 264 (consecutive and concurrent terms) do not apply in relation to the sentences mentioned in sub-paragraph (1).

(3) For the purposes of any reference in this Chapter, however expressed, to the term of imprisonment to which P has been sentenced or which, or part of which, P has served—

(a) the terms mentioned in sub-paragraph (1) are to be treated as a single term, and

(b) that single term is to be treated as if it were a 1967 Act sentence.

(4) If one or more of the sentences is a section 85 extended sentence—

(a) for the purpose of determining the single term mentioned in sub-paragraph (3), the extension period or periods is or are to be disregarded, and

(b) the period for which P is to be on licence in respect of the single term is to be increased in accordance with sub-paragraph (5).

(5) That period is to be increased—

(a) if only one of the sentences is a section 85 extended sentence, by the extension period;

(b) if there is more than one such sentence and they are wholly or partly concurrent, by the longest of the extension periods;

(c) if there is more than one such sentence and they are consecutive, by the aggregate of the extension periods.

(6) If P is also serving a 2003 Act sentence, sub-paragraph (3) is to be applied before the period mentioned in section 263(2)(c) (concurrent terms) or paragraph 33(3) (consecutive terms) is calculated.

33 (1) This paragraph applies where two or more sentences are to be served consecutively on each other and—

(a) one or more of those sentences is a 1967 Act sentence, and

(b) one or more of them is a 2003 Act sentence.

(2) Section 264 does not affect the length of the period which P must serve in prison in respect of the 1967 Act sentence or sentences.

(3) Nothing in this Chapter requires the Secretary of State to release P until P has served a period equal in length to the aggregate of the length of the periods which P must serve in relation to each of the sentences mentioned in sub-paragraph (1).

PART 4

PROVISIONS APPLYING GENERALLY

Licence conditions

34 (1) This paragraph applies to any licence (a "Parole Board licence") which falls within sub-paragraph (2) or (3).

(2) A licence falls within this sub-paragraph if—

(a) it is or was granted to a person ("P") on P's release (at any time) on the recommendation or direction of the Board, and

(b) P has not been released otherwise than on such a recommendation or direction.

(3) A licence falls within this sub-paragraph if—

(a) it is or was granted to a person ("P") on P's release (at any time), and

(b) condition A or condition B is met.

(4) Condition A is that, before 2 August 2010, the Board exercised the function under section 37(5) of the 1991 Act of making recommendations as to any condition to be included or inserted as a condition in a licence granted to P (including by making a recommendation that no condition should be included in such a licence).

(5) Condition B is that, before 2 August 2010—

(a) P was released on licence under section 33(2), (3) or (3A) or 35(1) of the 1991 Act, and

(b) the Board exercised the function under section 37(5) of that Act of—

(i) making recommendations as to the inclusion or insertion of a condition in a licence granted to P (including by making a recommendation that no condition should be included in such a licence), or

(ii) making recommendations as to the variation or cancellation of any such condition (including a recommendation that the condition should not be varied or cancelled).

(6) The Secretary of State must not—

(a) include on release, or subsequently insert, a condition in a Parole Board licence, or

(b) vary or cancel any such condition,

except in accordance with directions of the Board.

Fine defaulters and contemnors

35 (1) This paragraph applies to any person if—

(a) the person has been committed to prison or to be detained under section 108 of the Sentencing Act—

(i) in default of payment of a sum adjudged to be paid by a conviction, or

(ii) for contempt of court or any kindred offence,

(b) the person was so committed or detained before 4 April 2005, and

(c) the term for which the person was committed or detained is 12 months or more.

(2) As soon as a person to whom this paragraph applies has served two-thirds of the term, it is the duty of the Secretary of State to release the person unconditionally.

(3) Sub-paragraph (2) applies in place of section 258(2) (early release of fine defaulters and contemnors).

Early removal of prisoners liable to removal from UK

36 (1) This paragraph applies to any person who—

(a) has served one-half of a sentence of imprisonment, and

(b) has not been released on licence under this Chapter.

(2) The reference in sub-paragraph (1)(a) to one-half of a sentence is—

(a) in the case of a section 85 extended sentence, a reference to one-half of the custodial term;

(b) in the case of an extended sentence imposed under section 227 or 228, a reference to one-half of the appropriate custodial term.

37 (1) If a person to whom paragraph 36 applies—

(a) is liable to removal from the United Kingdom, and

(b) has not been removed from prison under section 260 during the period mentioned in subsection (1) of that section,

the Secretary of State may remove the person from prison under that section at any time after the end of that period.

(2) Sub-paragraph (1) applies whether or not the Board has directed the person's release under paragraph 6, 15, 25 or 28."

SCHEDULE 18

Section 122

LIFE SENTENCE FOR SECOND LISTED OFFENCE ETC: NEW SCHEDULE 15B TO CRIMINAL JUSTICE ACT 2003

In the Criminal Justice Act 2003, after Schedule 15A insert—

"SCHEDULE 15B

Sections 224A, 226A and 246A

OFFENCES LISTED FOR THE PURPOSES OF SECTIONS 224A, 226A AND 246A

PART 1

OFFENCES UNDER THE LAW OF ENGLAND AND WALES LISTED FOR THE PURPOSES OF SECTIONS 224A(1), 224A(4), 226A AND 246A

The following offences to the extent that they are offences under the law of England and Wales—

1 Manslaughter.

2 An offence under section 4 of the Offences against the Person Act 1861 (soliciting murder).

3 An offence under section 18 of that Act (wounding with intent to cause grievous bodily harm).

4 An offence under section 16 of the Firearms Act 1968 (possession of a firearm with intent to endanger life).

5 An offence under section 17(1) of that Act (use of a firearm to resist arrest).

6 An offence under section 18 of that Act (carrying a firearm with criminal intent).

7 An offence of robbery under section 8 of the Theft Act 1968 where, at some time during the commission of the offence, the offender had in his possession a firearm or an imitation firearm within the meaning of the Firearms Act 1968.

8 An offence under section 1 of the Protection of Children Act 1978 (indecent images of children).

9 An offence under section 56 of the Terrorism Act 2000 (directing terrorist organisation).

10 An offence under section 57 of that Act (possession of article for terrorist purposes).

11 An offence under section 59 of that Act (inciting terrorism overseas) if the offender is liable on conviction on indictment to imprisonment for life.

12 An offence under section 47 of the Anti-terrorism, Crime and Security Act 2001 (use etc of nuclear weapons).

13 An offence under section 50 of that Act (assisting or inducing certain weapons-related acts overseas).

14 An offence under section 113 of that Act (use of noxious substance or thing to cause harm or intimidate).

15 An offence under section 1 of the Sexual Offences Act 2003 (rape).

16 An offence under section 2 of that Act (assault by penetration).

17 An offence under section 4 of that Act (causing a person to engage in sexual activity without consent) if the offender is liable on conviction on indictment to imprisonment for life.

18 An offence under section 5 of that Act (rape of a child under 13).

19 An offence under section 6 of that Act (assault of a child under 13 by penetration).

20 An offence under section 7 of that Act (sexual assault of a child under 13).

21 An offence under section 8 of that Act (causing or inciting a child under 13 to engage in sexual activity).

22 An offence under section 9 of that Act (sexual activity with a child).

23 An offence under section 10 of that Act (causing or inciting a child to engage in sexual activity).

24 An offence under section 11 of that Act (engaging in sexual activity in the presence of a child).

25 An offence under section 12 of that Act (causing a child to watch a sexual act).

26 An offence under section 14 of that Act (arranging or facilitating commission of a child sex offence).

27 An offence under section 15 of that Act (meeting a child following sexual grooming etc).

28 An offence under section 25 of that Act (sexual activity with a child family member) if the offender is aged 18 or over at the time of the offence.

29 An offence under section 26 of that Act (inciting a child family member to engage in sexual activity) if the offender is aged 18 or over at the time of the offence.

30 An offence under section 30 of that Act (sexual activity with a person with a mental disorder impeding choice) if the offender is liable on conviction on indictment to imprisonment for life.

31 An offence under section 31 of that Act (causing or inciting a person with a mental disorder to engage in sexual activity) if the offender is liable on conviction on indictment to imprisonment for life.

32 An offence under section 34 of that Act (inducement, threat or deception to procure sexual activity with a person with a mental disorder) if the offender is liable on conviction on indictment to imprisonment for life.

33 An offence under section 35 of that Act (causing a person with a mental disorder to engage in or agree to engage in sexual activity by inducement etc) if the offender is liable on conviction on indictment to imprisonment for life.

34 An offence under section 47 of that Act (paying for sexual services of a child) against a person aged under 16.

35 An offence under section 48 of that Act (causing or inciting child prostitution or pornography).

36 An offence under section 49 of that Act (controlling a child prostitute or a child involved in pornography).

37 An offence under section 50 of that Act (arranging or facilitating child prostitution or pornography).

38 An offence under section 62 of that Act (committing an offence with intent to commit a sexual offence) if the offender is liable on conviction on indictment to imprisonment for life.

39 An offence under section 5 of the Domestic Violence, Crime and Victims Act 2004 (causing or allowing the death of a child or vulnerable adult).

40 An offence under section 5 of the Terrorism Act 2006 (preparation of terrorist acts).

41 An offence under section 9 of that Act (making or possession of radioactive device or materials).

42 An offence under section 10 of that Act (misuse of radioactive devices or material and misuse and damage of facilities).

43 An offence under section 11 of that Act (terrorist threats relating to radioactive devices, materials or facilities).

44 (1) An attempt to commit an offence specified in the preceding paragraphs of this Part of this Schedule ("a listed offence") or murder.

(2) Conspiracy to commit a listed offence or murder.

(3) Incitement to commit a listed offence or murder.

(4) An offence under Part 2 of the Serious Crime Act 2007 in relation to which a listed offence or murder is the offence (or one of the offences) which the person intended or believed would be committed.

(5) Aiding, abetting, counselling or procuring the commission of a listed offence.

PART 2

FURTHER OFFENCES UNDER THE LAW OF ENGLAND AND WALES LISTED FOR THE PURPOSES OF SECTIONS 224A(4), 226A AND 246A

The following offences to the extent that they are offences under the law of England and Wales—

45 Murder.

46 (1) Any offence that—

(a) was abolished (with or without savings) before the coming into force of this Schedule, and

(b) would, if committed on the relevant day, have constituted an offence specified in Part 1 of this Schedule.

(2) "Relevant day", in relation to an offence, means—

(a) for the purposes of this paragraph as it applies for the purposes of section 246A(2), the day on which the offender was convicted of that offence, and

(b) for the purposes of this paragraph as it applies for the purposes of sections 224A(4) and 226A(2), the day on which the offender was convicted of the offence referred to in section 224A(1)(a) or 226A(1)(a) (as appropriate).

PART 3

OFFENCES UNDER SERVICE LAW LISTED FOR THE PURPOSES OF SECTIONS 224A(4), 226A AND 246A

47 An offence under section 70 of the Army Act 1955, section 70 of the Air Force Act 1955 or section 42 of the Naval Discipline Act 1957 as respects which the corresponding civil offence (within the meaning of the Act in question) is an offence specified in Part 1 or 2 of this Schedule.

48 (1) An offence under section 42 of the Armed Forces Act 2006 as respects which the corresponding offence under the law of England and Wales (within the meaning given by that section) is an offence specified in Part 1 or 2 of this Schedule.

(2) Section 48 of the Armed Forces Act 2006 (attempts, conspiracy etc) applies for the purposes of this paragraph as if the reference in subsection (3)(b) of that section to any of the following provisions of that Act were a reference to this paragraph.

PART 4

OFFENCES UNDER THE LAW OF SCOTLAND, NORTHERN IRELAND OR A MEMBER STATE OTHER THAN THE UNITED KINGDOM LISTED FOR THE PURPOSES OF SECTIONS 224A(4) AND 226A

49 An offence for which the person was convicted in Scotland, Northern Ireland or a member State other than the United Kingdom and which, if committed in England and Wales at the time of the conviction, would have constituted an offence specified in Part 1 or 2 of this Schedule.

PART 5

INTERPRETATION

50 In this Schedule "imprisonment for life" includes custody for life and detention for life."

SCHEDULE 19

Section 122

LIFE SENTENCE FOR SECOND LISTED OFFENCE: CONSEQUENTIAL AND TRANSITORY PROVISION

PART 1

CONSEQUENTIAL PROVISION

Mental Health Act 1983 (c. 20)

1 In section 37 of the Mental Health Act 1983 (powers of courts to order hospital admission), in subsection (1A), after paragraph (b) insert—

"(ba) under section 224A of the Criminal Justice Act 2003,".

Criminal Justice Act 1988 (c. 33)

2 In section 36 of the Criminal Justice Act 1988 (reviews of sentencing), in subsection (2)(b)(iii), after "section" insert "224A,".

Powers of Criminal Courts (Sentencing) Act 2000 (c. 6)

3 The Powers of Criminal Courts (Sentencing) Act 2000 is amended as follows.

4 In section 12 (absolute and conditional discharge), in subsection (1), before "225(2)" insert "224A,".

5 In section 130 (compensation orders against convicted persons), in subsection (2), before "225(2)" insert "224A,".

6 In section 146 (driving disqualification for any offence), in subsection (2), before "225(2)" insert "224A,".

7 In section 164 (interpretation), in subsection (3)(c), after "section" insert "224A,".

Criminal Justice Act 2003 (c. 44)

8 The Criminal Justice Act 2003 is amended as follows.

9 In section 142 (purposes of sentencing: offenders aged 18 and over), in subsection (2)(c)—

(a) after "weapon)" insert ", under section 224A of this Act (life sentence for second listed offence for certain dangerous offenders)", and

(b) for "(dangerous offenders)" substitute "(imprisonment or detention for life for certain dangerous offenders)".

10 In section 150 (community sentence not available where sentence fixed by law etc), at the end of paragraph (ca) (but before the "or") insert—

"(cb) falls to be imposed under section 224A of this Act (life sentence for second listed offence for certain dangerous offenders),".

11 In section 152 (general restrictions on imposing discretionary custodial sentence), in subsection (1)(b), before "225(2)" insert "224A,".

12 In section 153 (length of discretionary custodial sentences: general provision), in subsection (1), before "225" insert "224A,".

13 In section 156 (pre-sentence reports and other requirements), after subsection (8) insert—

"(9) References in subsections (1) and (3) to a court forming the opinions mentioned in sections 152(2) and 153(2) include a court forming those opinions for the purposes of section 224A(3)."

14 In section 163 (general power of Crown Court to fine offender convicted on indictment) before "225(2)" insert "224A,".

15 Before section 224 insert—

"Interpretation".

16 In section 224 (meaning of "specified offence" etc), in subsection (2)(b), for "225" substitute "224A".

17 After section 224 (and before section 224A) insert—

"Life sentences".

18 After section 226 insert—

"Extended sentences".

19 Before section 231 insert—

"Supplementary".

20 (1) Section 231 (appeals where convictions set aside) is amended as follows.

(2) Before subsection (1) insert—

"(A1) Subsection (2) applies where—

(a) a sentence has been imposed on a person under section 224A,

(b) a previous conviction of that person has been subsequently set aside on appeal, and

(c) without that conviction, the previous offence condition in section 224A(4) would not have been met."

(3) In subsection (1), for "This section" substitute "Subsection (2) also".

(4) After subsection (2) insert—

"(3) Subsection (4) applies where—

(a) a sentence has been imposed on a person under section 224A,

(b) a previous sentence imposed on that person has been subsequently modified on appeal, and

(c) taking account of that modification, the previous offence condition in section 224A(4) would not have been met.

(4) Notwithstanding anything in section 18 of the Criminal Appeal Act 1968, notice of appeal against the sentence mentioned in subsection (3)(a) may be given at any time within 28 days from the date on which the previous sentence was modified."

21 After section 232 insert—

"232A Certificates of conviction

Where—

(a) on any date after the commencement of Schedule 15B a person is convicted in England and Wales of an offence listed in that Schedule, and

(b) the court by or before which the person is so convicted states in open court that the person has been convicted of such an offence on that date, and

(c) that court subsequently certifies that fact,

that certificate is evidence, for the purposes of section 224A, that the person was convicted of such an offence on that date."

22 In section 305(4) (interpretation of Part 12), after paragraph (ba) insert—

"(bb) a sentence falls to be imposed under section 224A if the court is obliged by that section to pass a sentence of imprisonment for life,".

Coroners and Justice Act 2009 (c. 25)

23 In section 125(6) of the Coroners and Justice Act 2009 (sentencing guidelines: duty of court) after paragraph (d) insert—

"(da) section 224A of that Act (life sentence for second listed offence for certain dangerous offenders);".

PART 2

TRANSITORY PROVISION

24 (1) In relation to any time before the coming into force of section 61 of the Criminal Justice and Court Services Act 2000 (abolition of sentences of detention in a young offender institution, custody for life etc), Part 12 of the Criminal Justice Act 2003 (sentencing) has effect with the following modifications.

(2) In section 224A (life sentence for second listed offence)—

(a) in subsection (2), after "imprisonment for life" insert "or, in the case of a person aged at least 18 but under 21, custody for life under section 94 of the Sentencing Act", and

(b) in subsection (3), after "more" insert "or, if the person is aged at least 18 but under 21, a sentence of detention in a young offender institution for such a period".

(3) In section 305(4) (interpretation of Part 12), in paragraph (bb) (inserted by paragraph 22 of this Schedule), after "imprisonment for life" insert "or, if the person is aged at least 18 but under 21, custody for life".

SCHEDULE 20

Section 125

RELEASE OF NEW EXTENDED SENTENCE PRISONERS: CONSEQUENTIAL AMENDMENTS OF CHAPTER 6 OF PART 12 OF THE CRIMINAL JUSTICE ACT 2003

1 Chapter 6 of Part 12 of the Criminal Justice Act 2003 (sentencing: release and recall) (as amended by Chapter 4 of Part 3 of this Act) is amended as follows.

2 (1) Section 237 (meaning of "fixed-term prisoner" etc) is amended as follows.

(2) In subsection (1)(b), before "227" insert "226A, 226B,".

(3) In subsection (3), before "227" insert "226A or".

3 In section 238 (power of court to recommend licence conditions), in subsection (4), for "228" substitute "226B".

4 In section 240ZA (time remanded in custody to count as time served), in subsection (11), before "227" insert "226A, 226B,".

5 (1) Section 246 (power to release prisoners on licence) is amended as follows.

(2) In subsection (4)(a), after "section" insert "226A,".

(3) In subsection (6), in the definition of "term of imprisonment", before "227" insert "226A, 226B,".

6 (1) Section 250 (licence conditions) is amended as follows.

(2) In subsection (4)—

(a) before the first "227" insert "226A or", and

(b) before the second "227" insert "226A, 226B,".

(3) After subsection (5) insert—

"(5A) In respect of a prisoner serving an extended sentence imposed under section 226A or 226B whose release is directed by the Board under section 246A(5), a licence under—

(a) section 246A(5) (initial release), or

(b) section 255C (release after recall),

may not include conditions referred to in subsection (4)(b)(ii) unless the Board directs the Secretary of State to include them."

7 In section 255A (further release after recall), in subsection (7)(a) (meaning of "extended sentence prisoner"), after "section" insert "226A, 226B,".

8 In section 258 (early release of fine defaulters and contemnors), in subsection (3A), before "227" insert "226A, 226B,".

9 (1) Section 260 (early removal of prisoners liable to removal from UK) is amended as follows.

(2) After subsection (2) insert—

"(2A) If a fixed-term prisoner serving an extended sentence imposed under section 226A or 226B—

(a) is liable to removal from the United Kingdom, and

(b) has not been removed from prison under this section during the period mentioned in subsection (1),

the Secretary of State may remove the prisoner from prison under this section at any time after the end of that period.

(2B) Subsection (2A) applies whether or not the Board has directed the prisoner's release under section 246A."

(3) In subsection (5), after "244" (but before ", 247") insert ", 246A".

(4) In subsection (7), before paragraph (a) insert—

"(za) in relation to a prisoner serving an extended sentence imposed under section 226A or 226B, has the meaning given by paragraph (a) or (b) of the definition in section 246A(8);".

10 (1) Section 261 (re-entry to UK of offender removed early) is amended as follows.

(2) In subsection (5)(b), for "or 244" substitute ", 244 or 246A".

(3) In subsection (6), in the definition of "requisite custodial period", before paragraph (a) insert—

"(za) in relation to a prisoner serving an extended sentence imposed under section 226A or 226B, has the meaning given by paragraph (a) or (b) of the definition in section 246A(8);".

11 In section 263 (concurrent terms), in subsection (4), before "227" insert "226A, 226B,".

12 (1) Section 264 (consecutive terms) is amended as follows.

(2) In subsection (6)(a) (definition of "custodial period"), before sub-paragraph (i) insert—

"(zi) in relation to an extended sentence imposed under section 226A or 226B, means two-thirds of the appropriate custodial term determined by the court under that section,".

(3) In subsection (7), before "227" insert "226A, 226B,".

13 In section 265 (restriction on consecutive sentences for released prisoners), in subsection (2), before "227" insert "226A, 226B,".

SCHEDULE 21

Section 126

ABOLITION OF CERTAIN SENTENCES FOR DANGEROUS OFFENDERS AND NEW EXTENDED SENTENCES: CONSEQUENTIAL AND TRANSITORY PROVISION

PART 1

CONSEQUENTIAL PROVISION

Juries Act 1974 (c. 23)

1 In Part 2 of Schedule 1 to the Juries Act 1974 (persons disqualified from jury service) in paragraph 6(d), before "227" insert "226A, 226B,".

Rehabilitation of Offenders Act 1974 (c. 53)

2 In section 5 of the Rehabilitation of Offenders Act 1974 (sentences excluded from rehabilitation under that Act), in subsection (1)(f), before "227" insert "226A, 226B,".

Criminal Justice Act 1982 (c. 48)

3 In section 32 of the Criminal Justice Act 1982 (early release of prisoners), in subsection (1)(a), before "227" insert "226A or".

Road Traffic Offenders Act 1988 (c. 53)

4 (1) Section 35A of the Road Traffic Offenders Act 1988 (extension of disqualification where custodial sentence imposed as well as driving disqualification) is amended as follows.

(2) In subsection (4)(e)—

(a) for "227" substitute "226A",

(b) for "half" substitute "two-thirds of", and

(c) for "227(2C)(a)" substitute "226A(5)(a)".

(3) In subsection (4)(f)—

(a) for "228" substitute "226B",

(b) for "half" substitute "two-thirds of", and

(c) for "228(2B)(a)" substitute "226B(3)(a)".

(4) In subsection (8), omit "or 247(2)".

(5) In subsection (9), omit paragraph (b).

Crime (Sentences) Act 1997 (c. 43)

5 In Schedule 1 to the Crime (Sentences) Act 1997 (transfer of prisoners within the British Islands), in paragraph 9(2)(a), after "244," insert "246A,".

Crime and Disorder Act 1998 (c. 37)

6 In section 51A of the Crime and Disorder Act 1998 (sending cases to the Crown Court: children and young persons), in subsection (3)(d), for "226(3) or 228(2)" substitute "226B".

Powers of Criminal Courts (Sentencing) Act 2000 (c. 6)

7 The Powers of Criminal Courts (Sentencing) Act 2000 is amended as follows.

8 In section 3A (committal for sentence of dangerous adult offenders), in subsection (2), for "225(3) or 227(2)" substitute "226A".

9 In section 3C (committal for sentence of dangerous young offenders), in subsection (2), for "226(3) or 228(2)" substitute "226B".

10 In section 76 (meaning of "custodial sentence"), in subsection (1)(bc), after "section" insert "226B or".

11 (1) Section 82A (determination of tariffs of life prisoners) is amended as follows.

(2) Omit subsection (4A).

(3) In subsection (7), for the definition of "life sentence" substitute—

""life sentence" means a sentence mentioned in subsection (2) of section 34 of the Crime (Sentences) Act 1997 other than a sentence mentioned in paragraph (d) or (e) of that subsection."

12 (1) Section 99 (conversion of sentence of detention to sentence of imprisonment) is amended as follows.

(2) In subsection (3), omit the words from "; and" to the end.

(3) After that subsection insert—

"(3A) Where the Secretary of State gives a direction under subsection (1) above in relation to an offender serving an extended sentence of detention imposed under Chapter 5 of Part 12 of the Criminal Justice Act 2003—

(a) if the sentence was imposed under section 226B of that Act, the offender shall be treated as if the offender had been sentenced under section 226A of that Act, and

(b) if the sentence was imposed under section 228 of that Act, the offender shall be treated as if the offender had been sentenced under section 227 of that Act."

(4) In subsection (5)(c), after "section" insert "226B or".

13 In section 100 (offenders under 18: detention and training orders), in subsection (1), for "228" substitute "226B".

14 (1) Section 106A (interaction of detention and training orders with sentences of detention) is amended as follows.

(2) In subsection (1), in paragraph (b) of the definition of "sentence of detention", after "section" insert "226B or".

(3) In subsection (6)—

(a) before "228" insert "226B or", and

(b) after "Board under" insert "subsection (5)(b) of section 246A or (as the case may be)".

15 (1) Section 147A (extension of driving disqualification where custodial sentence also imposed) is amended as follows.

(2) In subsection (4)(e)—

(a) for "227" substitute "226A",

(b) for "half" substitute "two-thirds of", and

(c) for "227(2C)(a)" substitute "226A(5)(a)".

(3) In subsection (4)(f)—

(a) for "228" substitute "226B",

(b) for "half" substitute "two-thirds of", and

(c) for "228(2B)(a)" substitute "226B(3)(a)".

(4) In subsection (8), omit "or 247(2)".

(5) In subsection (9), omit paragraph (b).

Criminal Justice and Court Services Act 2000 (c. 43)

16 The Criminal Justice and Court Services Act 2000 is amended as follows.

17 In section 62 (release on licence etc: conditions as to monitoring), in subsection (5)(f), after "226" insert ", 226B".

18 In section 64 (release on licence: drug testing requirements), in subsection (5)(f), after "226" insert ", 226B".

Sexual Offences Act 2003 (c. 42)

19 In section 131 of the Sexual Offences Act 2003 (young offenders: application), in paragraph (l), before "228" insert "226B or".

Criminal Justice Act 2003 (c. 44)

20 The Criminal Justice Act 2003 is amended as follows.

21 In section 153 (length of discretionary custodial sentences: general provision), in subsection (2), for "227(2) and 228(2)" substitute "226A(4) and 226B(2)".

22 (1) Section 156 (pre-sentence reports and other requirements) is amended as follows.

(2) In subsection (3)(a), for "section 227(1)(b) or section 228(1)(b)(i)" substitute "section 226A(1)(b) or section 226B(1)(b)".

(3) After subsection (9) (inserted by paragraph 13 of Schedule 19) insert—

"(10) The reference in subsection (1) to a court forming the opinion mentioned in section 153(2) includes a court forming that opinion for the purposes of section 226A(6) or 226B(4)."

23 In the heading of section 225 (life sentence or imprisonment for public protection for serious offences) omit "or imprisonment for public protection".

24 In the heading of section 226 (detention for life or detention for public protection for serious offences by those aged under 18) omit "or detention for public protection".

25 In section 231 (appeals where convictions set aside), in subsection (1)—

(a) in paragraph (a), after "225(3)" insert ", 226A",

(b) in paragraph (b)—

(i) before "227(2A)" insert "226A(2) or", and

(ii) before "227(2B)" insert "226A(3) or", and

(c) in paragraph (c), after "may be)" insert "226A(2) or".

26 Omit section 232 (certificates of convictions for the purposes of sections 225 and 227).

27 In section 235 (detention under sections 226 and 228) after "226" insert ", 226B".

28 In the heading of that section after "226" insert ", 226B".

29 In section 327 (arrangements for assessing etc risks posed by certain offenders: interpretation), in subsection (3)(b)(vi), after "section" insert "226B or".

30 In section 330 (orders and rules), in subsection (5)(a), omit—

(a) "227(6),", and

(b) "228(7)".

31 Omit Schedule 15A (offences specified for the purposes of sections 225(3A) and 227(2A)).

Offender Management Act 2007 (c. 21)

32 (1) Section 28 of the Offender Management Act 2007 (application of polygraph conditions for certain offenders released on licence) is amended as follows.

(2) In subsection (3)(a), after "section" insert "226A or".

(3) In subsection (3)(f), after "226" insert ", 226B".

Counter-Terrorism Act 2008 (c. 28)

33 In section 45(1)(a) of the Counter-Terrorism Act 2008 (sentences or orders triggering notification requirements under Part 4 of that Act), after sub-paragraph (vi) (but before the "or" at the end of that sub-paragraph), insert—

"(via) detention under section 226B of that Act (extended sentence of detention for certain dangerous offenders aged under 18),".

Coroners and Justice Act 2009 (c. 25)

34 (1) Section 126 of the Coroners and Justice Act 2009 (determination of tariffs etc) is amended as follows.

(2) In subsection (1)—
(a) omit paragraphs (a) and (b),
(b) in paragraph (c), for "227 of that Act" substitute "226A of the Criminal Justice Act 2003", and
(c) in paragraph (d), for "228" substitute "226B".

(3) In subsection (2)—
(a) omit paragraph (b),
(b) in paragraph (c), for "227(3) of that Act" substitute "226A(6) of the Criminal Justice Act 2003", and
(c) in paragraph (d), for "228(3)" substitute "226B(4)".

(4) In subsection (4), for the words from "has" to the end substitute "means a sentence mentioned in subsection (2) of section 34 of the Crime (Sentences) Act 1997 other than a sentence mentioned in paragraph (d) or (e) of that subsection".

Consequential repeals

35 In consequence of amendments made by section 123, 124 or 125 or this Schedule—
(a) in the Criminal Justice Act 2003, omit paragraph 4 of Schedule 18, and
(b) in the Criminal Justice and Immigration Act 2008 omit—
(i) sections 13, 14, 15, 16 and 18(2);
(ii) Schedule 5;
(iii) in Schedule 26, paragraph 76.

PART 2

TRANSITORY PROVISION

36 (1) In relation to any time before the coming into force of section 61 of the Criminal Justice and Court Services Act 2000 (abolition of sentences of detention in a young offender institution, custody for life etc), Chapter 5 of Part 12 of the Criminal Justice Act 2003 (sentencing: dangerous offenders) has effect with the modifications in sub-paragraphs (2) and (3).

(2) In section 226A (extended sentence for certain violent or sexual offences: persons 18 or over), at the end insert—

"(12) In the case of a person aged at least 18 but under 21, this section has effect as if—

(a) the reference in subsection (1)(c) to imprisonment for life were to custody for life, and

(b) other references to imprisonment (including in the expression "extended sentence of imprisonment") were to detention in a young offender institution."

(3) In section 226B (extended sentence for certain violent or sexual offences: persons under 18), in subsection (7), for "18" substitute "21".

37 (1) In relation to any time before the repeal of section 30 of the Criminal Justice and Court Services Act 2000 (protection of children: supplemental) by Schedule 10 to the Safeguarding Vulnerable Groups Act 2006, that section has effect with the modification in sub-paragraph (2).

(2) In subsection (1), in paragraph (dd) of the definition of "qualifying sentence", after "226" insert ", 226B".

SCHEDULE 22

Section 127

DANGEROUS OFFENDERS SUBJECT TO SERVICE LAW ETC

PART 1

SENTENCES FOR DANGEROUS OFFENDERS SUBJECT TO SERVICE LAW ETC

Armed Forces Act 2006 (c. 52)

1 The Armed Forces Act 2006 is amended as follows.

2 After section 218 and the italic heading "Required or discretionary sentences for particular offences" insert—

"218A Life sentence for second listed offence

(1) This section applies where—

(a) a person aged 18 or over is convicted by the Court Martial of an offence under section 42 (criminal conduct);

(b) the corresponding offence under the law of England and Wales is an offence listed in Part 1 of Schedule 15B to the 2003 Act;

(c) the offence was committed after this section comes into force; and

(d) the sentence condition and the previous offence condition are met.

(2) Section 224A(2) of the 2003 Act applies in relation to the offender.

(3) In section 224A(2)(a) of that Act as applied by subsection (2)—

(a) the reference to "the offence" is to be read as a reference to the offence under section 42; and

(b) the reference to "the previous offence referred to in subsection (4)" is to be read as a reference to the previous offence referred to in subsection (5) of this section.

(4) The sentence condition is that, but for this section, the Court Martial would, in compliance with sections 260(2) and 261(2), impose a sentence of imprisonment for 10 years or more, disregarding any extension period imposed under section 226A of the 2003 Act as applied by section 219A of this Act.

(5) The previous offence condition is that—

(a) at the time the offence under section 42 was committed, the offender had been convicted of an offence listed in Schedule 15B to the 2003 Act ("the previous offence"); and

(b) a relevant life sentence or a relevant sentence of imprisonment or detention for a determinate period was imposed on the offender for the previous offence.

(6) A sentence is relevant for the purposes of subsection (5)(b) if it would be relevant for the purposes of section 224A(4)(b) of the 2003 Act (see subsections (5) to (10) of that section).

(7) A sentence required to be imposed by section 224A(2) of that Act as a result of this section is not to be regarded as a sentence fixed by law."

3 (1) Section 219 (dangerous offenders aged 18 or over) is amended as follows.

(2) For subsection (2) substitute—

"(2) Section 225(2) of the 2003 Act applies in relation to the offender."

(3) In subsection (3), omit "and (3A)".

4 In the heading of that section for "Dangerous" substitute "Life sentence for certain dangerous".

5 After that section insert—

"219A Extended sentence for certain violent or sexual offenders aged 18 or over

(1) This section applies where—

(a) a person aged 18 or over is convicted by the Court Martial of an offence under section 42 (criminal conduct) (whether the offence was committed before or after the commencement of this section);

(b) the corresponding offence under the law of England and Wales is a specified offence;

(c) the court is of the required opinion (defined by section 223);
(d) the court is not required to impose a sentence of imprisonment for life by section 224A(2) of the 2003 Act (as applied by section 218A of this Act) or section 225(2) of that Act (as applied by section 219 of this Act); and
(e) condition A or B is met.

(2) Condition A is that, at the time the offence under section 42 was committed, the offender had been convicted of an offence listed in Schedule 15B to the 2003 Act.

(3) Condition B is that, if the court were to impose an extended sentence of imprisonment under section 226A of the 2003 Act as a result of this section, the term that it would specify as the appropriate custodial term would be at least 4 years.

(4) Subsections (4) to (9) of section 226A of the 2003 Act apply in relation to the offender.

(5) In section 226A(4) to (9) of the 2003 Act as applied by this section—
(a) the reference in subsection (6) to section 153(2) of the 2003 Act is to be read as a reference to section 261(2) of this Act;
(b) the reference in subsection (7) to further specified offences includes a reference to further acts or omissions that would be specified offences if committed in England and Wales;
(c) the reference in subsection (8)(a) to a specified violent offence is to be read as a reference to an offence under section 42 as respects which the corresponding offence under the law of England and Wales is a specified violent offence; and
(d) the reference in subsection (8)(b) to a specified sexual offence is to be read as a reference to an offence under section 42 as respects which the corresponding offence under the law of England and Wales is a specified sexual offence.

(6) In this section "specified offence", "specified sexual offence" and "specified violent offence" have the meanings given by section 224 of the 2003 Act."

6 Omit section 220 (certain violent or sexual offenders aged 18 or over).

7 In section 221 (dangerous offenders aged under 18) for subsection (2) substitute—

"(2) Section 226(2) of the 2003 Act applies in relation to the offender."

8 In the heading of that section for "Dangerous" substitute "Life sentence for certain dangerous".

9 After that section insert—

"221A Extended sentence for certain violent or sexual offenders aged under 18

(1) This section applies where—
(a) a person aged under 18 is convicted by the Court Martial of an offence under section 42 (criminal conduct) (whether the offence was committed before or after the commencement of this section);

(b) the corresponding offence under the law of England and Wales is a specified offence;

(c) the court is of the required opinion (defined by section 223);

(d) the court is not required by section 226(2) of the 2003 Act (as applied by section 221 of this Act) to impose a sentence of detention for life under section 209 of this Act; and

(e) if the court were to impose an extended sentence of detention under section 226B of the 2003 Act as a result of this section, the term that it would specify as the appropriate custodial term would be at least 4 years.

(2) Subsections (2) to (7) of section 226B of the 2003 Act apply in relation to the offender.

(3) In section 226B(2) to (7) of the 2003 Act as applied by this section—

(a) the reference in subsection (4) to section 153(2) of the 2003 Act is to be read as a reference to section 261(2) of this Act;

(b) the reference in subsection (5) to further specified offences includes a reference to further acts or omissions that would be specified offences if committed in England and Wales;

(c) the reference in subsection (6)(a) to a specified violent offence is to be read as a reference to an offence under section 42 as respects which the corresponding offence under the law of England and Wales is a specified violent offence; and

(d) the reference in subsection (6)(b) to a specified sexual offence is to be read as a reference to an offence under section 42 as respects which the corresponding offence under the law of England and Wales is a specified sexual offence.

(4) In this section "specified offence", "specified sexual offence" and "specified violent offence" have the meanings given by section 224 of the 2003 Act."

10 Omit section 222 (offenders aged under 18: certain violent or sexual offences).

PART 2

CONSEQUENTIAL PROVISION

Juries Act 1974 (c. 23)

11 In Part 2 of Schedule 1 to the Juries Act 1974 (persons disqualified from jury service), in paragraph 6(d), after "2003" insert "(including such a sentence imposed as a result of section 219A, 220, 221A or 222 of the Armed Forces Act 2006)".

Rehabilitation of Offenders (Northern Ireland) Order 1978 (S.I. 1978/1908 (N.I. 27))

12 In article 6(1) of the Rehabilitation of Offenders (Northern Ireland) Order 1978 (sentences excluded from rehabilitation under the Order), in sub-paragraph (g)(iii), after "section" insert "226A, 226B,".

Criminal Justice Act 1982 (c. 48)

13 In section 32 of the Criminal Justice Act 1982 (early release of prisoners), in subsection (1A)—
(a) before "227" insert "226A or", and
(b) after "219" insert ", 219A".

Powers of Criminal Courts (Sentencing) Act 2000 (c. 6)

14 The Powers of Criminal Courts (Sentencing) Act 2000 is amended as follows.

15 In section 99 (conversion of sentence of detention to sentence of imprisonment), in subsection (6)—
(a) after "226" insert ", 226B", and
(b) after "221" insert ", 221A".

16 In section 106A(1) (interaction with sentence of detention), in the definition of "sentence of detention"—
(a) before "228", in the second place it appears, insert "226B or", and
(b) before "222" insert "221A or".

Criminal Justice and Court Services Act 2000 (c. 43)

17 The Criminal Justice and Court Services Act 2000 is amended as follows.

18 In section 62 (release on licence etc: conditions as to monitoring), in subsection (5)(f), after "221" insert ", 221A".

19 In section 64 (release on licence etc: drug testing requirements), in subsection (5)(f), after "221" insert ", 221A".

Sexual Offences Act 2003 (c. 42)

20 In section 131 of the Sexual Offences Act 2003 (young offenders: application), in paragraph (l), before "222" insert "221A or".

Criminal Justice Act 2003 (c. 44)

21 In section 237 of the Criminal Justice Act 2003 (meaning of fixed term prisoner etc), in subsection (1B), after paragraph (b) insert—
"(ba) references to a sentence under section 226A of this Act include a sentence under that section passed as a result of section 219A of the Armed Forces Act 2006;
(bb) references to a sentence under section 226B of this Act include a sentence under that section passed as a result of section 221A of the Armed Forces Act 2006;".

Armed Forces Act 2006 (c. 52)

22 The Armed Forces Act 2006 is amended as follows.

23 (1) Section 188 (consecutive custodial sentences) is amended as follows.

(2) In subsection (2), in paragraph (c)—
(a) for "228" substitute "226B", and

(b) for "222" substitute "221A".

(3) In subsection (4), in paragraph (c)—

(a) before "228" insert "226B or", and

(b) before "222" insert "221A or".

24 In section 209 (offenders aged under 18 convicted of certain serious offences: power to detain for specified period), in subsection (7)—

(a) for "section 226(2)" substitute "sections 224A and 226(2)", and

(b) for "section 221(2)" substitute "sections 218A and 221(2)".

25 In section 211 (offenders aged under 18: detention and training orders), in subsection (4)—

(a) after "218," insert "218A,", and

(b) for "222" substitute "221A".

26 In section 221(3) (dangerous offenders aged under 18), after "as applied" insert "by".

27 In section 223 (the "required opinion" for the purposes of sections 219 to 222), in subsection (1)—

(a) for "220(1)" substitute "219A(1)", and

(b) for "222(1)" substitute "221A(1)".

28 In the heading of that section for "222" substitute "221A".

29 For section 224 (place of detention under certain sentences) substitute—

"224 Place of detention under certain sentences

Section 235 of the 2003 Act (detention under sections 226, 226B and 228) applies to a person sentenced to be detained under section 226(3), 226B or 228 of that Act as applied by section 221, 221A or 222 of this Act."

30 (1) Section 228 (appeals where previous convictions set aside) is amended as follows.

(2) For subsection (1) substitute—

"(1A) Subsection (3) applies in the cases described in subsections (1B) to (2).

(1B) The first case is where—

(a) a sentence has been imposed on any person under section 224A of the 2003 Act (as applied by section 218A of this Act);

(b) a previous conviction of that person has been subsequently set aside on appeal; and

(c) without that conviction, the previous offence condition mentioned in section 218A(1)(d) would not have been met.

(1C) The second case is where—

(a) a sentence has been imposed on any person under section 225(3) of the 2003 Act (as applied by section 219(2) of this Act);

(b) the condition in section 225(3A) of the 2003 Act was met but the condition in section 225(3B) of that Act was not; and

(c) any previous conviction of the person without which the condition in section 225(3A) would not have been met is subsequently set aside on appeal.

(1D) The third case is where—

(a) a sentence has been imposed on any person under section 226A of the 2003 Act (as applied by section 219A of this Act);

(b) the condition in section 219A(2) was met, but the condition in section 219A(3) was not; and

(c) any previous conviction of the person without which the condition in section 219A(2) would not have been met is subsequently set aside on appeal.

(1E) The fourth case is where—

(a) a sentence has been imposed on any person under section 227(2) of the 2003 Act (as applied by section 220(2) of this Act);

(b) the condition in section 227(2A) of the 2003 Act was met but the condition in section 227(2B) of that Act was not; and

(c) any previous conviction of the person without which the condition in section 227(2A) would not have been met is subsequently set aside on appeal."

(3) In subsection (2)—

(a) for "Subsection (3) also applies" substitute "The fifth case is"; and

(b) in paragraph (a) after "226" insert "of this Act".

(4) After subsection (3) insert—

"(3A) Subsection (3B) applies where—

(a) a sentence has been imposed on a person under section 224A of the 2003 Act (as applied by section 218A of this Act);

(b) a previous sentence imposed on that person has been subsequently modified on appeal; and

(c) taking account of that modification, the previous offence condition mentioned in section 218A(1)(d) would not have been met.

(3B) An application for leave to appeal against the sentence mentioned in subsection (3A)(a) may be lodged at any time within 29 days beginning with the day on which the previous sentence was modified."

(5) In subsection (4), for "Subsection (3) has" substitute "Subsections (3) and (3B) have".

31 In section 237 (duty to have regard to the purposes of sentencing etc), in subsection (3)(b)—

(a) after "sections" insert "218A,", and

(b) before "225(2)" insert "224A,".

32 In section 246 (crediting of time in service custody: terms of imprisonment and detention), in subsection (6)(b)—

(a) before "228" insert "226B or", and

(b) before "222" insert "221A or".

33 (1) Section 256 (pre-sentence reports) is amended as follows.

(2) In subsection (1)(c)—

(a) for "220(1)" substitute "219A(1)", and

(b) for "222(1)" substitute "221A(1)".

(3) After subsection (9) insert—

"(10) The reference in subsection (1)(a) to a court forming any such opinion as is mentioned in section 260(2) or 261(2) includes a court forming such an opinion for the purposes of section 218A(4)."

34 (1) Section 260 (discretionary custodial sentences: general restrictions) is amended as follows.

(2) In subsection (1)(b)—

(a) before "225(2)" insert "224A,", and

(b) before "219(2)" insert "218A,".

(3) After subsection (4) insert—

"(4A) The reference in subsection (4) to a court forming any such opinion as is mentioned in subsection (2) or section 261(2) includes a court forming such an opinion for the purposes of section 218A(4).

(4B) The reference in subsection (4) to a court forming any such opinion as is mentioned in section 261(2) also includes a court forming such an opinion for the purposes of section 226A(6) or 226B(4) of the 2003 Act (as applied by section 219A or 221A of this Act)."

35 (1) Section 261 (length of discretionary custodial sentences: general provision) is amended as follows.

(2) In subsection (1)—

(a) before "225" insert "224A,", and

(b) before "219(2)" insert "218A,".

(3) In subsection (3), for "220, 222" substitute "219A, 221A".

36 In section 273 (review of unduly lenient sentence by Court Martial Appeal Court), in subsection (6)(b)—

(a) before "225(2)" insert "224A,", and

(b) before "219(2)" insert "218A,".

37 In section 374 (definitions applying for purposes of the whole Act), in the definition of "custodial sentence", after paragraph (e) (but before the "or" at the end of that paragraph) insert—

"(ea) a sentence of detention under section 226B of that Act passed as a result of section 221A of this Act;".

Counter-Terrorism Act 2008 (c. 28)

38 In Schedule 6 to the Counter-Terrorism Act 2008 (notification requirements: application to service offences), in paragraph 5(1)(a), after sub-paragraph (vi) (but before the "or" at the end of that sub-paragraph) insert—

"(via) detention under section 226B of that Act (extended sentence of detention for certain dangerous offenders aged under 18);".

PART 3

TRANSITORY PROVISION

39 (1) In relation to any time before the repeal of section 30 of the Criminal Justice and Court Services Act 2000 (protection of children: supplemental) by Schedule 10 to the Safeguarding Vulnerable Groups Act 2006, that section has effect with the modification in sub-paragraph (2).

(2) In subsection (1), in paragraph (dd) of the definition of "qualifying sentence", after "2003" insert "(including such a sentence imposed as a result of section 221, 221A or 222 of the Armed Forces Act 2006)".

SCHEDULE 23

Section 132

PENALTY NOTICES FOR DISORDERLY BEHAVIOUR

Criminal Justice and Police Act 2001 (c. 16)

1 Chapter 1 of Part 1 of the Criminal Justice and Police Act 2001 (on the spot penalties for disorderly behaviour) is amended as follows.

2 In section 1 (offences leading to penalties on the spot) omit subsections (4) and (5) (provision about orders under subsections (2) and (3) of that section).

3 (1) Section 2 (penalty notices) is amended as follows

(2) In subsection (1) for "10" substitute "18".

(3) After subsection (1) insert—

"(1A) If the offence mentioned in subsection (1) is a relevant penalty offence, the constable may give the person a penalty notice with an education option."

(4) Omit subsection (2) (requirement that constable giving a penalty notice other than at a police station be in uniform).

(5) Omit subsection (3) (requirement that constable giving a penalty notice at a police station be an authorised constable).

(6) In subsection (4)—

(a) after "Chapter", in the first place it appears, insert "—

"approved educational course" means an educational course run as part of an educational course scheme established by—

(a) in the case of a notice given by a constable of the British Transport Police Force, the Chief Constable of that force, and

(b) in any other case, the chief officer of police for the area in which the notice is given;

"educational course scheme" means a scheme established by a chief officer of police under section 2A;", and

(b) at the end insert ";

"penalty notice with an education option" means a penalty notice that also offers the opportunity to discharge any liability to be convicted of the offence to which the notice relates by—

(a) completing an approved educational course, and

(b) paying the course fee."

(7) After subsection (4) insert—

"(4A) In this section, "relevant penalty offence" means a penalty offence in relation to which there is an approved educational course.

(4B) The Secretary of State may by regulations make provision about the revocation of penalty notices."

(8) Omit subsection (5) (definition of "authorised constable").

(9) Omit subsections (6) to (9) (Secretary of State order making power and associated provision).

4 After section 2 (penalty notices) insert—

"2A Educational course schemes

(1) A chief officer of police may establish an educational course scheme under this section in relation to one or more kinds of penalty offence committed in the chief officer's area.

(2) An educational course scheme must include arrangements—

(a) for educational courses relating to the penalty offences to which the scheme relates to be provided to persons who are given penalty notices with an education option, and

(b) for a course fee set by the chief officer of police—

(i) to be paid by a person who attends an educational course, and

(ii) to be refunded in such circumstances (if any) as the chief officer considers appropriate.

(3) The purpose of an educational course mentioned in subsection (2) must be to reduce the likelihood of those who take the course committing the penalty offence, or penalty offences, to which the course relates.

(4) An educational course may be provided by any person who, and have any content that, the chief officer of police considers appropriate given its purpose.

(5) The Secretary of State may by regulations—

(a) provide that the fee mentioned in subsection (2)(b) may not be—

(i) less than an amount specified in the regulations, or

(ii) more than an amount so specified;

(b) make provision for and in connection with the disclosure, for the purpose of running an educational course scheme, of relevant personal information between—

(i) a person who is involved in the provision of an educational course under the scheme,

(ii) the chief officer of police who established the scheme, and

(iii) any other person specified or described in the regulations;

(c) make provision about the use of relevant personal information for that purpose;

(d) place restrictions on the disclosure or use of relevant personal information.

(6) In subsection (5) "relevant personal information" means any information that relates to, and identifies, a person who has been given a penalty notice with an education option.

(7) In this section's application in relation to the Chief Constable of the British Transport Police Force, subsection (1) has effect as if the reference to one or more kinds of penalty offence committed in a chief officer of police's area were a reference to one or more kinds of penalty offence—

(a) committed at, or in relation to, any of the places mentioned in section 31(1)(a) to (f) of the Railways and Transport Safety Act 2003 (places where a constable of the British Transport Police Force has the powers of a constable), or

(b) otherwise relating to a railway.

(8) In subsection (7) "railway" means—

(a) a railway within the meaning given by section 67(1) of the Transport and Works Act 1992 (interpretation), or

(b) a tramway within the meaning given by that section."

5 (1) Section 3 (amount of penalty and form of penalty notice) is amended as follows.

(2) Omit subsection (1A) (Secretary of State may specify different penalties for persons of different ages).

(3) After subsection (3) insert—

"(3A) The Secretary of State may by regulations require information in addition to that mentioned in subsection (3) to be included in, or to be provided with, a penalty notice with an education option."

(4) Omit subsections (5) and (6) (provision relating to orders under that section).

6 (1) Section 4 (effect of penalty notice) is amended as follows.

(2) In subsection (5) for "If" substitute "In the case of a penalty notice that is not a penalty notice with an education option, if".

(3) After subsection (5) insert—

"(6) In the case of a penalty notice with an education option, a sum equal to one and a half times the amount of the penalty may be registered under section 8 for enforcement against A as a fine if subsection (7) or (8) applies.

(7) This subsection applies if, by the end of the suspended enforcement period, A does not—
  (a) ask to attend an approved educational course relating to the offence to which the notice relates,
  (b) pay the penalty, or
  (c) request to be tried.

(8) This subsection applies if—
  (a) A has asked, by the end of the suspended enforcement period, to attend an approved educational course of the kind mentioned in subsection (7)(a), and
  (b) A does not, in accordance with regulations made under subsection (9)—
    (i) pay the course fee,
    (ii) start such a course, or
    (iii) complete such a course.

(9) The Secretary of State may by regulations make provision—
  (a) as to the time by which A is required to do each of the things mentioned in subsection (8)(b)(i) to (iii) (including provision allowing those times to be specified by a chief officer of police for the purposes of an educational course scheme established by that officer);
  (b) allowing A to request an extension of the time to do the things mentioned in subsection (8)(b)(i) to (iii) (including provision as to who should determine such a request and on what basis);
  (c) as to the procedure to be followed in relation to requests for extensions of time (including provision allowing the procedure to be determined by a chief officer of police for the purposes of an educational course scheme established by that officer);
  (d) as to the consequences of a request for an extension of time being granted (including provision specifying circumstances in which a chief officer of police may require a course fee to be paid again in order to avoid a sum being registered for enforcement as a fine under section 8);
  (e) as to the consequences of A failing to attend a course that A has arranged to attend (including provision as to who should determine what those consequences are and on what basis);
  (f) specifying circumstances in which A is, for the purposes of this Chapter, to be regarded as having completed, or having not completed, an approved educational course (including provision as to who should determine whether those circumstances have arisen and how that should be determined).

(10) Regulations made under subsection (9)(b), (e) or (f) may permit a person to delegate the function of making a determination."

7 (1) Section 5 (general restriction on proceedings) is amended as follows.

(2) In subsection (1) for "until the end of" substitute "during".

(3) After subsection (2) insert—

"(2A) Proceedings for an offence to which a penalty notice with an education option relates may not be brought against a person who has, by the end of the suspended enforcement period, asked to attend an approved educational course relating to the offence, unless section 4(8) applies.

(2B) If the person to whom a penalty notice with an education option is given—

(a) completes, in accordance with regulations made under section 4(9), an approved educational course relating to the offence to which the notice relates, and

(b) pays the course fee in accordance with those regulations,

no proceedings may be brought for the offence."

8 In section 6 (Secretary of State's guidance) after paragraph (b) insert—

"(ba) about educational course schemes;".

9 In section 8(4) (registration certificates) after "section 4(5)" insert "or (6)".

10 (1) Section 10 (enforcement of fines) is amended as follows.

(2) In subsection (6) for "If" substitute "Subject to any regulations made under subsection (7), if".

(3) After subsection (6) insert—

"(7) The Secretary of State may by regulations make provision as to the directions that the court may, or must, give or the orders it may, or must, make if it sets aside a fine relating to a sum registered under section 8 on the basis that section 4(8) applies."

11 After section 10 insert—

"Orders and regulations

10A Orders and regulations under Chapter 1

(1) Any power of the Secretary of State to make an order or regulations under this Chapter is exercisable by statutory instrument.

(2) Any power of the Secretary of State to make an order or regulations under this Chapter includes—

(a) power to make different provision for different cases, circumstances or areas, and

(b) power to make incidental, supplementary, consequential, transitional or transitory provision or savings.

(3) The Secretary of State may not make an order under section 1(2) unless a draft of the statutory instrument containing the order (whether alone or with other provisions) has been laid before, and approved by a resolution of, each House of Parliament.

(4) A statutory instrument that contains an order or regulations made under this Chapter and is not subject to any requirement that a draft of the instrument be laid before, and approved by a resolution of,

both Houses of Parliament, is subject to annulment in pursuance of a resolution of either House of Parliament."

12 (1) Section 11 (interpretation of Chapter 1) is amended as follows.

(2) Before the definition of "chief officer of police" insert—

""approved educational course" has the meaning given in section 2(4);".

(3) After the definition of "defaulter" insert—

""educational course scheme" has the meaning given in section 2(4);".

(4) After the definition of "penalty notice" insert—

""penalty notice with an education option" has the meaning given in section 2(4);".

Consequential amendments

13 In section 64A of the Police and Criminal Evidence Act 1984 (photographing of suspects etc) in subsection (1B)(d) omit "in uniform" in the first place those words appear.

14 (1) The Police Reform Act 2002 is amended as follows.

(2) In section 43(7) (railway safety accreditation schemes: Secretary of State power to give an accredited person the powers of a constable in uniform, or an authorised constable, to issue fixed penalty notices) omit "in uniform and of an authorised constable".

(3) In paragraph 1 of Schedule 4 (community support officers' powers to issue fixed penalty notices) in sub-paragraph (2)(a) omit "in uniform and of an authorised constable".

(4) In paragraph 1 of Schedule 5 (accredited persons' powers to issue fixed penalty notices) in sub-paragraph (2)(aa) omit "in uniform".

(5) In paragraph 1 of Schedule 5A (accredited inspectors' powers to issue fixed penalty notices) in sub-paragraph (2) omit "in uniform".

15 In consequence of the amendments made by paragraphs 3 and 5 of this Schedule, omit section 87 of the Anti-social Behaviour Act 2003.

SCHEDULE 24

Section 135

YOUTH CAUTIONS: CONSEQUENTIAL AMENDMENTS

Rehabilitation of Offenders Act 1974 (c. 53)

1 The Rehabilitation of Offenders Act 1974 is amended as follows.

2 In section 8A(2) (meaning of "caution")—

(a) omit paragraph (c), and

(b) in paragraph (d)—

(i) omit ", reprimand or warning", and

(ii) for "paragraphs (a) to (c)" substitute "paragraph (a) or (b)".

3 In Schedule 2 (protection for spent cautions) in paragraph 2(1)(e) (meaning of "ancillary circumstances": things done in connection with a rehabilitation programme)—
(a) for "warning under section 65" substitute "youth caution given under section 66ZA", and
(b) for "66(2)" substitute "66ZB(2) or (3)".

Police and Criminal Evidence Act 1984 (c. 60)

4 The Police and Criminal Evidence Act 1984 is amended as follows.

5 In section 34(5)(b) (requirement to release without bail unless proceedings may be taken or person may be reprimanded or warned), for the words from "reprimanded" to "65" substitute "given a youth caution under section 66ZA".

6 In section 37B(9)(b) (consultation with Director of Public Prosecutions: meaning of "caution"), for "warning or reprimand under section 65" substitute "youth caution under section 66ZA".

7 (1) Section 61 (fingerprinting) is amended as follows.

(2) In subsection (6) (power to fingerprint without consent in case of conviction etc for recordable offence)—
(a) at the end of paragraph (a) insert "or",
(b) for "or" at the end of paragraph (b) substitute "and", and
(c) omit paragraph (c) and the "and" at the end of that paragraph.

(3) In subsection (6ZA)(a) (conditions for application of subsection (6)), for ", cautioned or warned or reprimanded" substitute "or cautioned".

8 (1) Section 63 (non-intimate samples) is amended as follows.

(2) In subsection (3B) (power to take non-intimate sample without consent in case of conviction etc for recordable offence)—
(a) at the end of paragraph (a) insert "or",
(b) for "or" at the end of paragraph (b) substitute "and", and
(c) omit paragraph (c) and the "and" at the end of that paragraph.

(3) In subsection (3BA)(a) (conditions for application of subsection (3B)), for ", cautioned or warned or reprimanded" substitute "or cautioned".

9 In section 64ZC(6)(a) (destruction of data relating to a person subject to a control order: persons to be treated as having been convicted of an offence)—
(a) for "or" at the end of sub-paragraph (i) substitute "and", and
(b) omit sub-paragraph (ii) and the "and" at the end of that sub-paragraph.

10 In section 64ZI(3) (persons to be treated as having been convicted of an offence for the purposes of sections 64ZB and 64ZD to 64ZH) omit paragraph (b) and the "or" preceding that paragraph.

11 (1) Schedule 2A (fingerprinting and samples: power to require attendance at police station) is amended as follows.

(2) In paragraph 3 (attendance for fingerprinting: persons convicted etc of an offence in England and Wales)—

(a) in sub-paragraph (2)(a) for ", cautioned or warned or reprimanded" substitute "or cautioned", and

(b) in sub-paragraph (5) for ", caution or warning or reprimand" substitute "or caution".

(3) In paragraph 11 (attendance for taking of non-intimate sample: persons convicted etc of an offence in England and Wales)—

(a) in sub-paragraph (2)(a) for ", cautioned or warned or reprimanded" substitute "or cautioned", and

(b) in sub-paragraph (5)(a) for ", caution or warning or reprimand" substitute "or caution".

Police and Criminal Evidence (Northern Ireland) Order 1989 (S.I. 1989/1341 (N.I. 12))

12 In Article 64ZC(6)(a) of the Police and Criminal Evidence (Northern Ireland) Order 1989 (persons to be treated as having been convicted of an offence for the purposes of paragraph (1))—

(a) for "or" at the end of paragraph (i) substitute "and", and

(b) omit paragraph (ii) and the "and" at the end of that paragraph.

Jobseekers Act 1995 (c. 18)

13 In section 20D(6) of the Jobseekers Act 1995 (meaning of "cautioned" for the purposes of section 20C) omit paragraph (b) and the "or" preceding that paragraph.

Crime and Disorder Act 1998 (c. 37)

14 The Crime and Disorder Act 1998 is amended as follows.

15 In section 38(4) (meaning of "youth justice services")—

(a) for paragraph (aa) substitute—

"(aa) the provision of assistance to persons determining whether youth cautions should be given under section 66ZA below;", and

(b) in paragraph (b) for "66(2)" substitute "66ZB(2) or (3)".

16 In section 66H (interpretation)—

(a) in paragraph (a) (definition of "appropriate adult") for "65(7)" substitute "66ZA(7)", and

(b) after paragraph (e) insert—

"(ea) "youth caution" has the meaning given by section 66ZA(1);".

17 In section 121(6) (provisions extending to Scotland) omit paragraph (c).

Powers of Criminal Courts (Sentencing) Act 2000 (c. 6)

18 The Powers of Criminal Courts (Sentencing) Act 2000 is amended as follows.

19 In section 12(2) (which makes the provision for conditional discharge in that section subject to section 66(4) of the Crime and Disorder Act 1998)—

(a) for "66(4)" substitute "66ZB(6)", and

(b) for "reprimands and warnings" substitute "youth cautions".

20 In Schedule 9 (consequential amendments) omit paragraph 198.

Terrorism Act 2000 (c. 11)

21 Schedule 8 to the Terrorism Act 2000 (detention) is amended as follows.

22 In paragraph 14F(3) (persons to be treated as having been convicted of an offence for the purposes of paragraphs 14B to 14E) omit paragraph (b) and the "or" preceding that paragraph.

23 In paragraph 20F(3) (persons to be treated as having been convicted of an offence for the purposes of paragraphs 20B to 20E) omit ", or has been warned or reprimanded,".

Criminal Justice and Court Services Act 2000 (c. 43)

24 In section 56 of the Criminal Justice and Court Services Act 2000 (young offenders: reprimands and warnings) omit subsection (1).

Sexual Offences Act 2003 (c. 42)

25 In section 133(1) of the Sexual Offences Act 2003 (interpretation of Part 2), in the definition of "cautioned" omit paragraph (b) and the "or" preceding that paragraph.

Criminal Justice Act 2003 (c. 44)

26 In section 327B(9) of the Criminal Justice Act 2003 (meaning of "cautioned" for the purposes of that section) omit paragraph (b) and the "or" preceding that paragraph.

Childcare Act 2006 (c. 21)

27 In section 75(6) of the Childcare Act 2006 (disqualification from registration: interpretation) omit the definition of "caution".

Criminal Justice and Immigration Act 2008 (c. 4)

28 The Criminal Justice and Immigration Act 2008 is amended as follows.

29 In section 48(1) (which introduces Schedule 9 to that Act) omit paragraph (b) and the "and" preceding that paragraph.

30 In Schedule 9 (alternatives to prosecution for persons under 18) omit paragraph 2.

Counter-Terrorism Act 2008 (c. 28)

31 In section 18A(4) of the Counter-Terrorism Act 2008 (persons to be treated as having been convicted of an offence for the purposes of section 18(3B) and (3C)), omit paragraph (b) and the "or" preceding that paragraph.

Terrorism Prevention and Investigation Measures Act 2011 (c. 23)

32 In Schedule 6 to the Terrorism Prevention and Investigation Measures Act 2011 (fingerprints and samples), in paragraph 10(1)(a) (circumstances when an individual is to be treated as having been convicted of an offence)—

(a) at the end of sub-paragraph (ii) insert "or", and

(b) omit sub-paragraph (iv) and the "or" preceding that sub-paragraph.

SCHEDULE 25

Section 141

REHABILITATION OF OFFENDERS: CONSEQUENTIAL PROVISION

PART 1

REHABILITATION OF OFFENDERS: GENERAL

Rehabilitation of Offenders Act 1974: England and Wales

1 The Rehabilitation of Offenders Act 1974 is amended as follows.

2 In section 1(4)(a) (references in Act to a conviction) for "Great Britain" substitute "England and Wales".

3 In section 2(5) (rehabilitation of persons dealt with in service disciplinary proceedings) for "Great Britain" substitute "England and Wales".

4 Omit section 3 (special provision with respect to certain disposals by children's hearings under the Social Work (Scotland) Act 1968).

5 In section 4(1)(a) (effect of rehabilitation) for "Great Britain" substitute "England and Wales".

6 (1) Section 7 (limitations on rehabilitation under the Act) is amended as follows.

(2) In subsection (2)(a) for "Great Britain" substitute "England and Wales".

(3) In subsection (3) for "Great Britain" substitute "England and Wales".

7 Omit section 8(8) (defamation actions: application of section to Scotland).

8 In section 8A(2)(d) (definition of "caution") after "Wales" insert "and which is not an alternative to prosecution (within the meaning of section 8AA)".

9 (1) Section 9 (unauthorised disclosure of spent convictions) is amended as follows.

(2) In subsection (3) omit "(or, in Scotland, the accused person)".

(3) In subsection (8) omit ", in England and Wales,".

10 After section 10(1) (orders) insert—

"(1A) Any power of the Secretary of State to make an order under any provision of this Act includes power—

(a) to make different provision for different purposes, and

(b) to make incidental, consequential, supplementary, transitional, transitory or saving provision.

(1B) The power of the Secretary of State to make an order under section 5(6) includes power to make consequential provision which amends or repeals any provision of this Act or any other enactment."

11 Omit Schedule 1 (service disciplinary convictions referred to in section 6(6)(bb) of that Act).

Rehabilitation of Offenders Act 1974: Scotland

12 The Rehabilitation of Offenders Act 1974 is amended as follows.

13 In section 1(4)(a) (references in Act to a conviction) for "Great Britain" substitute "Scotland".

14 In section 2(5) (rehabilitation of persons dealt with in service disciplinary proceedings) for "Great Britain" substitute "Scotland".

15 In section 4(1)(a) (effect of rehabilitation) for "Great Britain" substitute "Scotland".

16 (1) Section 7 (limitations on rehabilitation under the Act) is amended as follows.

(2) In subsection (2)(a) for "Great Britain" substitute "Scotland".

(3) In subsection (3) for "Great Britain" substitute "Scotland".

17 (1) Section 9 (unauthorised disclosure of spent convictions) is amended as follows.

(2) In subsection (3) for "defendant (or, in Scotland, the accused person)" substitute "accused person".

(3) Omit subsection (8).

PART 2

REHABILITATION OF OFFENDERS: CONSEQUENTIAL REPEALS

Short title	*Extent of repeal*
Armed Forces Act 1976 (c. 52)	In Schedule 9, paragraph 21.
Criminal Law Act 1977 (c. 45)	In section 63(2), the words "Rehabilitation of Offenders Act 1974;". In Schedule 12, the entry relating to the Rehabilitation of Offenders Act 1974.
Magistrates' Courts Act 1980 (c. 43)	In Schedule 7, paragraph 134.
Armed Forces Act 1981 (c. 55)	In Schedule 4, paragraph 2(2).
Criminal Justice Act 1982 (c. 48)	In Schedule 14, paragraph 37.
Mental Health (Amendment) Act 1982 (c. 51)	In Schedule 3, paragraph 49.
Mental Health Act 1983 (c. 20)	In Schedule 4, paragraph 39.
Criminal Justice Act 1988 (c. 33)	In Schedule 8, paragraph 9(b).
Children Act 1989 (c. 41)	In Schedule 14, paragraph 36(7).

Short title	*Extent of repeal*
Criminal Justice Act 1991 (c. 53)	In section 68, paragraph (c) (but not the word "and" at the end of the paragraph). In Schedule 8, paragraph 5. In Schedule 12, paragraph 22(2).
Criminal Justice and Public Order Act 1994 (c. 33)	In Schedule 9, paragraph 11. In Schedule 10, paragraph 30.
Armed Forces Act 1996 (c. 46)	Section 13(3) and (4). Schedule 4.
Crime and Disorder Act 1998 (c. 37)	In Schedule 8, paragraph 35.
Youth Justice and Criminal Evidence Act 1999 (c. 23)	In Schedule 4, paragraph 6.
Powers of Criminal Courts (Sentencing) Act 2000 (c. 6)	In Schedule 9, paragraph 48(3) to (10). In Schedule 11, paragraph 13.
Criminal Justice and Court Services Act 2000 (c. 43)	In Schedule 7, paragraph 49.
Criminal Justice Act 2003 (c. 44)	In Part 1 of Schedule 32, paragraph 18(3).
Armed Forces Act 2006 (c. 52)	In Schedule 16, paragraphs 65(4) to (8) and 66.
Criminal Justice and Immigration Act 2008 (c. 4)	In Part 1 of Schedule 4, paragraph 21. In Schedule 10, paragraphs 2 and 5.
Policing and Crime Act 2009 (c. 26)	Section 18(2).

SCHEDULE 26

Section 142

KNIVES AND OFFENSIVE WEAPONS: MINOR AND CONSEQUENTIAL AMENDMENTS

Prevention of Crime Act 1953 (c. 14)

1 In section 2(3) of the Prevention of Crime Act 1953 (extent) for "shall not extend to Northern Ireland" substitute "extends to England and Wales only".

Mental Health Act 1983 (c. 20)

2 (1) Section 37(1A) of the Mental Health Act 1983 (powers of courts to order hospital admission or guardianship) is amended as follows.

(2) Before paragraph (a) insert—

"(za) under section 1A(5) of the Prevention of Crime Act 1953,".

(3) After paragraph (a) insert—

"(aa) under section 139AA(7) of the Criminal Justice Act 1988,".

Police and Criminal Evidence Act 1984 (c. 60)

3 In section 1(8A) of the Police and Criminal Evidence Act 1984 (power of constable to stop and search persons, vehicles etc) after "139" insert "or 139AA".

Criminal Justice Act 1988 (c. 33)

4 The Criminal Justice Act 1988 is amended as follows.

5 (1) Section 36(2)(b) (reviews of sentencing) is amended as follows.

(2) Before sub-paragraph (i) insert—

"(zi) section 1A(5) of the Prevention of Crime Act 1953;".

(3) After sub-paragraph (i) insert—

"(ia) section 139AA(7) of this Act;".

6 (1) Section 139B (power of entry to search for articles with a blade or point and offensive weapons) is amended as follows.

(2) In subsection (1) after "139A" insert "or 139AA".

(3) In subsection (4)—

(a) after "In the application of this section to Northern Ireland" insert "—

"(a) ";

(b) at the end add ", and

(b) the reference in subsection (1) to section 139AA is omitted."

7 In section 172(3) (provisions extending to Northern Ireland) for "sections 139 to 139B" substitute—

"section 139;
section 139A;
section 139B;".

Youth Justice and Criminal Evidence Act 1999 (c. 23)

8 (1) Schedule 1A to the Youth Justice and Criminal Evidence Act 1999 (relevant offences for the purposes of section 17: witnesses eligible for assistance on grounds of fear or distress about testifying) is amended as follows.

(2) After paragraph 9 insert—

"9A An offence under section 1A of that Act (threatening with offensive weapon in public)."

(3) After paragraph 26 insert—

"26A An offence under section 139AA of that Act (threatening with article with blade or point or offensive weapon)."

Powers of Criminal Courts (Sentencing) Act 2000 (c. 6)

9 The Powers of Criminal Courts (Sentencing) Act 2000 is amended as follows.

10 In section 12(1) (absolute and conditional discharge) for "section 51A(2) of the Firearms Act 1968" substitute "section 1A(5) of the Prevention of Crime

Act 1953, section 51A(2) of the Firearms Act 1968, section 139AA(7) of the Criminal Justice Act 1988".

11 In section 100 (offenders under 18: detention and training orders) after subsection (1) insert—

"(1A) Subsection (1) applies with the omission of paragraph (b) in the case of an offence the sentence for which falls to be imposed under these provisions—

(a) section 1A(5) of the Prevention of Crime Act 1953 (minimum sentence for offence of threatening with offensive weapon in public);

(b) section 139AA(7) of the Criminal Justice Act 1988 (minimum sentence for offence of threatening with article with blade or point or offensive weapon)."

12 In section 130(2) (compensation orders against convicted persons) for "section 51A(2) of the Firearms Act 1968" substitute "section 1A(5) of the Prevention of Crime Act 1953, section 51A(2) of the Firearms Act 1968, section 139AA(7) of the Criminal Justice Act 1988".

13 In section 146(2) (driving disqualification for any offence) for "section 51A(2) of the Firearms Act 1968" substitute "section 1A(5) of the Prevention of Crime Act 1953, section 51A(2) of the Firearms Act 1968, section 139AA(7) of the Criminal Justice Act 1988".

14 (1) Section 164(3) (further interpretative provisions) is amended as follows.

(2) After paragraph (a) insert—

"(aa) under section 1A(5) of the Prevention of Crime Act 1953,".

(3) After paragraph (b) insert—

"(ba) under section 139AA(7) of the Criminal Justice Act 1988,".

Criminal Justice Act 2003 (c 44)

15 The Criminal Justice Act 2003 is amended as follows.

16 (1) Section 142(2)(c) (purposes of sentencing: offenders aged 18 or over) is amended as follows.

(2) After "falls to be imposed" insert "under section 1A(5) of the Prevention of Crime Act 1953 (minimum sentence for offence of threatening with offensive weapon in public),".

(3) After "firearms offences)," insert "under section 139AA(7) of the Criminal Justice Act 1988 (minimum sentence for offence of threatening with article with blade or point or offensive weapon),".

17 (1) Section 142A(4)(b) (purposes of sentencing: offenders under 18) is amended as follows.

(2) Before sub-paragraph (i) insert—

"(zi) section 1A(5) of the Prevention of Crime Act 1953 (minimum sentence for offence of threatening with offensive weapon in public),".

(3) After sub-paragraph (i) insert—

"(ia) section 139AA(7) of the Criminal Justice Act 1988 (minimum sentence for offence of threatening with article with blade or point or offensive weapon),".

18 (1) Section 144 (reduction in sentences for early guilty pleas) is amended as follows.

(2) In subsection (2)—

(a) for "subsection (2) of section 110 or 111 of the Sentencing Act" substitute "a provision mentioned in subsection (3)";

(b) for "that subsection" in each place substitute "that provision".

(3) After that subsection insert—

"(3) The provisions referred to in subsection (2) are—

section 1A(6)(a) of the Prevention of Crime Act 1953;
section 110(2) of the Sentencing Act;
section 111(2) of the Sentencing Act;
section 139AA(8)(a) of the Criminal Justice Act 1988.

(4) In the case of an offence the sentence for which falls to be imposed under a provision mentioned in subsection (5), nothing in that provision prevents the court from imposing any sentence that it considers appropriate after taking into account any matter referred to in subsection (1) of this section.

(5) The provisions referred to in subsection (4) are—

section 1A(6)(b) of the Prevention of Crime Act 1953;
section 139AA(8)(b) of the Criminal Justice Act 1988."

19 (1) Section 150 (community sentence not available where sentence fixed by law etc) is amended as follows.

(2) After paragraph (a) insert—

"(aa) falls to be imposed under section 1A(5) of the Prevention of Crime Act 1953 (minimum sentence for offence of threatening with offensive weapon in public),".

(3) After paragraph (b) insert—

"(ba) falls to be imposed under section 139AA(7) of the Criminal Justice Act 1988 (minimum sentence for offence of threatening with article with blade or point or offensive weapon),".

20 In section 152(1)(b) (general restrictions on imposing discretionary custodial sentences) for "under section 51A(2) of the Firearms Act 1968 (c. 27)," substitute "under section 1A(5) of the Prevention of Crime Act 1953, under section 51A(2) of the Firearms Act 1968, under section 139AA(7) of the Criminal Justice Act 1988,".

21 In section 153(2) (length of discretionary custodial sentences: general provision) for "section 51A(2) of the Firearms Act 1968 (c. 27)," substitute "section 1A(5) of the Prevention of Crime Act 1953, section 51A(2) of the Firearms Act 1968, section 139AA(7) of the Criminal Justice Act 1988,".

22 (1) Section 305(4) (interpretation of Part 12) is amended as follows.

(2) Before paragraph (a) insert—

"(za) a sentence falls to be imposed under subsection (5) of section 1A of the Prevention of Crime Act 1953 if it is required by that subsection and the court is not of the opinion there mentioned,".

(3) After paragraph (a) insert—

"(aa) a sentence falls to be imposed under subsection (7) of section 139AA of the Criminal Justice Act 1988 if it is required by that subsection and the court is not of the opinion there mentioned,".

Armed Forces Act 2006 (c. 52)

23 The Armed Forces Act 2006 is amended as follows.

24 After section 227 (firearms offences) insert—

"227A Offences of threatening with a weapon in public or on school premises

(1) This section applies if—

(a) a person aged 18 or over is convicted by a court of an offence under section 42 (criminal conduct); and

(b) the corresponding offence under the law of England and Wales is an offence under section 1A of the Prevention of Crime Act 1953 or section 139AA of the Criminal Justice Act 1988 (threatening with article with blade or point or offensive weapon in public or on school premises).

(2) The court must impose a sentence of imprisonment for a term of at least 6 months unless the court is of the opinion that there are particular circumstances which—

(a) relate to the offence or to the offender, and

(b) would make it unjust to do so in all the circumstances.

(3) In relation to times before the coming into force of section 61 of the Criminal Justice and Court Services Act 2000, the reference in subsection (2) to a sentence of imprisonment, in relation to an offender aged under 21 at the time of conviction, is to be read as a reference to a sentence of detention in a young offender institution."

25 In section 237(3) (duty to have regard to purposes of sentencing etc) after paragraph (b) insert ";

(c) an offence the sentence for which falls to be imposed under section 227A(2)."

26 In section 239 (reduction in sentences for guilty pleas) at the end insert—

"(6) Nothing in section 227A(2) prevents the court, after taking into account any matter mentioned in subsection (2) of this section, from imposing any sentence which is at least 80% of that specified in section 227A(2)."

27 In section 260(1)(b) (discretionary custodial sentences: general restrictions) for "227" substitute "227A".

28 In section 261(3) (length of discretionary custodial sentences: general provision) for "and 227" substitute ", 227 and 227A".

29 In section 273(6)(b) (review of unduly lenient sentence by Court Martial Appeal Court) for "or 227" substitute ", 227 or 227A".

30 (1) Paragraph 12 of Schedule 2 ("Schedule 2 offences") is amended as follows.

(2) After sub-paragraph (r) insert—

"(ra) an offence under section 1A of the Prevention of Crime Act 1953 (threatening with offensive weapon in public);".

(3) In sub-paragraph (ai)—

(a) after "134" insert ", 139AA";

(b) after "torture," insert "threatening with article with blade or point or offensive weapon,".

Coroners and Justice Act 2009 (c. 25)

31 (1) Section 125(6) of the Coroners and Justice Act 2009 (sentencing guidelines: duty of court) is amended as follows.

(2) After paragraph (e) insert—

"(ea) section 1A(5) of the Prevention of Crime Act 1953 (minimum sentence for offence of threatening with offensive weapon in public);".

(3) After paragraph (f) insert—

"(fa) section 139AA(7) of the Criminal Justice Act 1988 (minimum sentence for offence of threatening with article with blade or point or offensive weapon);".

SCHEDULE 27

Section 143

CAUSING SERIOUS INJURY BY DANGEROUS DRIVING: MINOR AND CONSEQUENTIAL AMENDMENTS

Road Traffic Act 1988 (c. 52)

1 In section 13A(1) of the Road Traffic Act 1988 (disapplication of sections 1 to 3 for authorised motoring events) after "sections 1," insert "1A,".

Road Traffic Offenders Act 1988 (c. 53)

2 The Road Traffic Offenders Act 1988 is amended as follows.

3 In section 23(1A) (alternative verdicts in Scotland) after paragraph (a) insert—

"(aa) an offence under section 1A of that Act (causing serious injury by dangerous driving),".

4 (1) Section 24 (alternative verdicts: general) is amended as follows.

(2) In subsection (A2) after paragraph (a) insert—

"(aa) an offence under section 1A of that Act (causing serious injury by dangerous driving),".

(3) In the table in subsection (1) in the appropriate place insert—

"Section 1A (causing serious injury by dangerous driving)	Section 2 (dangerous driving)
	Section 3 (careless, and inconsiderate, driving)".

5 In section 34(4) (disqualification for certain offences) after paragraph (a)(ii) and the "or" after it insert—

"(iia) an offence under section 1A of that Act (causing serious injury by dangerous driving), or".

6 In section 36(2)(b) (disqualification until test is passed) after "(causing death by dangerous driving)" insert ", section 1A (causing serious injury by dangerous driving)".

7 In section 45(6) (effect of endorsement of counterparts) (until its repeal by the Road Safety Act 2006 comes into force)—

(a) after "section 1" insert ", 1A";

(b) after "causing death by dangerous driving" insert ", causing serious injury by dangerous driving".

8 In section 45A(4) (effect of endorsement of driving records) as substituted by the Road Safety Act 2006—

(a) after "section 1" insert ", 1A";

(b) after "causing death by dangerous driving" insert ", causing serious injury by dangerous driving".

9 In the table in Schedule 1 (application of provisions including sections 11 and 12(1): evidence as to driver and proof of identity) in the appropriate place insert—

"RTA section 1A	Causing serious injury by dangerous driving.	Sections 11 and 12(1) of this Act."

Crime (International Co-operation) Act 2003 (c. 32)

10 In paragraph 3 of Schedule 3 to the Crime (International Co-operation) Act 2003 (application of duty to give notice to foreign authorities of driving disqualification of a non-UK resident) after sub-paragraph (a) insert—

"(aa) section 1A (causing serious injury by dangerous driving),".

Armed Forces Act 2006 (c. 52)

11 In paragraph 12(aj) of Schedule 2 to the Armed Forces Act 2006 ("Schedule 2 offences")—

(a) after "section 1," insert "1A,";

(b) after “causing death by dangerous driving,” insert “causing serious injury by dangerous driving,”.

Printed in the UK by The Stationery Office Limited under the authority and superintendence of Carol Tullo, Controller of Her Majesty’s Stationery Office and Queen’s Printer of Acts of Parliament

5/2012 20517 19585